Maya Angelou

Maya Angelou

Adventurous Spirit

From *I Know Why the Caged Bird Sings* (1970)
to *Rainbow in the Cloud, The Wisdom and Spirit of
Maya Angelou* (2014)

Linda Wagner-Martin

Bloomsbury Academic
An imprint of Bloomsbury Publishing Inc

B L O O M S B U R Y
NEW YORK · LONDON · OXFORD · NEW DELHI · SYDNEY

Bloomsbury Academic

An imprint of Bloomsbury Publishing Inc

1385 Broadway	50 Bedford Square
New York	London
NY 10018	WC1B 3DP
USA	UK

www.bloomsbury.com

**BLOOMSBURY and the Diana logo are trademarks of
Bloomsbury Publishing Plc**

First published 2016

Library of Congress Cataloging-in-Publication Data
Wagner-Martin, Linda.
Maya Angelou : adventurous spirit / Linda Wagner-Martin.
pages cm
ISBN 978-1-5013-0785-0 (hardback) – ISBN 978-1-5013-0784-3 (paperback)
1. Angelou, Maya. 2. Authors, American–20th century–Biography.
3. African American authors–Biography. 4. Civil rights workers–Biography.
5. Angelou, Maya–Criticism and interpretation. I. Title.
PS3551.N464Z96   2015
818'.5409–dc22
[B]
2015009347

ISBN: HB: 978-1-5013-0785-0
PB: 978-1-5013-0784-3
epub: 978-1-5013-0787-4
ePDF: 978-1-5013-0786-7

Typeset by Newgen Knowledge Works (P) Ltd., Chennai, India
Printed and bound in the United States of America

For Tommy, Elizabeth, and Isabelle Wagner

Contents

Illustrations

Acknowledgments

A bbreviations used within the book are mostly self-explanatory; a key word from a book title will be followed by the appropriate page number. Because there is only one collection of interviews with Maya Angelou (*Conversations*), I have used the abbreviation "Con" to indicate that collection. The extensive bibliography has a complete listing of all materials consulted and quoted from.

Throughout this study I have referred to Angelou's son as "Guy." He was named *Clyde* at birth but after she had been traveling with the *Porgy and Bess* opera company for a year, he asked her when she returned if he might instead use the name *Guy*. She agreed. References to Angelou herself change as the study proceeds: when readers are considering the first several books of her autobiography, I use "Marguerite" rather than "Maya Angelou." Depending on which persona is being discussed, the author's name may vary.

Because there is one central poem collection for the study of Angelou's poetry, *The Complete Collected Poems of Maya Angelou*, published in 1994, I have used no titles or page numbers in the chapters about her poetry (chapters 5 and 10). By omitting a cumbersome reference system, this study allows more space for quotations from the poems themselves.

Thanks to the various collections, archives, and photography sites that made this research possible. Thanks too to Haaris Naqvi of Bloomsbury Press who encouraged this project.

Preface

This book about Maya Angelou and her lives in music, acting, believing, organizing, cooking, teaching, and writing could be wonderfully and effectively published in surround-sound. *Maya* the calypso singer and the six-foot-tall jazz dancer, *Maya* the actress, *Maya* the young mother of her talented son Guy, *Maya* the head of Martin Luther King, Junior's Northern office in New York City, *Maya* the diligent Christian believer, *Maya* the autobiographer and poet whose books are translated into countless languages and read around the world—not to mention *Maya* the teacher and the Maya who learned, through exposure and her amazing ear, to speak many languages, from Fanti in Ghana, through Spanish, French, Italian, to the medley of various California dialects she grew up hearing. There was also the Maya Angelou whose career as writer, director, and actor in television and film productions was often a surprising first for a woman, and even more often a surprising first for a woman of color. And perhaps most beloved of all, the *Maya* of *Letter to My Daughter* who knew how to be, continuously, a welcoming and nonjudging woman.

How does the author of an academic book capture the radiant and effulgent mind, attitude, and sound that was Maya Angelou? When Maya Angelou took your hand and looked deeply into your eyes, your life knew it had been changed. Perhaps more importantly, how does an author capture the far-reaching effects of Maya Angelou's eight memoirs and as many poem collections, as well as her countless essays, letters, interviews, and even more personal writings? The hundreds of thousands of copies of her books, translated into more than forty languages, spread over the globe as if she were composing a new kind of literacy quilt, a message of grace and love, of charity and of persisting in, and overcoming, the most difficult of life's circumstances.

How, too, does any account of this woman's life avoid over-reaching or exaggerating the gap between the sheer physical poverty of her childhood—a literally dirt-poor existence in Arkansas, when she and her brother Bailey lived with their grandmother Annie Henderson at the back of the isolated frame store, while their disabled Uncle Willie hid in the dark vegetable bin to avoid Ku Klux Klan night riders—and the truly international acclaim that brought one former president of the United States, along with the wife of the sitting United States President and one of the wealthiest professional women in this country to speak at her North Carolina memorial service (June 7, 2014). Tears of loss at Maya Angelou's death flooded the reaches of the world: the buoyant, and truly *phenomenal*, woman had been one of America's most effective ambassadors. She had looked into lives that should have been closed to her empathy. She had spoken to people who should have viewed her tall blackness—softened with her surprisingly down-home eloquence—with diffidence. She was the approachable woman who had spoken of recipes, of family, and of spiritual beliefs in the midst of iconic civil rights proselytizing: she did not disguise either her sharp intellect or her loving heart.

Yet therein lies an unusual story. Maya Angelou had begun her childhood as a victim of rape by her mother's boyfriend, and in her silent years that followed that violation—when she was seven and a half—she was moved from Missouri to Arkansas to California to

Mexico: she came close to being a "throw-away" child. Quietly, the child Maya Angelou observed the world around her. Just as quietly, she listened. She sometimes spoke to Bailey, her beloved brother, but she chose—during these seminal years—to be mute. And less than a decade later, when she had once again resumed speaking, she spent her senior year in a public San Francisco high school pregnant with the child she had already determined she—alone—would keep and raise. Her son was born one month after her graduation: then she worked, found child care, did without, and worked, found child care, did without, and worked. . . .

At the start, her wide-ranging career as dancer, singer, actor, street car conductor, and kitchen help, cook, cleaning person, music store clerk, prostitute, and sometimes madam was prompted by the sheer physical need to earn money. Maya Angelou was the sole support of not only herself but also her son. As personable as she was talented, she won fellowships to study in arts schools and with New York professional dancers. Perhaps more significant, she was open to *accepting* the help of people she met: part of her ability to accept assistance stemmed from her constant profession of faith. Encouraged by her African American friends John O. Killens and James Baldwin, Rosa Guy and Paule Marshall, and directed by these and others at the Harlem Writers Guild, Maya Angelou eventually tried the difficult profession of writing. Led first to Robert Loomis, the Random House editor who both encouraged her and (as she said in the preface to *I Know Why the Caged Bird Sings*) "gently prodded [her] back into the lost years," Maya Angelou published a book of autobiography or poetry or essay nearly every subsequent year of her life. The acclaim that greeted her first work, *I Know Why the Caged Bird Sings*, in 1970 was overwhelming. It was also world-wide, and it was never-ending. Angelou's first book was also nominated for a National Book Award. Similar warm receptions greeted her second autobiography, *Gather*

Together in My Name (1974) and her third, *Singin' and Swingin' and Gettin' Merry Like Christmas* (1976), along with the books of poems (some of them adapted from her earlier songs), *Just Give Me a Cool Drink of Water 'Fore I Diiie* (1971), nominated for the Pulitzer Prize in Poetry; *Oh Pray My Wings Are Gonna Fit Me Well* (1975); *And Still I Rise* (1978); *Shaker, Why Don't You Sing?* (1983), and many others.

In January 1993, Maya Angelou read her poem "On the Pulse of Morning" at the invitation of the president of the United States. The inauguration of President William Jefferson Clinton was graced with this distinguished woman's art and the reminder of what she had herself overcome in her life. As the eyes of millions of viewers trained on her expressive face, Maya Angelou was the first American woman—and the first poet of color—ever to be so honored. As she said in her glowingly hopeful lines:

> . . . You, created only a little lower than
> The angels, have crouched too long in
> The bruising darkness . . .

The poet does not omit herself from this implied challenge: "You, who gave me my first name, you,/Pawnee, Apache, Seneca, you,/Cherokee Nation, who rested with me." Signaling a new spirit, an unbounded promise, Angelou's impressive poem reminds her audience, comprised of this vast mixture of American people, to hope:

> Lift up your eyes
> Upon this day breaking for you.
> Give birth again
> To the dream . . .
> Lift up your hearts.
> Each new hour holds new chances
> For a new beginning . . .

> ("Pulse," *Collected*, 271–2).

Delivering the Inaugural poem "On the Pulse of Morning" at the William Jefferson Clinton Inauguration, January 1993. Photographer: Sharon Farmer. Credit: William J. Clinton Presidential Library.

Maya Angelou's story in total speaks for the promise of a charitable and loving spirit, for the power of family to shape lives that all-too-often disappear into the annals of neglect, and for the genuine belief that constancy will solve a myriad of problems.

In Maya Angelou's story, the best of careful nurture and keen attention come together to create an *American* life, filled with the promise of which she speaks:

Lift up your hearts.
Each new hour holds new chances
For a new beginning . . .

1

Marguerite Annie Johnson, April 4, 1928

In 1970, when she was 41, Maya Angelou became one of the world's most visible writers. What is it that brings readers to some books, readers who have perhaps looked into a book only once every few years—if then? Why do other books remain closed to even those people who are fascinated by language?

What is the *synergy* of story?   The *radiance* of the word?

The *attraction* of recognition?

Maya Angelou's *I Know Why the Caged Bird Sings* was *not* a story people wanted to read. Raped when she was seven and a half by her mother's boyfriend, the child Marguerite Johnson barely survived. The violation brought her close to death; she separated herself from everyone except her brother. She dissociated herself from her mother and her St. Louis family—the mark of that dissociation was her chosen muteness. Later, recollecting that she would sometimes speak to Bailey, she describes her silence as the mark that her voice was "eluding" her. Instead of speaking, she wrote songs and taught them to Bailey; he in turn taught her songs to the children who were their friends. For five years, Bailey became her voice (Order 148).

Maya Angelou traced her life as writer back to those silent years. She said, "We all bring almost unnameable information from childhood . . . If we are lucky, we make transitions, and don't live in that time of pain and rejection and loneliness and desolation. But there will understandably be bits of it which adhere to us" (Con 221).

When Angelou chose the most positive stanza from Paul Laurence Dunbar's 1899 poem "Sympathy" to serve as the title of her first book, she was already focused on the role of compassion in human lives.

> *I know why the caged bird sings, ah me,*
> *when his wing is bruised and his bosom sore, . . .*
> *It is not a carol of joy or glee,*
> *But a prayer that he sends from his heart's deep core, But a plea, that*
> *upward to Heaven he flings—I know why the caged bird sings!*

Even in the midst of rage and pain, the writer, the singer, that allegorical bird, must create a legacy that endures, and one that comforts. Angelou often said, in various interviews, that as a writer she learned to choose to describe episodes that would give hope to readers; her intent in writing autobiography was not to *maim* either people or their memories:

> What I have left out of *Caged Bird* and all the books is a lot of unkindness. I've never wanted to hurt anybody. So many of the people are still alive. The most difficult part for me has always been the selection of the incidents. To find one which is dramatic without being melodramatic or maudlin, and yet will give me that chance to show that aspect of personality, of life which impacted on me . . . from which I drew and grew (Order 139).

With rare insight into the way telling stories works (whether orally or in print), Angelou couched her aims as writer in relation to the theater: "I see the incident in which I was a participant, and maybe the only participant, as drama . . . And I've used, or tried to use, the form of the Black minister in storytelling so that each event I write about has a beginning, a middle, and an end. And I have tried to make the selections graduate so that each episode is a level, whether of narration or drama . . . a level of comprehension like a staircase" (ibid. 140).

In 1970 when Random House published *I Know Why the Caged Bird Sings* (which quickly became a best-seller and was translated into many languages), Angelou's methods were unique. There was very little autobiography or memoir being published, and there had been almost no autobiography published that was written by African Americans since the days of slave narratives. In the late 1960s, publishers were looking for fiction, a few were taking on novels by outspoken feminist writers (such as Erica Jong's best-selling book *Fear of Flying* or Marilyn French's *The Women's Room*); and they were content to stay with mainstream (i.e., white) writers. There was very little interest in books about marital or domestic strife—no category yet existed for "domestic abuse" nonfiction. The term hardly existed.

Although Ralph Ellison's novel *Invisible Man* had been published in 1952 and had quickly become *the* contemporary novel by a writer of color to appear in course syllabi, it was the only book by an African American that most readers had even heard of. (Richard Wright's 1940 *Native Son* and his own autobiography to come later, *Black Boy*, were considered decidedly radical—thoroughly unpleasant, dangerously and frighteningly intent on blaming mainstream white culture for whatever ailed black characters and black culture.) With the impetus that Civil Rights activity had created during the 1960s, some readers had found the plays and essays of James Baldwin, but they were in the minority. Even such a figure as Martin Luther King, Jr. was considered a speaker, a preacher, more than he was seen to be a literary figure. Only Maya Angelou's friend Malcolm Little, the man later known as el-Hajj Malik el-Shabazz and before that as Malcolm X, had based his literary career on memoir. His collaborative autobiography—*The Autobiography of Malcolm X*—was published in 1965, shortly after his assassination; Alex Haley was the co-writer of this autobiography, but Haley's friendship with Maya, and his fame from *Roots*, lay in the future.

Even as late as 1970, publishers had not recognized the need for book categories based on skin color, gender, or politics. Historians assumed that the Civil Rights efforts of the 1960s had changed reading habits, but they were wrong. Books were labeled "non-fiction" and "fiction" with little regard for gender or race. The evolving category of "women's fiction" might have looked important, but it was not: when Toni Morrison—later to win the Nobel Prize for Literature—published her first novel, *The Bluest Eye*, in 1970, it quickly went out of print. Following her second novel, *Sula*, in 1973, Morrison achieved some recognition; but it was not until 1977, when her third book, *Song of Solomon*, won a major literary prize, that she began to receive the kind of recognition that had become Maya Angelou's with the 1970 appearance of her first book, *I Know Why the Caged Bird Sings*.

In 1970, the only other American woman writer who was publishing autobiography—and autobiography in serial fashion, itself a rarity—was playwright Lillian Hellman. Long established on the Broadway and off-Broadway stage, Hellman's fame made her first memoir—*An Unfinished Woman*, published in 1969 and winner of the National Book Award in 1970—a best-seller. When *Pentimento* appeared in 1973, readers felt bewildered: were these episodes memoir or fiction? With the adaptation of several of these segments into *Julia*, a popular 1977 movie, Hellman's career as an autobiographer started to diminish. With her third autobiography, *Scoundrel Time*, in 1976, readership increased because Hellman and her long-time partner, Dashiell Hammett, had been blacklisted by the House Committee on Un-American Activities in the early 1950s and this memoir focused directly on those years. In 1980 when Hellman published her enigmatic fourth book, *Maybe*, she lost credibility as an autobiographer (she was testing the limits of the traditional memoir, as she had throughout her book series, but her readers were largely puzzled).

The visibility of Hellman's successive memoirs may have intrigued Angelou's editor at Random House, Robert Loomis. Hellman was well known, mainstream, and heterosexual, unlike some authors in the early 1970s who vaunted the legitimacy of lesbianism. (Consider the changes incipient then in US culture: sexual preference linked with issues of gender and race, but people considered all such issues "radical." It was not until 1967 with *Loving v. Virginia* that interracial marriage became legal. *Roe v. Wade* dated from 1973. *Ms Magazine* began publication in 1971. In 1974 President Gerald Ford signed legislation that allowed girls to play Little League baseball.)

Maya Angelou's appeal in her autobiographical writing was much less literary than Hellman's. She had no celebrity status, though she had appeared on stage and in clubs: the heart of her memoir writing was, in fact, the *commonality* of her life. Hellman was white; Angelou was not only African American but African American from the Southern United States—and Angelou was largely uneducated in any formal sense. She also wrote, without apology, about the bleak events in the early years of her life—and she did so without blaming mainstream culture—that is, white culture—for those events. *I Know Why the Caged Bird Sings* was an unanticipated kind of book. Its politics was comparatively mild; its energy was devoted to expressing the family love that had saved Maya and her brother; its narrative patterning alternated the serious, and the chilling, with the tranquil and the exuberant. The book was structured around scenes and episodes so that it read like a story. Its readers may not have known what a "memoir" was or how it differed from an "autobiography." What they knew was that they were eager to read Angelou's story.

That Angelou had created a kind of unique voice in the midst of what appeared to be "autobiography" or "self-narrative" was not the subject of the reviews and appreciations. Rather, in the words of James Baldwin, Angelou had written what he termed "testimony from a black sister," writing which "liberates the reader into life simply because Maya Angelou confronts her own life with such a moving wonder, such a luminous dignity." Newspaper reviewers responded to *I Know Why the Caged Bird Sings* as "simultaneously touching and comic," "a heroic and beautiful book," "an unconditionally involving memoir for our time or any time." In the words of critic Julian Mayfield, who did not fear relating to the book as an African American reader, and seeing in it the vicissitudes of African American life, it was "a work of art which eludes description because the black aesthetic—another way of saying 'the black experience'—has too long been neglected to be formalized by weary clichés . . . Anyone who doesn't read Maya Angelou doesn't want to know where it was, much less where it's at."

Appearing in 1970, when such important African American poets as Audre Lorde, Nikki Giovanni, and Sonia Sanchez were publishing their first poem collections, Angelou's memoir served as a preface to her own first book of poems, which would appear in 1971. Angelou's *Just Give Me a Cool Drink of Water 'Fore I Diiie*, though it was nominated for the Pulitzer Prize in Poetry, appeared from Random House—whereas works by many African American poets were being published by Dudley Randall at Detroit's Broadside Press. (Broadside published Langston Hughes, Gwendolyn Brooks, and Randall himself, as well as Alice Walker, June Jordan, LeRoi Jones—later Amiri Baraka; African American critics expected black poets and playwrights to appear from African American venues.) In Angelou's poems, as in her memoir, she created a voice and a form that was idiosyncratic, using both the traditional poem forms of James Weldon Johnson and individually appropriate stanzas drawing from song rhythms, jazz, hymns, and spoken emphases. In both her poetry and her memoir, then, Angelou forged her own directions—and as a result her aesthetic achievements were sometimes unappreciated or overlooked.

To read Maya Angelou's works—from these early 1970s books as well as the later—demands that the reader know her autobiography, her essays, her recipes (for her recipes are often embedded in family stories), and her poems. One of her favorite topics is the generosity of her tough paternal grandmother, Annie Henderson, to whom her mother had sent her, along with her brother, after the rape and the subsequent trial—and then the murder of the rapist. The reader comes to know this beloved grandmother figure in vignettes about Annie Henderson's earning the money to build the shack-like store: she made and fried meat pies every day at noon for men who worked at the two factories in Stamps, Arkansas—rotating the fresh pies day by day, charging five cents for the first-made pies and three cents for the left-overs—walking miles from her kitchen to the first factory, carrying all her equipment. Then she walked to the second site and sold pies there.

Years passed.

When she had saved enough money, divorced mother of two boys that she was, she built a cooking shack midway between the factories. At that point, her customers came to her. That shed eventually became the store that supported her, her grandchildren and her disabled son. Angelou creates the ambience of the loving and yet relentless grandmother, whether she writes in autobiography or in poetry.

Because Bailey and Marguerite had lived with Annie Henderson years before, when their parents were in the process of getting a divorce, they were accustomed to calling her "Momma," and they considered living in the back of the store a place of privilege. Almost from the beginning of *I Know Why the Caged Bird Sings*, Annie Henderson dominates its narrative. Waking up at 4:00 a.m., with no alarm clock, she is there to sell breakfast to her customers during picking season. We hear her sleep-filled voice as she goes to her knees in thanks, "Our Father, thank you for letting me see this New Day" (*Caged* 11). Next she issues orders to her grandchildren, and then Angelou as writer brings the reader directly into the store itself: "The lamplight in the Store gave a soft make-believe feeling to our world which made me want to whisper and walk about on tiptoe. The odors of onions and oranges and kerosene had been mixing all night and wouldn't be disturbed until the wooded slat was removed from the door and the early morning air forced its way in with the bodies of people who had walked miles to reach the pickup place." Immediately, Angelou uses characters' voices to create the scene:

"Sister, I'll have two cans of sardines."
"I'm gonna work so fast today I'm gonna make you look like you standing still."
"Lemme have a hunk uh cheese and some sody crackers."

The reader feels the peace. There are no locks, only the wooden slab that holds the doors shut. There is no fear among people who all work as hard as possible to secure some kind of living, and whose religion spreads throughout the town, offering support as well as joy. When Maya Angelou recalls the weekly church service, she compares it to ecstasy—her silent grandmother cares well for her but expressiveness is not Annie Henderson's strong suite: it is the black preacher who extols the love of God. "I decided when I was very young to read the whole Bible and I did so twice. I loved its cadence. And in church when the minister would make the Bible come alive . . . when he would elaborate on the story—whether it was the story of the Prodigal Son or of Dry Bones in the Valley—it would go through the top of my head. *I could see it.* And the tonality, and the music, and the old people . . . all that. For me, it was going to the opera" (in Order 10).

Language as performance was an energy that accrued from both reading the King James Bible, filled as it is with metaphor after metaphor, and listening to the empowering music of both language and singing. The lasting resonance of her Stamps, Arkansas, church melds with her grandmother's love, and leaves Maya Angelou content: "All of my work, my life, everything I do is about survival, not just bare, awful, plodding survival, but survival with grace and faith. While one may encounter many defeats, one must not be defeated. In fact that encountering may be the very experience which creates the vitality and the power to endure" (Order 11).

Candid as the author is, she recalled that—years later—coming back to Arkansas was recognizing that terrible poverty—"flesh-real and swollen-belly poor"—even as she, as she matured, saw her own "trying-on of roles" as a means of gaining "an instinctive self-education." Growing up in the segregated South was never easy. It was, in fact, purposefully created to *make* growing up hard. Tall and angular as the young Marguerite was, she wrote years later to her New York friend Rosa Guy, "My belief [as a child] that I was ugly was absolute, and nobody tried to disabuse me—not even Momma. Momma's love enfolded me like an umbrella but at no time did she try to dissuade me of my belief that I was an ugly child." (February 4, 1966, letter, Wake Forest archive). Perhaps the sense that Momma loved not only Marguerite but many other good people was itself comforting: as Angelou wrote in *Caged Bird*, "a deep brooding love hung over everything she [Annie] touched" (*Caged* 47).

Annie Henderson spoke of *God's* love rather than her own, but her granddaughter recognized the love in everything she did. When Angelou recalled the care with which Momma made the Sunday breakfasts—which needed to fill her grandchildren so full that they would not be hungry until 3:00 p.m., when church finally ended, she described the way food was prepared with attention to loving details: "She fried thick pink slabs of home-cured ham and poured the grease over sliced red tomatoes. Eggs over easy, fried potatoes and onions, yellow hominy and crisp perch fried so hard we would pop them in our mouths and chew bones, fins and all. Her cathead biscuits were at least three inches in diameter and two inches thick" (*Caged* 33). One of the pervasive emphases within this first memoir is the givingness of the African American community. In Angelou's words, "Although there was always generosity in the Negro neighborhood, it was indulged on pain of sacrifice. Whatever was given by Black people to other Blacks was most probably needed as desperately by the donor as by the receiver. A fact which made the giving or receiving a rich exchange" (ibid. 41).

In her later writings, Angelou told stories that showed the noble spirit of her grandmother more vividly. The story that accompanies her recipe for Annie Henderson's caramel cake, in *Hallelujah!, The Welcome Table*, her first recipe book, describes the painful process of her own coming back to speech. Having been sent back to Stamps to live, the silent Marguerite was an accepted (if strange) child—spoken for, as we have seen, by Bailey and allowed by most of her teachers to write answers on the chalkboard. A new teacher was forced to accept the child's behavior, but she attributed it to the fact that the Hendersons were store-proud, that Marguerite felt a sense of privilege because her grandmother owned the store. Unfortunately, this young teacher tried to correct the girl's behavior. She would not allow her to answer in writing; she slapped the tall child across the face when Marguerite would not conform. The child ran home, crying.

The usually gentle Annie Henderson insisted that she return to the school with her granddaughter. Wearing a fresh apron, she walked serenely to the building and asked Miss Williams, "Are you somebody's grandbaby?"

Miss Williams answered, "I am someone's granddaughter."

Momma said, "Well, this child here is my grandbaby." Then she slapped her. Not full force but hard enough for the sound to go around the room and to elicit gasps from the students.

"Now, Sister, nobody has the right to hit nobody in the face. So I am wrong this time, but I'm teaching a lesson." She looked at me. "Now find yourself a seat and sit down and get your lesson."

Momma left the room and it was suddenly empty and very quiet (*Table* 15–16).

The after-school celebration back home was marked by Annie's carefully made caramel cake, a task that took four to five hours because she had no brown sugar, and had to make caramel syrup by hand. No other cook in Stamps, Arkansas, ever attempted *Annie Henderson's Caramel Cake*, which looked "like paradise, oozing sweetness" (ibid. 17). The name of the delicacy was always capitalized.

Yet, even as Annie Henderson was Bailey's and Marguerite's beloved Momma, they yearned for their own chic maternal figure, Vivian Baxter. In later books of her memoirs, as well as in her 2013 *Mom and Me and Mom*, Angelou clarifies the roots of her little girl admiration for her mother. Taken by their father into St. Louis once they are old enough to live without constant care, "Bibbie's darling babies" shared the awe the urban culture gave to the light-skinned and talented Vivian Baxter. Angelou recalled that she "loved her most" when she danced, alone, in the Seeburg-haunted bar: "She was like a pretty kite that floated just above my head. If I liked, I could pull it in to me by saying I had to go to the toilet or by starting a fight with Bailey. I never did either, but the power made me tender to her" (*Caged* 53). Even though Angelou knew she had this control over her mother's affections, she was content to simply bask in her nearness: "To describe my mother would be to write about a hurricane in its perfect power. Or the climbing, falling colors of a rainbow . . . My mother's beauty literally assailed me. Her red lips (Momma said it was a sin to wear lipstick) split to show even white teeth and her fresh-butter color looked see-through clean. Her smile widened her mouth beyond her cheeks beyond her ears and seemingly through the walls to the street outside. I was struck dumb" (ibid. 49–50).

More of Vivian Baxter's character, and her influence on Marguerite, appears in the second and third of Angelou's memoirs . . . charting the years when her mother was, first, a professional gambler in San Francisco, and then a landlady after she bought a fourteen-room house there. Later, Marguerite and Bailey attend George Washington High School in San Francisco, and Marguerite takes dance and drama lessons at the California Labor School. It is during her early high school years that Angelou talks her way into becoming the first black woman streetcar conductor in the city, a spirited role that seems to be reflected from the indomitable force that *is* her mother. When she graduates in 1945 from Mission High School and a month later gives birth to her son, Angelou next insists she must leave her mother's home and care for the baby on her own. The image she then creates for her readers is Vivian Baxter, supportive and feisty, as in Angelou's second essay collection, *Even the Stars Look Lonesome*. The essay "Mother and Freedom" opens:

> She stood before me, a dolled-up, pretty yellow woman, seven inches shorter than my six-foot bony frame. Her eyes were soft and her voice was brittle. "You're determined to leave? Your mind's made up?"
>
> I was seventeen and burning with passionate rebelliousness. I was also her daughter, so whatever independent spirit I had inherited

had been nurtured by living with her and observing her for the past four years. "You're leaving my house?"

I collected myself inside myself and answered, "Yes. Yes, I've found a room." "And you're taking the baby?" "Yes."

She gave me a smile, half proud and half pitying. "All right, you're a woman. You don't have a husband, but you've got a three-month-old baby. I just want you to remember one thing. From the moment you leave this house, don't let anybody raise you. Every time you get into a relationship you will have to make concessions, compromises, and there's nothing wrong with that. But keep in mind Grandmother Henderson in Arkansas and I have given you every law you need to live by. Follow what's right. You've been raised" (*Stars* 47–8).

Angelou's memory of that conversation may be more accurate than a reader supposes. The essay continues:

More than forty years have passed since Vivian Baxter liberated me and handed me over to life . . . I have taken life as my mother gave it to me on that strange graduation day all those decades ago . . . My mother raised me, and then freed me (ibid. 48).

Angelou's mother recognized the gift that Annie Henderson had given her daughter: she couples *their* raising Marguerite as if the fusion was only, ever, a benefit. Angelou, too, notes that the power of these two women's loves propelled her through years of disdain and discomfort: with her sharp memory of what she had learned from Vivian Baxter, "that life had no right to beat me to the ground, to batter my teeth down my throat, to make me knuckle down and call it Uncle" (*Stars* 48).

It is the force of *both* Maya Angelou's mother figures—Annie Henderson and Vivian Baxter—that dominates her last collection of essays, titled *Letter to My Daughter* (always with the explanation that she had only her son, Guy, and no daughters—except her metaphoric daughters throughout the world). In the closing essay of this 2008 book, Angelou combines her constant love of these two women with her stunningly achieved belief in God. Titled "Keep the Faith," this essay describes that the search for religious belief is a continuous struggle, and that Angelou has achieved her belief through envisioning Momma Annie Henderson at the apex of heaven. She reminisces, "One of my earliest memories of my grandmother, who was called 'Momma,' is a glimpse of that tall, cinnamon-colored woman with a deep, soft voice, standing thousands of feet up in the air with nothing visible beneath her."

Transferring the suspended figure back to earth in Arkansas, Angelou described the woman's responding to any challenge by clasping her hands behind her back and drawing herself up to her full six-foot height. "She would tell her family in particular, and the world in general, 'I don't know how to find the things we need, but I will step out on the word of God. I am trying to be a Christian and I will just step out on the word of God.'"

In her child's imagination, the author saw her beloved grandmother "flung into space, moons at her feet and stars at her head, comets swirling around her shoulders. Naturally, since she was over six feet tall, and stood out on the word of God, she was a giant in heaven. It wasn't difficult for me to see Momma as powerful, because she had the word of God beneath her feet" (*Letter* 166). Angelou's gospel song, written for Annie Henderson, repeats those phrases:

> *You* said to lean on your arm
> And I am *leaning*
> *You* said to trust in your love

And I am *trusting*
You said to call on your name
And I am *calling*
I'm stepping out on *your* word.

The essay closes with Angelou's mature and consistently aging vision: "there, right there, between the sun and moon, stands my grandmother, singing a long meter hymn, a song somewhere between a moan and a lullaby and I know faith is the evidence of things unseen" (ibid.).

2

Ambivalence is not so easy

In some ways, the unusual success of Maya Angelou's *I Know Why the Caged Bird Sings* presented her with difficulties that were almost as significant as the income from the book's sales and its translations into other languages. This first memoir covered only her childhood years. When it was published, she was a woman in her early forties, already twice married, already something of a world figure on stage and in the political arena. In the early 1970s, the recriminations of her profile—of being born in the poverty of the American South, of being a rape victim, of being a young and unwed mother, were lasting; when these descriptions were placed within an African American culture, readers assumed that they knew more about her life experiences than she had told them. As she said in one interview, "I'm often asked: 'How did you escape it all: the poverty, the rape at an early age, a broken home, growing up black in the South?' My natural response is to say: 'How the hell do you know I *did* escape? You don't know what demons I wrestle with'" (Con 14).

There are evidences of Angelou's anger throughout her interviews. She knows how power-hungry some African American men can be (she worked side by side with political leaders during the 1960s; she understood that her role as secretary and organizer was nothing compared with the men's roles in attaining civil rights). In one interview she noted, "I'm going to write about all those black men with their fists balled up who talk about nation-buildin' time and then go home to rape their nieces and step-daughters and all the little teen-age girls who don't know beans about life. I'm goin' to tell it because rape and incest are rife in the black community" (Con 9). In terms of her own autobiography, Angelou continued that she had planned, for the second book *Gather Together in My Name*, that there would be a black woman character who had *not* escaped. "So what I'm doing is writing the autobiography but carrying a fictional character along—the woman who *didn't* escape. So that each time I reached a crossroads, and because somebody loved me, I went [she hooks her two index fingers, then twists them] this way, and she goes that way. And then another crisis came along, and, because I was lucky, I went that way, but she goes the other way" (ibid. 14).

Without carrying through this plan, Angelou was becoming prominent enough that she was interviewed frequently—imposing in her regal carriage, using her expressive voice as a well-trained actor would—and through the medium of her self-celebration, she was able to influence listeners and readers. The tendency with some readers of *I Know Why the Caged Bird Sings* was to sentimentalize the protagonist's struggles: in answer to one such leading question, Angelou agreed that black American women were "the quintessential survivors." This kind of romanticized view of Marguerite's grief and shame undercut what the memoir in itself achieved. Angelou said, "The black American female has nursed a nation of strangers—literally. And has remained compassionate. This, to me, is survival. She is strong. And she is inclusive, as opposed to exclusive. She has included all the rest of humanity in her life and has often been excluded from their lives" (Con 17). In a later comment about her friend the widowed

Coretta King, Angelou emphasized how much injustice remains in the modern world: "Coretta . . . said the greatest violence is seeing a child go to bed hungry. These are the great violences: assaults on the body and soul. Hunger, poverty, fear, dirt, and guilt . . . That is what my life is about: highlighting these things and, hopefully, encouraging others to help make things better" (ibid. 37). There is much, much work to be done; Angelou says succinctly, "If the woods are on fire, you don't worry if your slip is showing. You know, you just don't have time" (Con 117).

In her interview with Bill Moyers, Angelou made her anger one of her recurrent themes: "When I pick up the pen to write, I have to scrape it across these scars to sharpen the point" (Moyers 4). A few years later, in the *Paris Review* interview (which George Plimpton asked her to "perform" before a standing-room-only audience at the YMHA on Manhattan's Upper East Side), she contextualizes that emotional state in discussing how difficult it has been for African American writers to be published. She emphasizes that she writes simply, so that the reader feels no barriers, but that she is aiming for what the West African (Ghanaise) culture would call "deep talk." Angelou explains that "I write for myself and for the reader who will pay the dues. There's a saying: 'The trouble for the thief is not how to steal the chief's bugle but where to blow it.' Now, on the face of it, one understands that. But when you really think about it, it takes you deeper" (Paris 245). She complains that critics and reviewers (chiefly the New York ones, she jibes) talk about how easily *she* writes. She, in reality, works terribly hard for that effect. In 1990, she notes that *I Know Why the Caged Bird Sings* is in its twenty-first printing in hard cover and in its twenty-ninth in paperback; it has never been out of print. "All my books are still in print . . . because people go back and say, Let me read that. Did she really say that?" (Paris 246).

By 1990, Angelou had come to consider herself a spokesperson for African Americans, something of a public intellectual. When George Plimpton asked her to return to discussing the difficulty of finding publishers, Angelou segues to racial stamina. "I knew I was going to do something. The real reason black people exist at all today is because there is a resistance to a larger society that says you can't do it—you can't survive. And if you survive, you certainly can't thrive. And if you thrive, you can't thrive with any passion or compassion or humor or style. There's a saying, a song that says, 'Don't you let nobody turn you 'round, turn you 'round. Don't you let nobody turn you 'round.' Well, I've always believed that. So knowing that, knowing that nobody could turn me 'round, if I didn't publish, well, I would design this theater we're sitting in. Yes. Why not? Some human being did it. I agree with Terence. Terence said *homo sum: humani nihil a me alienum pute*. I am a human being. Nothing human can be alien to me" (Paris 256). As in her writings, Angelou here does not stress the difficulties so much as the people's capacity to overcome those difficulties.

Angelou frequently describes the way writing centers her life. She says that had she not found the avenue of writing, she would be bereft. Her entire life, including her dreams, relates to whether or not she writes—or, perhaps more accurately, whether or not she writes well.

There is a dream which I delight in and long for when I'm writing . . . I dream of a very tall building. It's in the process of being built and there are scaffolds and steps. It looks sort of like the inside of the Arc de Triomphe. I'm climbing with alacrity and joy and laughter. Quite often it's day but it's not very bright because I'm inside the structure going up. I have no sense of dizziness or discomfort or vertigo. I'm just climbing. I can't tell you how delicious that is!

I began, I guess, twenty years ago to notice that when my dream came, it always meant that the work was going well . . .

There's another dream which also has to do with work. I don't seem to have any just plain delight dreams or dreams about love or anything personal. The other dream is also a good dream. That is when I wake from it, I feel that things are all right. It's not ecstatic, it's not as delicious . . . but it's okay. It has to do with a particular area . . . it seems like a small town with nice, just modest, homes. I seem to know the area very well and feel quite at home there (Epel 26).

Whether she is discussing writing or dreams or life's happenings, it seems clear that Maya Angelou is the great narrator of human experience. Even though the reader carries away from her autobiographies a tone of stability, of comfort, many of her narratives are shaded *away* from the pleasant.

When she discusses Annie Henderson's store and "cleanly-swept" yard, for instance, the pleasantness seems dominant: "The back yard was the real living area . . . my grandmother had a table built around the chinaberry tree so people could sit there under it. On Saturdays, women would come there and get their hair done and ladies would come, hairdressers. Men would barber around this chinaberry tree . . . We had lawn here, where we could play croquet, in the back, because in the front of the house was dirt. I raked the dirt."

Then, the somnolent mood of the summer afternoon shatters. "Now the [white] girls came along this road, and they'd walk in front of the house, in front of the store. Whenever Momma or anybody saw white girls coming, they'd call Uncle Willie and tell him to hide. Because these girls, or women, for that matter, could come in the store and say, 'I'll have two pounds of this . . . I'll have ten pounds of this . . . I'll have so and so.' And then they would say, 'Put it on my bill,

Willie.' And my uncle could not say, 'You don't have a bill' because all
they would have to do is say, 'He tried to touch me.'"

"They knew they couldn't blackmail Grandmother. There was
no point coming into the store and getting candy or trying to. They
showed out because my grandmother was so impregnable. She was a
fortress that could not be entered into." Angelou added then that both
Bailey and Uncle Willie lived under what she accurately terms this
"implied threat" (Braxton 9–10).

Despite its biblical-sounding title, *Gather Together in My Name*
was the bleakest story Angelou could have told: the young mother,
searching in the California cities for respect and a livelihood, found
herself tricked into versions of a high life that included drugs,
endangering her son, and prostitution. As *I Know Why the Caged
Bird Sings* came to its close, Angelou was seemingly poised to create a
new existence for herself and her baby Guy; she had left her mother's
house with her blessing. But what that first memoir obscured was the
innocence of the teenage mother. Marguerite Annie Johnson was still
the wide-eyed girl who thought the constant love she had known—
both in Stamps, Arkansas, and in California—was a given. What she
was to learn in this second volume was that every innocent girl was
likely to become someone's prey.

The chronology of these several years narrated in *Gather Together*
seems marked by the various cooking jobs Angelou held—all poorly
paid, all intended to place her in a public eye. Episodes are blurred
as predators, both male and female, try to coerce the tall black
girl into a lifestyle she has not expected. Finally, midway through
the book, Angelou returns with her little boy to Stamps. Readers
expect some replayed scenes—the voice that has told the stories of
I Know Why the Caged Bird Sings seems to take over the narrative.
Annie Henderson's tears of joy as she welcomes Marguerite set
the tone; Uncle Willie is even more grateful that she has returned.

(In a descriptive paragraph, Angelou says more about this man's disability than has previously been told: "He had been crippled in early childhood, and his affliction was never mentioned. The right side of his body had undergone severe paralysis, but his left arm and hand were huge and powerful.") As he holds Guy, his muscles react and he fears that he will harm the baby. "Then Momma called from the kitchen."

The reader is taken into Angelou's comfortable acceptance. "We were in the Store; I had grown up in its stronghold. Just seeing the shelves loaded with weenie sausages and Brown Plug chewing tobacco, salmon and mackerel and sardines all in their old places softened my heart and tears stood at the ready just behind my lids. But the kitchen, where Momma with her great height bent to pull cakes from the wood-burning stove and arrange the familiar food on well-known plates, erased my control and the tears slipped out and down my face to plop onto the baby's blanket" (*Gather* 281).

Being home comforts Marguerite. She waits on customers, orders a Simplicity pattern from the main general store (and is told it will take 3 days for it to come from "exotic" Texarkana), and then—to her surprise—is invited to go out with the African American girls who had never been her friends. The invitation is a trick: her "friends" leave her alone in the bar and she is rescued by a boy she had known in high school, a farm kid whose alcoholic father keeps him tied to their small livelihood. He teaches her to vomit, gives her sen-sen, and drops her off, safely, at the Store. (She adds, "The following year I heard that he had blown his brains out with a shotgun on the day of his father's funeral.")

In more danger at home than being left at the bar, Marguerite next unwittingly complains at the general store about her dress pattern: she has become an "uppity black" in the midst of an all-white establishment. When she returns to Annie's, her grandmother berates

her for causing the disturbance and—worst of all—slaps her across
the face. Twice. Three times. Her grandmother minces no words:

> You think 'cause you've been to California these crazy people won't
> kill you? You think them lunatic cracker boys won't try to catch
> you in the road and violate you? You think because of your all-fired
> principle some of the men won't feel like putting their white sheets
> on and riding over here to stir up trouble? You do, you're wrong.
> Ain't nothing to protect you and us except the good Lord and some
> miles. I packed you and the baby's things, and Brother Wilson is
> coming to drive you to Louisville (*Gather* 294).

Saddened by this loss of her one true home, and her beloved
grandmother and uncle, Angelou returns to her cooking job in San
Francisco. The vast difference between her exposition of these jobs in
Gather Together in My Name and retrospectively, in her interviews,
is dramatic. In the latter, she tersely explains, "After high school, I
took odd jobs. I had a day & night restaurant in Stockton, California.
After I lost that I used to peel paint off cars with my hands. I had a
son to support and I had to find work to support him" (Con 4). In the
memoir, however, she describes and repeats, rehearses and repeats,
both the anxiety of her finding work and of her first breakthroughs
into dancing as a means of earning a living. "I was in a state again
that was blood line familiar. Up a tree, out on a limb, in a pickle, in a
mess but I didn't pack my bags (or leave them) and go back to Mother.
Survival was all around me but it didn't take hold. Women nearly as
young as I, with flocks of children, were creating their lives daily. A
few hustled (I had obviously little aptitude for that); some worked as
housemaids (becoming one of a strange white family was impossible.
I would keep my negative Southern exposures to whites before me
like a defensive hand); some wrestled with old lady Welfare (my neck
wouldn't bend for that)" (*Gather* 378).

One of the most effective scenes in this second book of Angelou's memoirs is her thinking that one of her occasional lovers might marry her. Instead, Troubadour Martin takes her to visit an addicts' center, a cheap motel room where homeless people buy hits. Angelou does not know about Troub's addiction; he takes her into the bathroom and shows her how to tie off a vein. He administers the heroin, and asks if she wants to try. From the romantic haze she has used to envision him as a possible spouse to the wrenching revelation of his life of addiction, Angelou promises him that she will stay straight. "No one had ever cared for me so much," she recalled. "He had exposed himself to me to teach me a lesson and I learned it as I sat in the dark car inhaling the odors of the wharf. The life of the underworld was truly a rat race, and most of its inhabitants scurried like rodents in the sewers and gutters of the world. I had walked the precipice and seen it all; and at the critical moment, one man's generosity pushed me safely away from the edge" (*Gather* 284).

Seeing Angelou's method here as in *I Know Why the Caged Bird Sings* as relating linked stories leads the reader to question: Why *this* form? *Why* autobiography? When Plimpton asked her about the fascination with memoir, she lauded its capacity, saying "Autobiography is awfully seductive—it's wonderful . . . It has caught me. I'm using the first person singular and trying to make that the first person plural, so that anybody can read the work and say, Hmm, that's the truth, yes, uh-huh, and live in the work. It's a large, ambitious dream. But I love the form" (Paris 247). She later traces her understanding of memoir to Frederick Douglass's work, "always saying *I* meaning *we*. And what a responsibility! Trying to work with that form, the autobiographical mode, to change it, to make it bigger, richer, finer, and more inclusive in the twentieth century has been a great challenge for me . . . The greatest compliment I receive is when people walk up to me on the street or in airports and say, Miss Angelou, I *wrote* your books last year and I really—I mean I *read* . . . That is it—that the person has come into the books so seriously, so completely, that he or she, black or white, male or female, feels *that's my story. I told it. I'm making it up on the spot.* That's the greatest compliment. I didn't expect, originally, that I was going to continue with the form" (Paris 242).

One of Angelou's consistent principles for good writing was to build in dramatic moments. Her grandmother's chastising her about the dangers of being black—especially since Annie Henderson was usually "very quiet"—holds a central place in *Gather Together in My Name* (Order 144). That speech, accompanied by her slapping her grown granddaughter, also taught Marguerite the perils of opening her African American family members to the white hostility and rage that could so easily destroy them, especially her crippled Uncle Willie, whose life had previously been threatened—often—by the Klan.

If Angelou's aim in writing her autobiographies was to describe "a time and an ethos," then the Stamps, Arkansas, setting and characters so vividly drawn in *I Know Why the Caged Bird Sings* keeps resonating throughout all the books (Order 161). The author's carefully contrasting choice, as developed in *Gather Together in My Name,* to make Marguerite's return to Stamps a pivotal episode, reinforces the early time and its ethos, but it also changes those elements. Being driven away from Stamps—as she and baby Guy were at her grandmother's arranging—signaled the end of that homelike existence. That scene is made more plausible by the protagonist's real despair at the end of *Gather Together.* There Angelou insists, "My head stayed high from habit, but my last hope was gone. Every way out of the maze had proved to be a false exit. My once lively imagination would not come up with one more fantasy. My courage was dwindling . . . For the first time in my life I sat down defenseless to await life's next assault" (*Gather* 378).

Such despair is unusual for the Marguerite-Maya persona. More frequently, Angelou looks for ways to incorporate positive—even spiritual—import. When she writes, as she frequently has, about her grandmother's years of earning money for the store, she has the Annie Henderson character say, "I looked up the road I was going and back the way I came, and since I wasn't satisfied, I decided to step off the road and cut me a new path" (in Williams 206).

Maya Angelou the writer would like to convey those same positive thoughts, and in all her autobiographies except *Gather Together* she manages to do so. It seems to be second nature, in fact, as when she was asked about the role her subconscious life played in her existence as writer. In *Writers Dreaming*, she very briefly described her rape, and then shared this imaginative fantasy with her interviewer:

> You know, from the age of 7 1/2 to 12 ½ I was mute. I believed at the time that I could make myself, my whole body, an ear. And I could absorb all sound. Those years I must have done something to my brain, or with it, so that the part of the brain which would have been occupied in the articulation of speech and the creation of sound, those electrical synapses, did something else with themselves. They just reinvented themselves so that I'm able to remember incredible amounts of data. I would say I get along reasonably well in seven or eight languages. I have spoken as many as twelve. I have taught in three. I seem to have total recall or none at all. And so, when I need to get inside myself, I can do it without going to sleep (Epel 27).

There is nothing positive about denying the physical and psychological damage that rape and incest leave behind, however. In Angelou's interview with Joanne Braxton, she tells her friend candidly that her memoir had to begin with her rape.

> The rape of a child is the cruelest action because it has so many implications. The child is, herself, himself, the potential rapist. Many people who have been raped quite often go on to violate everything: themselves first, and, then, their families, their lovers,

then the community and the society. It is so awful. I can say, honestly, that I don't believe a day has passed that I haven't thought about it, in something I do, in my own sexuality, in my own practices. So I thought to myself, "You write so that perhaps people who hadn't raped anybody yet might be discouraged, people who had might be informed, people who have not been raped might understand something, and people who have been raped might forgive themselves."

That's why I wrote about the rape.

Everything counts . . . everything counts, everything, all the time. I am always amazed to see photographs of myself. I always look like I'm about to cry, and I have a reason for it (Braxton 12–13).

3

I Know Why the Caged Bird Sings

Joanne Braxton, Angelou's critic and friend, gives readers a succinct yet apt metaphor for the writer's autobiographical method. She compares what she calls Angelou's "discontinuous narrative form" to the creation of a memory jar, "a monument honoring a deceased loved one." Somewhat like making a quilt (using fragments of clothing or other material that in themselves evoke memories), a memory jar consists of layers, with small objects embedded within one layer or another, all surrounded by a plaster that holds the design in place.

In contrast to an autobiography that works toward political argument, or one that narrates the achievement of a single subject, Maya Angelou's serial autobiographies, according to Braxton, create stories of both her culture and what Braxton terms "the Maya-myth" (Braxton 20). One of the reasons critics have been so attracted by Angelou's accomplishment in autobiography is the versatility—and the unusualness—of her method. Critic Francoise Lionnet points out early that Angelou "intertwines in a harmonious way her individual experiences with the collective social history of African Americans." In *I Know Why the Caged Bird Sings*, such reciprocity reveals "the dignity and mutual support that rural blacks extended to one another during the depression" (Lionnet 19). Placing Angelou's first memoir in the history of autobiography by African American women, historian Estelle Jelinek notes that after the Civil Rights decade, the 1960s, women autobiographers became "more outspoken about their pride in their race and in themselves as women." Jelinek pairs Angelou with Anne Moody in this respect, but she also privileges the quality of Angelou's *Caged Bird* because of its author's "poetic" temperament (Jelinek 149). In Angelou's hands, the language of the narrative became much more than an identifiable character's voice, just as it conveyed more than a factual personal chronology.

Whether a critic was male or female, white or African American, the unique autobiographies of, first, Gertrude Stein (her *Autobiography of Alice B. Toklas* published in the mid-1930s) and then Angelou's *I Know Why the Caged Bird Sings*, 1970, became important and illustrative texts; neither conformed to the outline of the expected contemporary autobiography. In Stein's case, the book was "about" Stein's relationship with Toklas; the book, however, contains comparatively little information about Toklas, even though the title honors her. In Angelou's case, the focus was on her culture—her relatives and their circumstances in the small, segregated Arkansas town, and then in urban areas where religion played a smaller part. The "character" of herself as the young Marguerite Johnson was intended to be only one figure among many others. The writers' power in creating unusual effects, some of them comic, and in finding a wide readership to praise those effects, links the roles of these two twentieth-century women autobiographers.

Braxton writes her full description of the *memory jar* as she is discussing Angelou's first five memoirs; she uses the layering effect visible in the first book to create a panorama that draws together all the autobiographies:

Like the multiple surfaces overlapping the brown glass of the memory jar, Angelou's five narratives build one upon the other, occasionally overlapping the poetry and autobiographical essays. For the writer, one of the unique advantages of the 'layered' form of the accretive narrative is that it allows other voices to speak and more than one story to be told. Accretive forms occur naturally in the folk discourse of oral cultures; if one speaker lays down the thread of a well-known narrative, another might pick it up. In Angelou's larger narrative, the emerging Mayas carry the story, engaging in a call and response both with the imagined reader and with earlier selves, sometimes within the same text (Braxton 20).

These comments parallel remarks Angelou herself frequently made—that she was consistently drawing on the practices of the African American church (the call-and-response, the multiple narratives occurring as chants or choruses), just as she was trying to create the effect of oral storytelling.

She spoke to this wide-ranging point in her *Paris Review* interview, that the language of the Bible buttressed her, that she often read aloud from the Bible, savoring its sounds. She also said, "I loved the black American minister. I loved the melody of the voice and imagery, so rich and almost impossible. The minister in my church in Arkansas, when I was very young, would use phrases such as, God stepped out, the sun over his right shoulder, the moon nestling in the palm of his hand. I mean I just loved it, and I loved the black poets, and I loved Shakespeare, and Edgar Allan Poe,—I liked Matthew Arnold a lot— still do. Being mute for a number of years, I read and memorized, and all those people have had tremendous influence."

Angelou spoke often about the way she selects her language, linking her choices in words with the ultimate purpose of autobiography, or of self-writing:

[W]hen I'm writing, I'm trying to find out who I am, who we are, what we're capable of, how we feel, how we lose and stand up, and go on from darkness into darkness. I'm trying for that. But I'm also trying for the language. I'm trying to see how it can really sound. I really love language. I love it for what it does for us, how it allows us to explain the pain and the glory, the nuances and the delicacies of our existence. And then it allows us to laugh, allows us to show wit. Real wit is shown in language. We need language (Paris 248).

While Maya Angelou here made less of the fact that she was writing as an African American woman, her race was perhaps the most dominant consideration in her life as writer. Whenever she spoke of the power of language, whenever she emphasized its orality (and her constant privileging of a writer's trying to re-create the oral), she was taking her readers into the realm of African American (and sometimes African) speech. As she answered another of Plimpton's questions, when he asked what necessities were most important to the writer, "*Ears. Ears.* To hear the language. But there's no one piece of equipment that is most necessary. Courage, first" (Paris 255).

Angelou would have agreed with Robert Stepto, one of the foremost observers of African American literature, when he stated that African American literature is marked by the inclusion of the oral. He further described that one strand in the national literature is "storytelling about storytelling," which gives readers a new form: "storytelling has developed its own store of artistic conventions. They are 'artistic' conventions, not strictly 'literary' ones, chiefly because they have their origins in both oral and written art" (Stepto 213). Most important in Stepto's prolegomenon is his recognition that written language by African Americans more than likely will involve mainstream culture, white culture. He further says that: "The basic written tale is fundamentally a framed tale in which either the framed or framing narrative depicts a black storyteller's white listener socially and morally maturing into competency. In thus presenting a very particular reader in the text, the basic written tale squarely addresses the issue of its probable audience while raising an issue for some or most of its readers regarding the extent to which they can or will identify; with the text's 'reader' while pursuing (if not always completing) their own act of reading" (Stepto 207). Given that Angelou's *I Know Why the Caged Bird Sings* has throughout its history met opposition, even banning, because of its sexual frankness as well as its depictions of strident racism and persecution, Stepto's aesthetic suggested here goes some way to explain the wide differences in the book's reception.

George Kent, premier African American critic, placed *I Know Why the Caged Bird Sings* into its accurate fold within African American literature. It "fits importantly into the varied ranges of black autobiography, especially in its dominant strain, which he defines as 'a journey through chaos.'" He speaks also to the role of the so-called American dream in the African American imagination: "The Black must believe in the American Dream or destroy much that is of value within him. The optimism of such books can be seen as embracing the after-beat of rhythms picked up from those established by the abolitionist perspective in slave narratives. As weapons in the struggle, the narratives absorbed the tenets of Christianity, the Ideals of the Enlightenment and of the American Constitution. Things were terrible, but the Great Day would come when the ideals were actualized." For Angelou, her way out of the chaos that blurred the promise of American life lay in her characters, what Kent calls "her special stance toward the self, the community, and the universe, and by a form exploiting the full measure of imagination necessary to acknowledge both beauty and absurdity" (Kent 19–20).

In this first autobiography, Kent notes that Angelou's characters function in two ways: "as mirrors of both the vigor and the unsteadiness of childhood innocence, and imagination, and as nearly independent vibrations of the spirit of black life" (Kent 15). He also charts the important characters of *Caged Bird* as stemming from two main strands of African American life: the character of Momma Henderson represents "the religious tradition," whereas that of Vivian Baxter draws from the "blues-street tradition." Encompassing the fluidity of the African and African American culture, the presence of the two women helps Angelou control the narrative as she alternates between Stamps, Arkansas, and St. Louis, Missouri, followed by San Francisco. Kent says, "Grandmother's religion gives her power to order her being, that of the children, and usually the immediate space surrounding her. The spirit of the religion combined with simple, traditional maxims shapes the course of existence and the rituals of facing up to something called decency . . . In this world, children cannot be impudent; they must respect religious piety; they need to obey" (Kent 20–1).

Much as Marguerite and Bailey may love Vivian Baxter, their mother represents instability—since she sends them away from her several times. Even though traveling alone by train, a note attached to their clothing, was *not* rare for African American children, in *I Know Why the Caged Bird Sings* Angelou makes it seem scandalous—probably because the Marguerite character was so little, and obviously so afraid to travel alone, with only Bailey, all that distance. Being sent away from their mother is, narratively, given nearly as much space as the child's rape. Bailey's running away from Arkansas to search for his mother elsewhere constitutes the only bad behavior of his young life. Creating a tapestry of the children's emotional life, rather than their chronological life, is one of the unusual strategies Angelou incorporates. According to biographical theorist Sven Birkerts, "Memoirs are neither open ended nor provisional . . . they present not the line of the life but the life remembered." And, expanding that idea, he notes that the memoirist is after "the story or stories that have given that life its internal shape" (Birkerts 53).

Some critics have discussed the alternation of places as Angelou tells her story—Valerie Baisnee not only counts pages devoted to each location but describes the alternation in nongeographical ways ("light and dark scenes, sadness and happiness"). She focuses on the point that Angelou does not tell this story chronologically (Baisnee 63, 66). The author instead creates an emotional construct, so that Marguerite's feelings of abandonment on the train parallel her physical destruction as she is being pursued—at first gently—and finally raped. Bailey's feelings of abandonment may be less explicit, but his running away from Stamps speaks volumes.

Carefully disguised in layers of narrative, the rape of the character of little Marguerite takes control as the core of the autobiography. *I Know Why the Caged Bird Sings*, however, begins innocuously. When the daughter tries to recite at the Stamps black church, seeing herself as a pretty white child, dressed in a fancy purple taffeta dress, the imaginary scene turns to disaster: Marguerite challenges the audience ("what you looking at me for?") and then, running out of the building, pees her pants. From beauty—and whiteness—to shame, Angelou sets up the mockery that the child as outsider, as only *grandchild* rather than child, will come to know well. Sent away from St. Louis by train, Bailey and Marguerite will spend most of their youth in Stamps, Arkansas, and even though Angelou reminds the reader of the importance of place, events do not consistently bear out that importance. "All of childhood's unanswered questions must finally be passed back to the town and answered there" (*Caged* 15).

Marguerite and Bailey at work in the store; Marguerite and Bailey reciting from James Weldon Johnson's "The Creation" rather than their beloved Shakespeare (Momma Henderson allows no white writers in their ken); Marguerite and Bailey knowing that cleanliness, even

on cold mornings, remains next to the all-important Godliness—
these distinct scenes lead to the most comic section of the memoir,
the Reverend Howard Thomas's sharing the Sunday meal with the
Henderson family, and Bailey's mockery of the preacher.

The idyll that is life in Stamps, Arkansas, darkens when their father
Bailey appears, and decides they are old enough to travel with him
to their mother's. Angelou opens this chapter, after their arrival,
with Marguerite saying "I had decided that St. Louis was a foreign
country." Sixty pages into the memoir, the oddly assorted lifestyles of
Vivian Baxter and her boyfriend, the older Mr. Freeman, take center
stage, cushioned by the dramatically powerful Grandmother Baxter
and her sons. Marguerite and Bailey attend the Toussaint L'Ouverture
Grammar School; Bailey calls Vivian "Mother Dear," shortened to
"M'Dear" but filled, nevertheless, with longing.

Only a little over ten pages will be devoted to the lustful advances
of Mr. Freeman, but the deft seduction—even as it culminates in
the actual violation of rape—is described in all its jarring detail.
The reader comes into this sequence unaware; events unfold
starkly. Then Marguerite is raped. Then comes the aftermath of
Marguerite's confession to Bailey, Mr. Freeman's arrest, Marguerite's
hospitalization, the courtroom trial and conviction, and then—a
few hours before he begins his jail sentence of a year and a day—the
discovery of Freeman's body, the man assumed to have been kicked
to death.

Abruptly, Bailey and Marguerite are sent back to Stamps (Angelou
refers to this as "our retreat from St. Louis"). The threnody of the
guardedly pastoral life resumes. Angelou muses, "Weekdays revolved
on a sameness wheel" (*Caged* 93). Marguerite works, unsatisfactorily,
for Mrs. Viola Cullinan (a white woman who would not bother to
learn her name). She describes the effectiveness, and the comedy, of
a large-scale revival meeting; she chronicles the hysteria of the Joe

Louis fight ("Champion of the world. A Black boy," *Caged* 114). She includes the typical summer picnic and fish fry, and then segues into a longer section about Bailey's own processes of seduction and his finally meeting his match with the older, more mature Joyce. The Stamps section draws to a conclusion with the ritual of Sister Florida's funeral, and the ghostly visits that are its aftermath. Angelou observes, "Naturally, I believed in hants and ghosts and 'thangs.' Having been raised by a super-religious Southern Negro grandmother, it would have been abnormal had I not been superstitious" (*Caged* 140).

The final two episodes illustrate Angelou's alternation in mood: first comes Marguerite's graduation from the Lafayette County Training School, complete with luxury and pomp, as well as racial insult from the white speakers; that scene is followed with Annie Henderson's meek, servile behavior when she takes Marguerite to the white dentist. Even though the man has borrowed money from her grandmother, he pridefully declares that he will not put his hands into a black person's mouth. Annie does not object, but Marguerite is violently offended.

In this pastiche of scenes and behaviors, Angelou gives the reader cause to interrogate the issue of guilt. Bailey apparently feels no guilt for the sex play he indulges in during adolescence. Yet Marguerite is torn by the guilt, along with the shame, she feels because she had enjoyed some of Mr. Freeman's foreplay. She adopted voluntary mutism because she was sure that her testimony had caused both his conviction and his death. She could never erase the memory of what her voice, her words, had done. To have been herself a spectacle, she knew, was unforgivable.

Marguerite wonders about this business of being a role model, of finding someone she might use to show her correct behaviors. She thinks about Momma Henderson: "Knowing Momma, I knew that I never knew Momma. Her African-bush secretiveness and suspiciousness had been compounded by slavery and confirmed by centuries of promises made, and promises broken. We have a saying among Black Americans which describes Momma's caution, 'If you ask a Negro where he's been, he'll tell you where he's going'" (*Caged* 164). Difficult as Annie Henderson's behavior is to read, she soon announces that she is making a trip to California with Bailey and Marguerite, because she is old and Uncle Willie, crippled. What the reader understands from this moving scene is that Bailey is too often frightened by other boys when he ventures into the white parts of town; and that, as in the scene of the discovered dead body, he cannot quell his eagerness to protest, to speak against unfairness. She takes the children, rents an apartment and lives with them for six months, allowing Vivian Baxter to make plans to move them into her house. It is a brusque but amazing act.

Although the late scenes of Bailey's and Marguerite's life in California are interesting in a different way (and they are recounted comparatively quickly), the heart of *I Know Why the Caged Bird Sings* must be located in Stamps, Arkansas, with Annie Henderson as its central character. The undeniable core event remains Marguerite's rape and her years of guilty silence while she lives as a mute. Whether or not Maya Angelou was attempting to write a therapeutically sound treatise, she wrote a child's story in this first autobiography that gave readers a quantity of wisdom about pain and trauma.

While today's readers may think of "trauma" in connection with the ravages of war, Kali Tal defines the state of trauma more inclusively. "An individual is traumatized by a life-threatening event that displaces his or her preconceived notions about the world. Trauma is enacted in a liminal state, outside of the bounds of 'normal' human experience, and the subject is radically ungrounded" (Tal 15). Recovery is often unpredictable. "Because the theory of a literature of trauma is based on the reintegrative process—a series of discrete events that occur over a period of time—we can reasonably assume that a chronological approach would provide the clearest picture of this development. Shifts in theme, voice and subject can then be plotted along a time line . . . [But] this is no simple project . . . since there are several separate chronologies that must be maintained. Retellings appear at different stages, and it is essential to consider each retelling as a part of the larger process of revision" (Tal 18). Psychologist Judith Herman points out that contact with "a single, caring, comforting person may be a lifeline . . . The reward of mourning is realized as the survivor sheds her [his] stigmatized identity" (Herman 133, 194).

Readers might then consider how abruptly the young Marguerite is taken out of her mother's home and returned to Stamps, with the somewhat undemonstrative Annie Henderson as her primary caregiver. Whereas Annie, Uncle Willie, and Bailey supplied unquestioning love, the small Arkansas town was not a sophisticated place; Angelou evidently worked through the combination of trauma and guilt by enforcing her schema of intense reading and memorizing, writing songs, and living in her self-imposed silence. Tal calls this recovery finding a route into "mythologization," so that the traumatic event is reduced "to a set of standardizing narratives, which become the 'story' of the trauma." The event then becomes "a contained and predictable narrative" (Tal 6).

Suzette A. Henke points out that Angelou has achieved this containment in her description in *I Know Why the Caged Bird Sings*. "Angelou's adult narrative voice recounts the experience of rape in a controlled style that is taut, laconic, and deliberately restrained by biblical allusion. She articulates the trauma in carefully modulated testimonial tones that compensate psychologically for the horror of the child's excruciating pain" (Henke 111). This critic emphasizes that part of the child's pain results from the rapist's threat to kill her beloved brother, his means of keeping his victim quiet. And Henke also pairs what Marguerite fears—the loss of her mother's love—with her personal physical violation. Her rapist, in fact, is her mother's lover; she has frequently seen Vivian Baxter sitting on the man's lap. When Mr. Freeman pulled the child into that same lap, as he did in the early stages of his molesting her, she read that act as a sign that he "liked" her in the same familiar way he "liked" her mother.

Henke quotes Angelou's words from *Caged Bird*: "What he did to me, and what I allowed, must have been very bad if already God let me hurt so much" (*Caged* 68). But the critic continues, that Marguerite is here "accusing herself of tacit complicity." After all, says Henke, "the child's only guide to sexuality is the New Testament"; she worries that *she* will be "stoned to death as an adulterous sinner" (Henke 111–12). She also knows that turning to Annie Henderson will bring no comfort, since her grandmother's devotion to God and His word circumscribes and directs her very life.

It is Henke who also brings the reader's attention to the fact that when Marguerite decides she needs to learn about sex, and asks the neighbor boy to have sex with her, she is taking control of her body which—in her sight—is *still* the body of a victim. In Henke's words, why does she think she needs to experience sex? Is this act masking "the etiology of psychosomantic vulnerability, a syndrome that gives way to masochistic revictimization. In the wake of post-traumatic stress disorder, the rape victim continues to suffer such low self-esteem that she unwittingly reduces her body to a specular object, an 'other' from which she feels coolly detached" (Henke 115).

To see *I Know Why the Caged Bird Sings* as a testimonial to a young daughter's rape, violated by a family friend, changes the dynamic of Angelou's apparent interest in African American communities, in family relationships, in the power of religious belief, and in children's joyous educations into books and learning, reading and writing. Joanne Braxton praises Angelou's conclusion to the memoir (calling it "comic and triumphant") because as Marguerite cares for her newly born son, she speaks in a convincing language comprised of "sass, invective, impertinence, and ritual invocation," language that enables her to "defend herself physically and psychologically" (Braxton 205–06).

Years later, George Plimpton complimented Angelou on the structure of the first several books of the autobiography in series. He said that "line by line" *Caged Bird* leads directly into the second volume, *Gather Together in My Name* (Paris 242). Yet except for the existence of Angelou's baby son, the two books are quite dissimilar: there is very little mention of Annie Henderson or Uncle Willie or Stamps (the only glimpse of this location and these people is in the scene when Annie makes Marguerite take her son and leave town); there is little mention of Vivian Baxter, even though most of the memoir is set in California; there is almost no mention of Bailey.

Maya Angelou receiving an honorary doctor of letters degree from Northeastern University. During her career, after the publication of her first book of autobiography, I Know Why the Caged Bird Sings, *Angelou was so honored by nearly fifty universities in the United States and abroad.*

What exists in *Gather Together in My Name* is a sometimes repetitious journey through sexual experiences as the Marguerite character pretends to know more than she does, somehow borrowing from the active sexual life she has watched her vivacious mother lead. Poverty, ingenuity, and her apparently deep love for her child drives the young character Marguerite through month after month of sparse living in single rooms. Published in 1974, this is the least written about volume of Angelou's autobiography.

4

Gather Together in My Name

Maya Angelou has frequently told the story of writer James Baldwin's taking her to dinner with Jules and Judy Feiffer. All three are lavish, energetic story tellers, and Maya, to get any of her own stories told, interrupts them candidly. She tells Plimpton, "I had to fight for the right to play it good. I had to insert myself to tell some stories too" (Paris 243). Judy Feiffer was so impressed with Angelou's stories that she later phoned Robert Loomis, an editor at Random House, and urged him to ask for a memoir from the tall African American woman, best known at the time as a singer and dancer (and a friend of James Baldwin's).

Angelou was not interested in writing any kind of memoir, even for Random House. She could see a promising future in writing for film and television; her occasional performance-oriented work was keeping her afloat financially. After several phone sessions, Loomis evidently talked with Baldwin about some more effective way to persuade Angelou. Because he knew that Maya was highly competitive, Baldwin urged Loomis (or so Angelou later guessed) to pretend to give up gracefully, to explain to her that writing a good "literary" autobiography was so difficult that most experienced writers would not take on such projects. Loomis was, accordingly, condescending to Angelou, and she recognized that attitude. So, as Baldwin had planned, she accepted the challenge. (And Loomis remained her editor from 1967 until the present.) (Paris 244).

Taking on the challenge to craft a good "literary" autobiography, Angelou became a member of the new and impressive Harlem Writers' Guild, to which Baldwin himself already belonged, as did John Henrik Clark, Alice Childress, Julian Mayfield, Ossie Davis, Lonnie Elder III, Sarah Wright, Rosa Guy, Paule Marshall and particularly John O. Killens, whose encouragement—and friendship—Angelou mentions in the dedication to *I Know Why the Caged Bird Sings*. (Besides Baldwin, the greatness of whose writing is unquestioned, Killens grew to be a truly fine novelist, known for his cultural acumen, his sharp satires, and his style.) By the time of *Gather Together in My Name* three years later, Angelou uses as dedication for that second autobiography her "blood brother, Bailey Johnson, and to the other *real* brothers who encouraged me to be bodacious enough to invent my own life daily." Angelou (now the experienced writer) chooses to use the slang "bodacious" without apology, and she then lists Baldwin and Killens as well as Julian Mayfield, Max Roach, Leo Maitland, and two Africans who were her friends—the poet Kwest Brew and the man people assumed was, for a time, her spouse, Vusumzi Make, among others.

As Angelou will narrate in the coming volumes of her autobiography, from *Singin' and Swingin' and Gettin' Merry Like Christmas* through *A Song Flung Up to Heaven*, after her son is born, she exists on truly menial jobs and then—having moved to New York—she marries a Greek suitor, Tosh Angelos (taking his name and changing it slightly). Then she begins her career as singer, song writer, dancer, and performer—finally taking a role in the American opera *Porgy and Bess* and touring twenty-two countries (hating the fact that Guy is being cared for by her mother, Vivian Baxter). She then cuts short her role and returns for Guy, moving to New York where she teaches dance and becomes more active in the Harlem Writers' Group, takes a role in the Off-Broadway production of *The Blacks*, and replaces Bayard Rustin as northern coordinator of Martin Luther King, Jr.'s Southern Christian Leadership Conference. She meets the African leader Vusumzi Make who proposes to her and then takes her and Guy to Egypt, Ghana, and other countries on the continent. Guy is eventually educated at University of Ghana. She works in journalism and acts in *Mother Courage* and other plays. Angelou meets Malcolm X, returns to New York and is saddened by his assassination, as she is later when Martin Luther King, Jr. is murdered. This brief summary is not intended to anticipate a reader's interest in the way Angelou will choose to write her autobiographical narratives, but for readers who are less familiar with this decade of Angelou's life, some of their questions may need to be answered.

Maya Angelou has taken her professional name—which is her legal name as well—from two men who have loved her. The surname of her first husband (the marriage to whom lasted three years) is coupled with the form of her Christian name used by her beloved brother, Bailey. *Marguerite*, in his child's speech, becomes *Ritzi* or *Mar* or *My*, and then forms itself into the name *Maya*. Considered mysterious and exotic when Angelou began singing professionally, the name was a cognomen of love.

Comparatively famous in 1970 after the publication of *I Know Why the Caged Bird Sings*, that first memoir followed the next year by her initial poem collection, *Just Give Me a Cool Drink of Water 'Fore I Diiie*—a book nominated for the Pulitzer Prize in Poetry, Angelou leads in this second autobiography with a rarely disguised tone of resentment. To write about these years, she immerses herself in the hard period of earning a living (with no training to do so), and indirectly illustrates what Kali Tal and other psychologists claim is latent anger at her earlier victimization. (Tal explains, "Bearing witness is an aggressive act. It is born out of a refusal to bow to outside pressure to revise or to repress experience, a decision to embrace conflict rather than conformity, to endure a lifetime of anger and pain rather than to submit to the seductive pull of revision and repression. Its goal is change . . . If survivors retain control over the interpretation of their trauma, they can sometimes force a shift in the social and political structure" [Tal 7].) With aggression, however, comes change—sometimes defiant change. Judith Herman speaks to the long-term effects of any trauma, an event which may well "shatter the construction of the self that is formed and sustained in relation to others" and, ultimately, "cast the victim into a state of existential crisis" (Herman 51).

Gather Together in My Name is the single book of Angelou's memoirs that shows her, several times, in crisis. It has an assertive, almost male flavor. It begins with a description of a bring-your-own-bottle party, celebrating the end of World War II. In Angelou's words—flaunting an absence of "political correctness"—"Hadn't we all joined together to kick the hell out of *der Gruber*, and that fat Italian, and put that little rice-eating Tojo in his place?" (*Gather* 227). As Angelou describes the civilian lives awaiting the black men who had fought this war, bitterness takes over:

Two months after V-Day, war plants began to shut down, to cut back, to lay off employees. Some workers were offered tickets back to their Southern homes. Back to the mules they had left tied to the tree on ole Mistah Doo Hickup farm. No good. Their expanded understanding could never again be accordioned into these narrow confines. They were free or at least nearer to freedom than ever before and they would not go back.

Those military heroes of a few months earlier, who were discharged from the Army in the city which knows how, began to be seen hanging on the ghetto corners like forgotten laundry left on a backyard fence. Their once starched khaki uniforms were gradually bastardized . . . The shoes remained. Only the shoes. The Army had made those shoes to last. And dammit, they did.

Thus we lived through a major war. The question in the ghettos was, Can we make it through a minor peace? (*Gather* 228–9).

Angelou quickly interjects her personal note: "I was seventeen, very old, embarrassingly young, with a son of two months, and I still lived with my mother and stepfather" (Ibid.).

The surroundings described in this second autobiography are not pastoral. As critic Selwyn Cudjoe pointed out, *Gather Together* reveals "a more selective vision of Afro-American life . . . the *declassed* elements of the society." He finds it hard to identify with the Marguerite character as she drifts through this period, and he objects to what he calls the book's "lack of moral weight and ethical center" (Cudjoe 17–19). For *New York Times Book Review* critic Annie Gottleib, *Gather Together* is a kind of continuation of *I Know Why the Caged Bird Sings* (a stance taken by many reviewers). She also, however, recognizes the harsh tone, commenting on the autobiographer's voice of "quiet pride, a painful candor and a clean anger" (Gottleib 16). She sees that Angelou's "soft mother talk" is laced with "salty street talk." She concludes that the author lays her own life open "without the reflex-covering gestures of melodrama or shame." For Sandi Russell, in this second memoir, Angelou is "careening from one bad involvement to another," and if her drug-addict lover had not shot up in front of her, *she* "might be silenced and we would have lost yet another beautiful black voice" (Russell 153).

No reviewer has enough space to convey the mixed tones in *Gather Together*. As Angelou's anger erupts again and again, she draws rationales from the life she is narrating. Explaining that her mother and step-father had offered to care for baby Guy while Angelou went to college, she shows her hostility toward this mother who had not cared for *her* while she was a child. Her mistrust was one piece "that made up the skin of my refusal, but the core was more painful, more solid, truer. A textured guilt was my familiar, my bedmate to whom I had turned by back. My daily companion whose hand I would not hold. The Christian teaching dinned into my ears in the small town in Arkansas would not be quieted by the big-city noise."

Angelou's answer to this offer is, "My son had no father—so what did that make me? According to the Book, bastards were not to be allowed into the congregation of the righteous. There it was. I would get a job, and a room of my own, and take my beautiful son out into the world. I thought I might even move to another town and change our names" (*Gather* 229). Defiant in her willed separation from her family, Angelou shows how precarious her anger makes her isolated and lonely situation.

The undercurrent throughout this second memoir is the religious benediction—or, rather, the lack of benediction, the *absence* of the blessing that Marguerite knows she is not going to receive. Annie Henderson could have supplied it, but Vivian Baxter (nor the Baxter family) does not have the force of belief that would allow her/them to give it. It is not only the returning soldiers who are left hanging unpleasantly in a supposedly civilized world, a world that cares little for people who struggle against social and racial prejudice.

The reader cannot escape the pain as Marguerite fails to get job after job—reading *Gather Together* is experiencing a long journey toward the teenager's failure. She has successfully applied to join the Army, when the courses she took in dance and drama at the California Labor School convince the board that she must be a Communist (the federal government does not charge her with fabrication because of her age). She then finds work as a tap-dancer with a man who trains her, until his former partner returns to California and then "Poole and Rita" leave the scene. (About her life dancing, Angelou exclaims "I loved it. I was a hungry person invited to a welcome table for the first time in her life" [*Gather* 316].) After each disappointment, she finds work as a short-order cook, roaming throughout the state and trying to continue to refuse help from Vivian Baxter.

As many critics have pointed out, Angelou's descriptions of her life with her son Guy link all the autobiographical volumes, beginning with his birth at the end of *I Know Why the Caged Bird Sings*. More pervasive is Angelou's attention to his needs for good care, for good education, and for some basic level of understanding about the child and his or her psychological needs (children collectively and in general, not only her son). One comment from her posthumously published *Rainbow in the Cloud*, for example, illustrates how wise, and how pervasive, her attention to children was:

> Of all the needs (there are none imaginary) a lonely child has, the one that must be satisfied, if there is going to be hope and a hope of wholeness, is the unshaking need for an unshakable God (*Rainbow* 6).

To personalize that abstraction a little, when her son Guy Johnson was publishing his novels during the late 1990s, he wrote a paragraph of praise to his (unnamed) mother, dedicating his mature life to her training and her example. This is that paragraph from the "Acknowledgments" page of his novel, *Standing at the Scratch Line*:

> To my mother, the lady with seven-league boots, you who have taught me there is no end to learning, to growing, to reaching higher, to preserving the right path, and perhaps greater, that all pursuits are lost if there is no love, no investment in others. I continue to emulate you. I continue to say your ideas are mine. I want to be like you: an artist in stride, moving with direction, purpose, and voice (*Standing* vii).

Here is one example of Angelou's consistent praise for her son, this in an earlier interview, "If I have a monument in this world, it is my son. He is a joy, a sheer delight; a good human being who belongs to himself . . . It's so thrilling to be here on this tiny blob of spit and sand, reading our own meaning into the stars" (Con 203).

Throughout *Gather Together*, the Marguerite character redeems herself (from her frequent temptations for finding love, drinking, even attempting to use drugs) by insisting that Guy's safety and well-being comes first. When she believes that she will be leaving for her military training, she quits her cooking job in order "to spend more time with Guy, to record his cherubic smile and be amazed at the beauty of his coordination. He seldom cried and seemed a budding introvert, for although he never thrust himself from company, he appeared to be equally amused alone. A baby's love for his mother is probably the sweetest emotion we can savor. When my son heard my voice at the downstairs door, he'd begin to sing, and when I arrived in his view he'd fall back on his fat legs, his behind would thud to the floor and he'd laugh, his big head rocking up and down . . . I knew it would be hard to leave him. Hard on me, but harder on him, for he had no way of understanding that I was gone to prepare a place for us. I hugged his sweetness to me and squeezed my love into his pores" (*Gather* 305).

Angelou's adapting the biblical phrase here ("to prepare a place for us") brings its own sweetness to her description. *Gather Together in My Name* is, in fact, often quietly steady. But there are countless moments of violence—when Vivian Baxter knifes one of her lovers who is trying to cut her in their bedroom; when Marguerite takes Guy by train to visit the Baxter aunts and uncles and finds them, in her words, "absolutely the meanest, coldest, craziest family in the world" (*Gather* 251); when Big Mary kidnaps Guy and hides him out on her brother's farm miles away. Many other of the tempestuous scenes accrue from Marguerite's own romantic involvements. Thinking she loves Charlie, a sailor about to be discharged, only to have him return home to marry his "sweetheart" (about his absence, she writes "I was one emotional runny sore" [*Gather* 244]); finding friendship in a lesbian household, and investing some of her wages into setting women up as prostitutes for women's pleasure; more seriously, being lied to by L. D., who is happily married and thinks of Angelou as herself a good candidate for prostitution, whose services he will pimp. Even though Angelou writes in *Rainbow in the Cloud* about the *pleasures* of sex, her late teens are spent "falling in love," having sex, and eventually, briefly, practicing prostitution.

> Parents who tell their offspring that sex is an act performed only for procreation do everyone a serious disservice (*Rainbow* 6).

And as she writes in this memoir about her life after Guy has been born, "I became pleased with my body because it gave me such pleasure" (*Gather* 242).

One of the lengthier scenes in *Gather Together in My Name* is Marguerite's early experience at the "house" of prostitution. She notes in the memoir, "The women's conversations interested me more than the tricks' visits" (*Gather* 350). Accordingly, she re-creates their dialogue, replete with street and sex idioms, and lets the reader imagine the confusion the character Marguerite is feeling:

> Bea looked up at me, disdain a mist across her face. "You a cherry, ain't you?"
>
> "Yes." Lying would get me nothing.
>
> "Well, that's a thirty-second business. When you turn the first trick, you'll be a 'ho. A stone 'ho. I mean for life." She grinned sourer than a rotten lemon, but her make-up and jewelry and air of abandoned sex gave her a glint of glamour.
>
> Clara wedged in a peacemaker's tone, "Well, that won't be so bad will it? I mean you're a whore."

"Hell, yes, I'm a damn good one. I'm a mud kicker. In the streets I make more money by accident than most bitches make on purpose." She rolled her head and twisted her body. "And it's more action, too. I mean the lights and tricking all night till the sun comes up."

I wondered why she left the streets.

"I just got too hot. I was getting busted two, three times a week. So my daddy brought me down to this crib. Let the heat get off. Then I'll go back switching and bitching and getting merry like Christmas" (*Gather* 345–6).

After Marguerite (now known as "Sugar") had been working for a week, she told Bea that she "won't be doing this long." Bea replies:

"Like hell. Wait till you make a nice piece of money. Then your daddy will give you a little white girl."

"A what? What would I do with a white girl?"

She laughed a tight little laugh. "Not 'a' white girl. You don't know what 'white girl' is?"

"I don't know what you mean."

"They call cocaine 'white girl.' Some people call horse 'white girl,' too. I don't mess with heroin, though. It makes me sick. But wait till your daddy gives you some coke. 'Kiss the baby!'" Hugging herself, she coasted away for a second on her thought.

I wouldn't tell her that L.D. didn't even want me to smoke pot, but she seemed to pick the thought out of my mind.

"They won't let you smoke hemp, though. They say it makes a 'ho too frisky.' 'Hos get their heads bad and forget about tending to business.'"

(*Gather* 350–1).

The alternation of moods helps to explain Marguerite's drawing away from prostitution; when she is called home because her mother has had surgery, she sees that Bailey—now employed as a railroad porter—is ill and depressed. His beloved wife Eunice has died from pneumonia, and he has resumed the drug habit that he had earlier practiced. Angelou tries to help him, but without Eunice, he cannot shake the habit; he does, however, discover what *she* has been doing and forbids her going back to prostitution. He threatens her, and L. D., and he tells her what to say to her pimp. Because she knows he is right, Angelou obeys him. Angelou tells her reader, at that point, "I lost part of my brother forever" (*Gather* 359).

At the center of *Gather Together in My Name*, Angelou places the frightening scene of her return to Stamps, Arkansas, taking her baby with her. The home that had so nurtured her in childhood seems to have remained the same. She writes, "Values among Southern rural blacks are not quite the same as those existing elsewhere. Age has more worth than wealth, and religious piety more value than beauty.//There were no sly looks over my fatherless child. No cutting insinuations kept me shut away from the community" (*Gather* 283). Within days, however, her "uppity" manner has gotten her in trouble with the white store clerks, and we have seen that Annie Henderson has arranged for Marguerite and the baby to be driven quickly out of the area. Rather than *returning* home, Angelou had been *sent away* from home. She meditates about her loneliness to the reader:

> I had written a juicy melodrama in which I was to be the star. Pathetic, poignant, isolated. I planned to drift out of the wings, a little girl martyr. It just so happened that life took my script away and upstaged me (*Gather* 251).

The writer's role seemed to be something less than reality. For Angelou, thinking back to her teenaged years, the reality of caring for Guy, earning a living, and maintaining some semblance of "normalcy," was overwhelming. Men she thought to be her friends, if not her lovers, were nothing short of evil. There, standing tall across the street from the diner where she worked her regular shift as a short-order cook, was a music store. There, tempting her to spend any spare money she had, were the vinyl records—Dial and Columbia Blue Label. There, she found a new dimension to her education as she bought the music of "Charlie 'Bird' Parker, Max Roach, Al Haig, Bud Powell, Dizzy Gillespie, and others" (*Gather* 296).

5

Music, poetry, and being alive

"Music was my refuge," Angelou writes as she opens her third memoir, *Singin' and Swingin' and Gettin' Merry Like Christmas*. Borrowing Bea's metaphor from the prostitutes' conversation, Angelou tells her story from behind her sly smile: how exploitative will her love for music be? What will she do to follow a career in dancing, singing? She writes about seeing that she had, as a tap-dancer, "scrambled around the foot of the success ladder" (*Gather* 316). But now she was once again working as a cook, and she writes, "I could crawl into the spaces between the notes and curl my back to loneliness.//In my rented room (cooking privileges down the hall), I would play a record, then put my arms around the shoulders of the song" (*Singin'* 391).

Angelou became a song writer. In 1971 a number of her songs became poems and her first collection of poetry, titled *Just Give Me A Cool Drink of Water 'Fore I Diiie*, was nominated for the Pulitzer Prize. A wide-ranging group of poems, many were originally copyrighted by Hirt Music (Gerard W. Purcell Associates of New York); others were based on the traditions of spoken idiom and the expected lyric forms of both quatrain and modernist free verse. Inflected in some cases with the rhythms of spirituals, jazz, and the blues, Angelou's poems collectively illustrate what critic Houston Baker describes as "folklore, vernacular crafts, magical realism, jazz, other performative models" (Baker 205). Reviews of the book, rather than focusing on the styles of the poems, emphasized the poet's street language, her political anger, and her sonorous love poems; no review could adequately discuss the great diversity of Angelou's poems.

In 1972, Stephen Henderson published one of the earliest studies of African American poetry under the title *Understanding the New Black Poetry: Black Speech and Black Music as Poetic Reference.* His emphasis falls on poets' uses of "oral tradition both rural and urban." He usefully places James Weldon Johnson and Paul Laurence Dunbar in the context of "the folk sermon and the spiritual," and then shows that more contemporary poets have "deliberately" appropriated what he calls "preaching techniques" (Henderson xi). (Angelou was reciting from those bodies of poetry, almost before she was reading.) She also loved the works of Sterling Brown and Langston Hughes, the latter pair illustrating what Henderson labeled the ballad and the blues, which together create a "soul field [where] the freshness and raciness of their language ring true to their sources of inspiration." Henderson notes that white culture has consistently had trouble accepting "the blues and the universal Black energy of jazz" (ibid. xii). These are starting points for modern black poets, but these writers may also incorporate "the street experience" (both the exploration of it and the appropriation of it), "and the formulation of an aesthetic and an ideology based in part upon it" (Henderson xii–xiii).

Given that Maya Angelou had been a professional entertainer— known as a calypso performer as well as a jazz singer and a blues singer, and spending a year touring as Ruby and as a lead dancer in the Gershwin opera *Porgy and Bess*—her gravitation toward the sounds of jazz and the blues was natural. (That she had grown up hearing spirituals and church anthems, and regularly participating in religious services, gave her a wealth of experience with serious lyric and dramatic delivery.) When she later interviewed Amiri Baraka (formerly LeRoi Jones, a writer known as *the* jazz poet of contemporary aesthetics), one of her first questions to him was that he explain the source of passion in his language. He answered, as if from *her* own experience, "When we grow up around music and oratory—you know, preaching—as we all do in the African-American community, we can recognize cultural utterance as a kind of style . . . Language is a kind of historical monument." Angelou replies to him about the ordinariness of the intrinsic rhythms of language: "the universe is rhythmic: the sun rises and sets, the tides go in and out, the moons and the seasons" (Baraka 260–1).

She later asks Baraka whether he is more a "jazz" poet than a "blues" poet. His answer is, "The way I look at it, I don't think you can really deal with jazz unless you have some feeling for the blues. Without the blues, jazz is a music without a memory—it has no national identity" (Baraka 263). He then reads his poem "Folklore," which begins "We are the blues . . . ourselves, . . . our favorite color" and closes with "X," his poem to Malcolm Little, which ends (in commemoration of his—and Angelou's—great love for Malcolm X): "and from that wound . . . pours Malcolm . . . Little . . . by . . . little" (Baraka 265).

Angelou as interviewer does not abandon her own voice or character. When she asks Baraka to read, she describes a poem as being "one last sound of your heart." She asks him about his career as playwright and seemingly enjoys his praise of Langston Hughes in the theater (he calls Hughes's play *Scottsboro Limited* "one of the great verse dramas). It's a jazz verse-drama that he wrote in the 1930s, but, because it was a little too much to the left, it's been sort of 'sequestered' in space." She talks about his politics and his establishment of "Spirit House." She identifies with his background, "having been raised as an African American, having internalized those rhythms and sounds and vowels." She also identifies with his experiences as a teacher, noting that, unfortunately, some professors are what she calls "anti-truth" teachers: such teachers only "cripple" their students. Such a person "breaks the student's legs and then says, 'Now go out and run me that hundred yard dash and bring me the award'" (Baraka 264).

Critic James H. Cone calls the blues "secular spirituals" because they "confine their attention solely to the immediate and affirm the bodily expression of the black soul." Yet they have a theological significance in the sense that they are "impelled by the same search for the truth of the black experience as the spiritual" (Cone 100). The later controversies about "jazz" influenced poetry and "blues" influenced verse constituted a later stage of self-consciousness as African American poets tried to straddle that line between writing from white traditions (to show off their formal educations) and speaking in more natural, and probably raced, language.

As novelist and critic Gayl Jones describes the conflicts of being African American writers, they are walking through their literary life trying to avoid "the Catch-22 . . . trapped between proving they can write traditionally and meeting the inventive demands of modernism" (Jones 13). In her praise of Jean Toomer's story "Karintha" from *Cane*, she illustrates the way the oral and the vernacular can provide formal shape. (She extends this discussion as she explores the way Sherley Williams achieves the characterization of Bessie Smith [and Ma Rainey] in Williams's poem "Someone Sweet Angel Child." Jones's point here is the way positioning single words creates meaningful syncopation.) (Jones 38–9).

Prior to Jones's discussion, Robert Stepto and Gene Bluestein had tied poems that they saw as *blues*-influenced back to both the African American call-and-response pattern and the cumulative effects of group play: jazz never existed as a solo mode. "The will to achieve the most eloquent expression of idea-emotion through the technical mastery of instruments . . . the give-and-take, the subtle rhythms, shaping and blending of ideas, tone and imagination demanded of group improvisation. The delicate balance struck between individual personality and the group during those early jam sessions was a marvel of social organization" (Bluestein 135–6).

Robert B. Stepto early defined jazz as the premier form of American music, based as it usually is on what he calls "the immersion narrative . . . a ritualized journey into a symbolic South in which the protagonist forsake[s] highly individualized mobility in the narrative's least oppressive social structure for a pasture of relative stasis in the most oppressive environment, a *loss* that is only occasionally assuaged by the newfound balms of group identity" (Stepto 167). More recently Andrew Scheiber, a theorist who probes deeply into the differences between jazz and the blues, thinks that content may have little to do with form and sound: "one soars by getting down, and the recursive path to the future always involves a transversing of the depths of the past" (Scheiber 43). He quotes from Toni Morrison's novel *Jazz* to incorporate into his argument the useful metaphor of life as "an abused record with no choice but to repeat itself at the crack" (Scheiber 39, *Jazz* 220).

For Scheiber, the blues format "does not represent a rational or a planned world. The appropriate form of mastery in this world is not *predict and plan* but *bob and weave*, and success comes through . . . a readiness of response that understands the broken guitar string, the natural disaster, the chance juxtaposition of numbers in a lottery . . . the course of events turns for no apparent reason (and often with no apparent preparation) toward encounters with repeated paradigmatic figures or situations" (Scheiber 40–2).

Angelou creates a number of successful jazz or blues poems, such as "Black Ode" ("Your beauty is a thunder/And I am set a wandering—a wandering/Deafened/ Down twilight tin-can alleys/

And moist sounds") but she also writes in a variety of other, somewhat more conventional forms. The reader might speculate that nearly every poem in this first collection needs to be heard for its greatest effect. The measured quatrains of "They Went Home," "The Gamut," "Remembering," and "In a Time" create their own meaningful song: "Soft you day, be velvet soft," opens "The Gamut" and sets a pace that recurs in longer stanzaic poems, such as "Late October," where some of the lines consist of only one or two words ("Carefully/the leaves of autumn/ . . . roil ceaselessly in/cobweb greys and turn/to black/for comfort.")

Angelou sometimes creates the shape of an entire stanza on the basis of a single word. Two of her poems of dedication (the collection dedicated to "Amber Sam and the Zorro Man") work in this way: "A Zorro Man" uses the single word first line for each stanza:

Here

In the wombed room . . .

and "To a Man" opens "My man is/Black Golden Amber/Changing." The metamorphosis that includes the human figure going in and out of a sensual amber state concludes:

My man is Amber

Changing

Always into itself

New. Now New.

Still itself.

Still.

The poem "Sounds Like Pearls" has a similar effect, and in its restraint, closes the first half of the book.

A handful of Angelou's early poems are designed to show street life expressed in street rhythms. "Letter to an Aspiring Junkie," according to critic Sandi Russell, "speaks with the syncopated sounds of black city-dwellers." Russell, in appreciation of Angelou's poetic craft, notes her versatility—that she "ranges from the language and cadences of black street talk to jazz" (Russell 157). "Times-Square-Shoeshine-Composition," while a street poem, shouts "experimentation" to the reader, as does "Miss Scarlett, Mr. Rhett and Other Latter-Day Saints." Angelou incorporates nonverbal elements in each—"(O Sing)" and "(Intone DIXIE)" occur in the latter poem, marking the satiric assumptions the poet intends to convey, and a rhythmic "(pow pow)" occurs two and three times in each verse as the "Times-Square-Shoeshine" voice speaks pridefully. ("Letter to an Aspiring Junkie," along with "No No No No," may work the best of all these early poems for Angelou's use of street language.) The latter poem begins with the single-word line ("No") and shocks the reader midway through each stanza with a crass diction (as well as behavior) designed to be far from poetic. The first stanza opens:

No

the two-legg'd beasts

that walk like men

play stink finger in their crusty asses . . .

whereas the third creates the abused woman, "No/the cocktailed afternoons/of what can I do."

In my white layered pink world

I've let your men cram my mouth

with their black throbbing hate

and I swallowed after . . .

Every one of the many stanzas includes an unexpectedly crude image: even the praying women in church are shown "picking undigested beans/from yesterday's shit." The United States White House is also corroded by its description of "rejections/on the cold marble steps/of America's White Out-House." This is the title poem of the collection, the only one that uses "Just Give Me a Cool Drink of Water 'Fore I Diiie" as a line within the poem.

Similarly, in "Riot: 60s," the street language conveys the atmosphere of unrelieved urban poverty that causes the destructive riot. The poem winds down into harsh racist epithets. It begins:

Our

YOUR FRIEND CHARLIE pawnshop

Was a glorious blaze

but the noncommittal tone changes and the poem heads toward its conclusion:

Chuggga chugga chigga

git me one nigga

lootin' n burnin'

he won't git far

moving to depict the "national guard nervous with his shiny gun/ goose the motor quicker":

here's my nigga picka

shoot him in the belly

shoot him while he run

Leaving the poem unended—no punctuation, the spoken words seemingly a brief afterword, a hasty end to the conflagration—makes it as immediate today as it was in 1971.

Angelou's political poems are nearly all effective, and sometimes relentless. "Harlem Hopscotch," less blatant than some of her poems, ends with scathing irony: "They think I lost. I think I won." This poem follows the paired satires on "the dozens": "The Thirteens (Black)" and "The Thirteens (White)" use the same structures, but change the content so that it is race-specific. Each of the six stanzas—three five-line stanzas in each poem—ends with the voiced "The thirteens. Right On." The power of the paired poems lies in the racially appropriate descriptions, all derogatory, all based on street behavior. Morally corrupt regardless of race, the characters Angelou draws in these poems are reprehensible ("Your brother jonesed your cousin" is a line from the white person's behavior; "Your cousin's taking smack," from the black).

Another effective political poem is "The Calling of Names." Here Angelou uses street language and insult interchangeably, progressing down the "correct" names for "Negro." The poem "No No No No" attempts to describe African American history, just as "My Guilt," a shorter treatment of slavery, assassinations, and lynching, brings recognizable names into the text ("dead Vesey, Turner, Gabriel/ dead Malcolm, Marcus, Martin King"), such specificity a rarity for Angelou.

Two of the most autobiographical-seeming poems are "When I Think about Myself," a relatively long poem of seven-line stanzas, laced with irony as well as good descriptions ("Too proud to bend,/ Too poor to break" balanced with "They grow the fruit,/But eat the rind"), and the sincere-sounding love poem, "To a Husband," capped with its moving lines, "You're Africa to me/At brightest dawn." It concludes:

I sit at home and see it all

Through you.

Aligning "To a Husband" with the poems of dedication ("A Zorro Man" and "To a Man") at the beginning of the book brings the general tone of the collection into a symmetry that helps to soften the harsh politics of the second part of *Just Give Me a Cool Drink of Water 'Fore I Diiie*. (Those politics surface again in her second collection, *Oh Pray My Wings Are Gonna Fit Me Well*). It is as if the sonority of the quiet lines, often about love or about the natural world, has set a pace that observant readers work hard to maintain. The conventions of poetry, in Angelou's first book, are not broken; if she begins writing a poem in quatrains, she stays in quatrains. Whereas there is considerable experimentation within the book as a whole, changes in form and language do not destroy the voice Angelou is able to create.

Angelou's poems are diverse; many of them are blues-based, but they are in many respects *general* poems. They are poems about *subjects*. They are not doing for Maya Angelou as author what *I Know Why the Caged Bird Sings* does. They do not bring the poet into the circumstances of the reader; they remain conventional and largely abstract poems. Later, after Angelou publishes a second large collection, and then a third, her poetry becomes more distinctively personal. By the time of "Phenomenal Woman," for example, she is writing much longer, somewhat sporadic and rhythmically intricate poems: *anthems* rather than lyrics. It is these anthems to herself and to other women—perhaps all women—that capture the spirit of the self-created Maya Angelou.

6

Singin' and Swingin' and Gettin' Merry Like Christmas

Angelou's third autobiography, one of the longest books in her series, incorporated some of the darkness of *Gather Together in My Name*. Despite its festive title, *Singin' and Swingin' and Gettin' Merry Like Christmas* was not entirely preoccupied with music and the routes Angelou took to make her living through dancing and singing. In fact, the memoir begins with Marguerite's still-desperate attempts to support herself and her son.

She has found the Melrose Record Shop on Fillmore Avenue, and there—in the time between her two jobs—she "could wallow, rutting in music" (*Singin'* 391). When Louise Cox, the shop's personable white owner, opens a charge account for her, Angelou is puzzled—she races home and gets money from her "emergency" fund in order to pay off her bill. Later, Louise offers her a full-time job with reasonable pay; again Angelou is puzzled. She stifles her racial misgivings, knowing that she can stop boarding Guy at the sitter's (five nights and six days a week), and luxuriates in what she describes at the shop as "the wealth of a world of music . . . Bartok and Schoenberg . . . the vocals of Billy Eckstine, Billie Holiday, Nat Cole, Louis Jordan and Bull

Moose Jackson . . . then the giants of bebop . . . Charlie Parker and Max Roach, Dizzy Gillespie, Sarah Vaughan and Al Haig and Howard McGhee. Blues" (*Singin'* 398).

Her reluctance to take the job, however, stems from one of Angelou's pervasive suspicions—that being offered the job was charity. She thought this even though she admitted to herself that she "had found no thread of prejudice" (ibid.).

With this increased income, Angelou brings Guy home to live and pays a sitter by the hour; then she approaches her mother about their moving back into her boarding house—as paying customers— until she can rent a house for herself and her baby. As she recalls, "At home . . . life shimmered with beautiful color" (*Singin'* 391).

Tosh Angelos becomes a regular customer at the store. A Greek, a former Navy man (now working as an electrician), a college-educated person well versed in African American music, Tosh begins to court Marguerite by planning activities with her son. Again, she mistrusts his interest; it is the early 1950s and miscegenation remains illegal (it will be 1967 before the courts in *Loving v. Virginia* legalize mixed-race marriage). When Angelos off-handedly proposes to her and she tells Vivian, her mother's reply is only, "A white man? A poor white man? How can you even consider it? . . . Think ahead. What the hell is he bringing you? The contempt of his people and the distrust of your own. That's a hell of a wedding gift" (*Singin'* 413). Hundreds of years of slavery, of white mistreatment of blacks, surged through her mother's response. Angelou had admitted to herself that Tosh was thoroughly Greek (and perhaps, therefore, less "white" than he appeared). She describes his "Greek community, where even Italians were considered foreign. His contact with Blacks had been restricted to the Negro sailors on his base and the music of the bebop originators" (*Singin'* 412). Being honest with herself, she could see "no common ground."

One of the greatest differences in their backgrounds turns out to be religious beliefs, or the lack of them. Angelou arranges events in this third memoir to show Marguerite's almost perpetual search for a comforting religion—since she no longer works two jobs, she has joined several Protestant churches and has been confirmed in one, she has gone with Louise and her mother to Christian Science services, and she has also visited a Jewish rabbi who gives her a reading list. In contrast, Tosh prides himself on being an atheist. (Angelou has earlier included a significant flashback to her son's horrified reaction to a street preacher, when he wants to run far away from the sermonizing. She realizes for the first time that the Methodist church where she and Bailey spent six hours every Sunday was unknown to Guy. Marguerite recognized that her son had had no religious experiences at all, torn as she had been by her long work hours and her separation from him as he grew up with one or another babysitter.)

After their marriage, Tosh insisted that Marguerite quit her job. He also disliked most of her friends, so she and Guy are made to exist in the "cocoon" of his protection: "My life began to resemble a *Good Housekeeping* advertisement. I cooked well-balanced meals and molded fabulous jello desserts" (*Singin'* 416). A few more months and Marguerite is suffocating; she keeps a dress at a friend's and sneaks off to church services every few weeks, reveling in "the spiritual and gospels songs, sweeter than sugar. I wanted to keep my mouth full of them and the sounds of my people singing fell like sweet oil in my ears" (*Singin'* 417). Eventually Tosh takes a phone call from one of the churches and hears the caller asking for Marguerite Angelos; Marguerite, however, continues to lie. "I made no protest, gave no confession—just stood silent. And allowed a little more of my territory to be taken away" (ibid. 423).

Differences in religious belief may have been more important to Angelou, but racial differences were more visible. After a year or so of marriage, she confessed to being bothered by "the public reactions to us . . . people stared, nudged each other and frowned when we three walked in the parks or went to the movies. The distaste on their faces called me back to a history of discrimination and murders of every type. Tosh, I told myself, was Greek, not white American; therefore I needn't feel I had betrayed my race by marrying one of the enemy, nor could white Americans believe that I had so forgiven them the past that I was ready to love a member of their tribe" (*Singin'* 418). Her behavior, however, shows more guilt than reason: "I dropped my eyes when we met Negroes. I couldn't explain to all of them that my husband had not been a part of our degradation. I fought against the guilt which was slipping into my closed life as insidiously as gas escaping into a sealed room" (ibid. 419).

The marriage eventually frays, though they do not divorce for another year. Increasingly given to angry outbursts, Tosh finally admits that he is "just tired of being married," and Marguerite goes through some bar-hopping and even more religious exploration— both secretly. Almost as an afterthought, Angelou describes her sudden attack of appendicitis—and surgery—but the importance of *her* hospitalization is that while *she* is recovering, Annie Henderson, her grandmother in Arkansas, dies, and Tosh does not tell her.

Marguerite's sure route back to both religious belief and African American community is gone. The formal process of honoring the beloved mother/grandmother has been not only disrupted but simply ignored. Tosh's behavior seems to be reason enough for Marguerite to give up on this man who remains oblivious to what she had grown up considering basic human values: the disparity between what Tosh considered moral behavior and what she knew to be true morality was an immeasurable chasm. "For days my mind staggered out of balance. I reeled on a precipice of knowledge that even if I were rich enough to travel all over the world, I would never find Momma. If I were as good as God's angels and as pure as the Mother of Christ, I could never have Momma's rough slow hands pat my cheek or braid my hair" (*Singin'* 430).

A year later they divorced; Guy was angry that he had lost his father. Marguerite worked hard to rebuild the child's trust and love. The more immediate problem, for her, was to find work. Following a hunch, she auditioned for a dance job at the Garden of Allah in San Francisco's International Settlement area. Although she had neither a costume nor a routine, she *could* dance. Being hired at $75 a week, plus drink profits (six shows nightly, six nights a week) solved her most pressing problem. But there would be many others: Marguerite was the first African American ever to dance in the club. (Whereas the other dancers were strippers, she was forbidden to use strip in her routine.)

After three months, she was making much more than her weekly salary. She had learned to tell the men interested in having a drink with her that buying a bottle of champagne would give them more time together (and she would get $2 of the cost of $8 champagne). *She* had become so successful, however, that the other dancers were jealous. Finally, management had no choice but to fire her, and because she had joined the union, they had to give her two weeks notice. No first-time dancer had ever made so much money.

Luckily for Marguerite, several days later, the management and the chanteuse of the Purple Onion came to see her performance. Jorie Remus was leaving for a New York engagement; eventually Marguerite sang a calypso song ("Run, Joe" as recorded by Louis Jordan) for an audition. They hired her as Jorie's replacement. Then they all began working on her, *with* her, to develop good routines. It is in this workshopping that she is named *Maya Angelou*; it is by studying the highly professional singing and comedy of Jorie Remus that Marguerite learns the bones of holding an audience, commanding the music, and attempting to become an effective singer. It is also here that the group suggests that she does not want to be a poor Southern African American; they suggest instead Cuba, Africa, or some mixture of origins and history so she can use her Spanish. (The rationale of the Purple Onion group is that "People were tired of the moss hanging from the magnolia trees and the corn pone and the lynchings and all that old stuff." Creating a new story would also keep listeners from feeling guilty about the treatment of Southern blacks.) Angelou thinks to herself, always conscious that her voice is not great, that she would sing calypso and jazz: she would prefer *not* to "compete with Josh White, or Odetta, who I thought was the greatest singer of American Negro folk songs, and who worked nearby" (*Singin'* 461).

The Purple Onion, located near Ferlinghetti's City Lights Bookstore, the site of Beat poetry readings, attracted a clientele of some sophistication. Performing with Maya Angelou was comic Phyllis Diller, also an unlikely crowd-pleaser from the Midwest. Visibility, her striking costumes, and her singing polished and unusual songs led to more and more notice of the tall African American woman. People who moved in near-celebrity circles came to see her; often those people invited her to parties and picnics and outings on boats (to which she took Guy). As she moved into these social circles, artists asked to paint her, and film makers found her voice—her speaking voice—interesting. California in the early 1950s was entertainment capitol of America, and Angelou wondered why so many doors were opening to her, even without her using any effort to open them. (Her height and her skin color, so long disadvantages in any occupation, now fueled cultural acceptance.)

Finally, when African American chanteuse Eartha Kitt was leaving the *New Faces of 1953* revue, Angelou was asked to audition. She did. But although she was given the offer, the Purple Onion would not let her break her contract. She reluctantly turned down the Kitt role.

Another revelation in Angelou's musical training occurred the night she saw George and Ira Gershwin's *Porgy and Bess* (from the DuBose Hayward novel). "I was stunned," she wrote with great honesty. With Leontyne Price as Bess, William Warfield as Porgy, and Cab Calloway as Sportin' Life (singing "It Ain't Necessarily So"), the 60-person company of this great American opera could not have been bettered. "*Porgy and Bess* had shown me the greatest array of Negro talent I had ever seen" (*Singin'* 497). Spurred by her exuberance over such musicianship, Angelou confesses, "I began making up music for poems I had written years before and writing new songs that fit the calypso form."

One evening after her act at the Purple Onion, Angelou was surprised when the talented actress who sang "The Strawberry Song" from *Porgy and Bess* came up to her and presented her with a red rose. She returned with the woman to her table of friends, overjoyed to find they all were from the cast. Other actors came to hear her at other times. It was through her friendship with the *Porgy and Bess* cast that Angelou met, and became a voice student of the great, and supportive, Frederick Wilkerson.

As she studies, as she begins to understand what professional life entails, Angelou becomes more and more observant. Art is something to strive for, and her life experiences grow less immediately personal. She writes, repeatedly, about what she sees:

The curtain began sliding open and pastel lights illuminated the set. A group of men, downstage left, were involved in a crap game; some knelt, others mimed throwing dice. Then Ned Wright, as Robbins, threw the dice and sang "Nine to Make, Come Nine." The pure tenor line lifted and held in the air for a second, and in a rush the pageant began.

The sopranos and tenors, bassos and baritones, acted as if they were indeed the poverty-stricken Southern Negroes whose lives

revolved around the dirt road encampment of Catfish Row. They
sang and listened, then harmonized with each other's tones so
closely that the stage became a wall of music without a single
opening unfilled.

Their self-hypnotism affected the audience and overwhelmed me.
I cried for Robbin's poor widow, Serena, who sang the mournful
aria "My Man's Gone Now." Helen Thigpen, a neat little quail of
a woman, sang the role with a conviction that burdened the soul.
Irene Williams sang Bess, sassily tossing her hips as effortlessly as
she flung the notes into the music of the orchestra. Leslie Scott,
handsome and as private as an African mask, sang Porgy and in
a full, rich baritone. When the first act was over, the audience
applauded long and loudly, and I found myself drenched with
perspiration and exhausted (*Singin'* 516).

With Angelou's turn to writing about music and musical
performance, consciously reflecting the new role music played in
her post-divorce life, the very *language* of her writing changes. There
is not only joy and excitement but a more select attention to details.
In paragraph after paragraph, the author shows her command of
observation and her knowledge of music performance. Here she
describes the singers in the cast readying themselves for the act of
singing:

I had heard the announcement of "Half-hour" earlier, but none of
the women responded. Now Martha [Flowers] turned away from
the mirror and her eyes glazed, began to sing "Do re me fa sol
la ti do." I didn't know whether I was expected to say something,
then Lillian also dropped her interest in our conversation and
an unseeing look came into her eyes, she stretched her lips in a
taut, false smile and holding her teeth closed, yelped "Ye, ya, yo,
you." Barbara Ann stood and began to sway slowly from side to

side. She started to lower and raise her jaw and then sang "Wooo Wooooooo."

They took no notice of me, but I couldn't do the same with them. I had never been so close to trained singers and the reverberations shook in my ears. I left the room and walked down the corridor to find my place in the wings. Sounds came out of each door I passed. One baritone roared like a wounded moose, another wailed like a freight train on a stormy night. The tenors yelped in high screeches. There were whines and growls and the siren of an engine on its way to a four-alarm fire. Grunts overlapped the high-pitched "ha ha ho ho's" and the total cacophony tickled me . . . These exquisite singers who would soon stand on the stage delivering the most lovely and liquid tones had first to creak like rusty scissors and wail like banshees (*Singin'* 515).

Angelou's writing as re-creation of her experiences on many levels—learning to be a singer, a performer, one who draws from the appreciation of the audience and takes risks from that appreciation—convinces the reader: the character Marguerite could not sight-read music, and her pitch was sometimes faulty. But she grew musically because she immersed herself in the people who constituted this theatrical world. She studied rehearsals, she chose to be a part of an excellent chorus and opera, and she learned from everything she experienced.

A few days before her Purple Onion contract ended, Saint Subber, the director of the new Broadway play *House of Flowers*, asked Angelou to audition for the role opposite the lead, which would be played by Pearl Bailey. Simultaneously, because the opera traveling group was ready to head to Europe, she was asked to try out for lead dancer (and the role of Ruby) in *Porgy and Bess*. She received both offers; she chose *Porgy and Bess*. In two days she traveled to Montreal, Canada, where the group was performing; she studied and rehearsed for the opening in Italy the following week. Within three days of the offers, she was abroad. (Because the United States State Department was the *Porgy and Bess* tour sponsor, that agency provided her a passport.)

Angelou writes much of this volume at the beautiful, serene, Rockefeller Study Center in Bellagio, Italy. She later describes the lush setting: "a large mansion snuggled into the hills above Bellagio. Fifteen artists at a time from around the world were invited to the enclave. Selected artists with companions had to make their way to Milan airport, and then magically they were swept up by tender arms and placed in a lap of luxury that few popular movie stars or rich corporate chiefs even dreamed existed" (*Hallelujah* 113). That Angelou was invited as a participant speaks to the prominence of her early writing; she has published only two autobiographies and one collection of poetry. Yet her work has already awakened the literary world to this matter-of-fact voice who is willing to share with readers the vicissitudes of a child's life in the poverty of the segregated American South—as well as the sometimes desperate searches for both money and love of the inexperienced young mother, living as a single parent and trying to provide for her young son. She writes in *Singin' and Swingin'* that "The tough texture of poverty in my life had been more real than sand wedged between my teeth" (18). In appreciation for her term at the Italian study center, she dedicates this third memoir to Bellagio.

One of the most pervasive questions critics and interviewers ask Angelou is how she chooses which events to include, and foreground, in each of her autobiographies. While in the case of *Singin' and Swingin' and Gettin' Merry Like Christmas*, most of the narrative will focus on Angelou's stage experiences, but still within the twenty-two countries of the *Porgy and Bess* tour, as well as numerous incidents of event and humor from the clubs, the author has to choose *what* to

Maya Angelou as a scholar and fellow at Bellagio Study Center, Bellagio, Italy, probably around 1974. Photo by Bellagio staff. Used with permission.

describe. As Angelou explained in a 1987 interview, "In truth, when I set out to write, I choose some sort of 'every-human being' emotion, themes. So I will choose generosity, meanness of spirit, romantic love, loss of love, families and love, ambition, greed, hate. And then I will set myself back in that time and try to see what incidents contained that particular theme. I may find seven. Some of them are too dramatic, I can't write them without being melodramatic, you understand, so I say *no, I won't write that one*. Some are too weak. But I find one and I think, aha, *this* one. Now let me enchant myself back to that day or that month, or those months, so I can remember everything about that one incident. In that way the work is episodic, you see, but if I'm lucky and work hard it should flow so that it looks like just a story being told" (Readings 33).

Several years later, she added, "I try to remember times in my life, incidents in which there was the dominating theme of cruelty, or

kindness, or generosity, or envy, or happiness, glee . . . perhaps four
incidents in the period I'm going to write about. Then I select one that
lends itself best to my device and that I can write as drama without
falling into melodrama" (Paris 244).

Mentioning "glee," as Angelou does here in this comment, brings
the reader back to a genuine appreciation for the exuberance she
creates in her descriptions of the *Porgy and Bess* European tour.
Even as New York director Saint Subber remarked with surprise
that Angelou turned down a Broadway play in order to go on tour
with a second-rate cast, her love for the Gershwin music, filled as it
was with blues and jazz and folk, drew her to choose the harder life.
Just as her solo dance in *Porgy and Bess* was not choreographed, so
the fluidity of the opera music struck resonance in Angelou's heart.
Critic Houston Baker describes the blues as music with "liberating
rhythms, re-inscribing (or replacing) Angelou's socialized sense of
placelessness with American literary prominence" (Baker 135). Poet
and dramatist Amiri Baraka also links her early autobiographies with
creating "the blues. It is young Maya's blues." He continues, "though
certain techniques and verses came to be standardized among blues
singers, the singing itself remained as arbitrary and personal as the
shout . . . The music remained that personal because it began with
the performers themselves, and not with formalized notions of how
it was to be performed" (Baraka 67). With cutting detail, Baraka
expands his concept of the practice of what he calls "blueing" the
notes. He refers to a technique based on "sliding and slurring effects
in Afro-American music, the basic 'aberrant' quality of a blues scale"
(Baraka 25). Critic Cherron Barnwell notes that: "The quoted lines
from song or poetry patterned into blues forms are textual signs in
Angelou's blues aesthetics" (Barnwell 136).

As critics responded to Angelou's personal role as chanteuse, the
analogies between her voiced narratives in the autobiographies and

musical blues as a form increased. Dolly McPherson, a close personal friend and early substantive critic of Angelou's work, emphasizes the ties. McPherson calls Angelou's memoirs "blues autobiography," and refers to Angelou as a "blues autobiographer." She discusses that, "One critic suggests that blues autobiographers depend, from the beginning of their works, upon some particular aspect of their character to act as a lens through which the confusion of experience can be perceived and the integrity of personality achieved" (McPherson 18). She concludes, "The process of discovering meaning in the blues autobiography is closely associated with the process of discovering personal consciousness" (ibid. 19).

McPherson also draws from critic Elizabeth Schultz's essay, "To Be Black and Blue," claiming that blues autobiography "expands the solo: the voice of the single individual singer retains the tone of the tribe. The blues autobiographer, by articulating the narrator's experiences—by lovingly absorbing these experiences in the narrator's consciousness—makes them comprehensible to the autobiographer and to those who listen" (McPherson 165, note 16).

When this critic deals specifically with *I Know Why the Caged Bird Sings*, she discusses what she sees as a theme of "ascension": "returning and leaving (motion) form a pattern . . . a making of peace with her past so that, in retrospect, . . . it is neither a sentimental haven nor a cage." McPherson continues, "What characterizes Angelou's circuitous journey—her movement toward self-knowledge—is *mutability*, emerging from and strengthened by her repeated movement, reorientation, and assimilation" (McPherson, 20). Critic Lean'tin Bracks echoes this sentiment, noting that "the importance of folktales, song, rituals, stories and family lore for reclaiming a silenced history" is crucial. Otherwise "history" as people understand comes almost exclusively "from mainstream (white) written history" (Bracks 10).

Glee, exuberance, even some humor mark the two-thirds of
Singin' and Swingin' that take readers into the wealth of Angelou's
graphic descriptions of seeing the countries and cities she had only
previously yearned for: Milan, Venice (for one glorious sold-out
week), Paris (where she takes on a second job, late-night singing
in a nightclub during the weeks of their French run), Zagreb, and
Belgrade. Before the cast sailed to Egypt, Angelou had to fend off a
desperate admirer. (She creates a pace for the story of the tour that
includes more comedy than she had chosen to use in her first two
autobiographies. Part of the humor in the Mr. Julian anecdote is
language-based.)

"Is this Mistress Maya Angelou?" The question was asked by a
voice I had never heard.

"Yes. I am Maya Angelou." I answered to a background of
disgruntled noises and curious looks from my roommates.

"Mistress Maya, I am being Mr. Julian. It's that last night I am seeing
you dance. I am watching you leap across the stage and looking at
your legs jumping through the air and, Mistress Maya, I am loving
you." The words ran together like dyes, and it was difficult for me
to separate them into comprehension.

"I beg your pardon?" Martha groaned. "Oh, my goodness, can't
he call you after the sun rises? Or does the sun never rise in
Yugoslavia?"

"It's I am loving you, Mistress Maya. It's that if you are hearing a
man is throwing his body into the Danube today, and dying in the
icy water, Mistress Maya, that man is being me. Drowning for the
love of you. You and your lovely legs jumping."

"Just a minute. Uh, what is your name?"

"I am being Mr. Julian, and I am loving you."

"Yes, well, Mr. Julian, why do you want to drown? Why would loving me make you want to die? I don't think that's very nice." Ethel and Martha were both leaning on their elbows watching me. Martha said, "Would he promise to die before sundown? Do you think he'll do it in time for us to get a little sleep?" Ethel said serenely, "Now Maya sees what her saintly lifesaving attitude has brought."

"Look, mister."

"It's being Mr. Julian."

"Yes, well, Mr. Julian, thanks for the telephone call—"

"May I please be seeing you? May I please be taking you to one expensive café and watching your lovely lips drinking down coffee with cream?"

"No, thank you. I am sorry, but I have to hang up now."

"Miss Maya, if you're not seeing me, if you're not letting me see your lips drinking down coffee with cream, then today, I am sending you my heart" (*Singin'* 553–4).

Angelou has told her readers that going to Europe had long been a dream of hers, but since she could barely pay her rent, such travel would remain a dream, and a remote one at that. The rapid progression from country to country, language to language, and currency to currency (there was no joint medium of exchange such as the *euro* during earlier decades) would have confused most performers, but for Angelou—knowing that Guy was well cared for by her mother and her aunt—travel with the *Porgy and Bess* company was nothing but a remarkable feast of experiences.

Angelou as narrator tells insightful stories about the European sites of the opera's performances, but her storytelling capacity expands noticeably once they travel to Egyptian and African cities. She creates immense drama as the ship docks: "As the ship neared land, streets and the details of buildings became more visible in the bright sunlight, and I fantasized the Africans who designed the houses and laid out the streets. Tall and dark-brown-skinned. Proud and handsome like my father. Bitter-chocolate black like my brother, lightly made and graceful. Or chunky and muscular, resembling my Uncle Tommy. Thick and sturdy, walking with a roll to their hips like boxers or gandy dancers. The fantasy was mesmerizing and before I knew it men were lashing the ship to the dock" (*Singin'* 578).

Not only Angelou was excitedly curious to see this "homeland." Lillian exclaimed, "'Look at the people, will you? Africans. My God. Now I have lived. Real Africans'" (*Singin'* 580). Later, as she walks in the streets alone, despite warnings about risks, Angelou announces, "I come from this country. I am only returning home" (*Singin'* 583). Followed by beggars—the underbelly of the African culture just as if it were a United States city she walked in, she returned to the protection of the hotel. She stayed within its walls, since the rout by the beggars had frightened her.

Driven to Cairo, a city still haunted by beggars, the troupe saw that, there, "more black-skinned people held positions of authority. The desk clerk in the Continental Hotel was the color of cinnamon; the manager was beige but had tight crinkly hair. The woman who supervised the running of the house was small and energetic and her complexion would never have allowed her to pass for white . . . I felt I was at last in Africa—in a continent at the moment reeling yet rising, released from the weight of colonialism, which had ridden its back for generations" (*Singin'* 586). After the group had its tour of the pyramids and rode camels, Angelou returned alone. ("I couldn't satisfy my longing to breathe in the entire country.") She asked the guides to allow her to be alone with the pyramids.

I took off my shoes and dug my feet into the hot sand.

Go down Moses, way down in Egypt land,

Tell old Pharaoh, to let my people go.

A Pharaonic tomb rose above my head and I shivered. Israelites and Nubians and slaves from Carthage and Mesopotamia had built it, sweating, bleeding, and finally dying for the mass of stones which would become in the twentieth century no more than the focus for tourists' cameras.

My grandmother had been a member of a secret Black American female society, and my mother and father were both active participants in the Masons and Eastern Star organizations. Their symbols, which I found hidden in linen closets and night stands, were drawings of the Pyramid at Giza, or Cheops' tomb.

I tried to think of a prayer or at least some dramatic words to say to the spirits of long-dead ancestors. But nothing apt came to mind. When the sun became unbearable, I took a taxi back to town.

North Africa made me more reflective. Other members of the cast reacted similarly to the Egyptian experience (*Singin'* 586–7).

As Angelou thought in retrospect, "We left Egypt undeniably changed. The exposure to extreme wealth and shocking poverty forced the frivolous to be level-headed and encouraged the sober to enjoy what they had taken for granted" (*Singin'* 590).

Once back on the Greek ship, looking ahead to performances in Morocco, Tel Aviv, Marseilles, Turin, and finally La Scala, the company felt its exhaustion. Angelou was scarcely surprised when she had a frightening letter from Vivian, reporting on her own financial losses and the seemingly serious skin condition and rash that Guy could not get rid of. Angelou promised she would return home in one month. Then she learned that she would have to not only transport herself back to the States, but she would also have to pay the travel costs—first class—for whoever would replace her in the cast.

Although she had been sending home every spare penny, and living in youth hostels rather than in hotels where possible, Angelou saw that those costs would amount to over a thousand dollars. She knew she could not earn that amount in a month, but she tried; she danced every night in Bricktop's club, and she also took a day job besides her *Porgy and Bess* obligations. Finally she had earned enough, and she took the nine-day trip back to New York on the *Cristoforo Colombo*—that trip was followed by a three-day train trip to San Francisco.

Stunned to see how distraught her son Guy was after her absence, Angelou realized she could never leave him again. His sobbing at night, fearful that she would leave him again, defeated her usual ebullience. His skin condition was serious: "it flaked with scales and his bedclothes had to be changed each day in an attempt to prevent new contagion" (*Singin'* 609). Without work, depressed by Guy's own depression, Angelou had a suicidal episode one afternoon. Luckily, she ordered Guy out of the house and away from her, and then took a cab to talk with a psychiatrist. He could not understand her misery; she attributed his lack of compassion to his being white.

Angelou left abruptly and went to see Frederick Wilkinson, her stable and kindly voice teacher. The upshot of her complaining to him, about the fact that she had ruined her 9-year-old son's life, was his ordering her to write—"what you have to be thankful for . . . Write, dammit! I mean write."

I picked up the pencil and began.

> I can hear.
> I can speak.
> I have a son.
> I have a mother.
> I have a brother.
> I can dance.
> I can sing.
> I can cook.
> I can read.
> I can write.

When I reached the end of the page I began to feel silly. I was alive and healthy. What on earth did I have to complain about? For two months in Rome I had said all I wanted was to be with my son. And now I could hug and kiss him anytime the need arose. What the hell was I whining about?

Wilkie said, "Now write, 'I am blessed. And I am grateful.'" I wrote the line (*Singin'* 612).

Weeks passed, with Angelou constantly reassuring Guy that she would not leave him. Much to her agent's surprise, she said she would take any work—anywhere—but the payment had to include transportation and housing for her young son. The next time she heard from the agent, it was to offer her a four-week singing engagement in Hawaii at The Clouds. She accepted the offer. Guy was ecstatic, and it was a good sojourn for both of them.

7

The Heart of a Woman

The title of Angelou's fourth autobiography comes from Georgia Douglas Johnson's famous poem, both stanzas of which begin with the title phrase:

The heart of a woman goes forth with the dawn

As a lone bird, soft winging, so restlessly on. . . .

The exuberance of this famous African American poem's opening sets the mood of achievement. Georgia Douglas Johnson wrote one of her best-known poems in 1918 and during the 1920s she was considered the premier woman poet of the Harlem Renaissance. With a college education, she took a government job, and her Washington, DC, address—1461 S Street NW—became a famous literary salon. Widowed in 1925, she worked tirelessly to support her children.

The second stanza of "The Heart of a Woman" reflects this hard economic life. Although the stanza again begins with the title phrase, it closes with the woman's relinquishing the promise she had earlier known, forgetting her earlier dream "of the stars,/While it [the heart] breaks, breaks, breaks on the sheltering bars."

Angelou reinforces the impression that this fourth autobiography is about the character Maya Angelou *as woman*. Approaching thirty, finally able in her musical career to support Guy and herself, she dedicates this autobiography to "a few of the many sister/friends whose love encouraged me to spell my name: WOMAN." As she had with earlier book dedications, she here makes a centered list, this time of fourteen names, ranging from Rosa Guy, Paule Marshall, and Louise Merriwether (all successful writers) to such African friends as Efuah Sutherland and A. B. (Banti) Williamson, as well as such scholars as Eleanor Traylor and Dolly McPherson. (She begins this dedication by giving the book to her first grandchild, Colin Ashanti Murphy-Johnson, born close to the publication date of this memoir, 1981.)

What Angelou creates in her fourth autobiography, a litany of true womanliness, she will extend in many later essays as well as in her 2008 nonfiction book *Letter to My Daughter* and, in 2014, in *Rainbow in the Cloud*, where she gives the reader a set of maxims about WOMAN:

> A woman is careful with judgment, is courteous, has courage, and is much given to kindness, support, and respect for other women.
>
> Each time a woman stands up for herself, without knowing it possibly, without claiming it, she stands up for all women.
>
> Being a woman is hard work. Not without joy and even ecstasy, but still relentless, unending work. Becoming an old female may require only being born with certain genitalia, inheriting long-living genes, and the fortune not to be run over by an out-of-control truck, but to become and remain a woman command the existence and employment of genius (*Rainbow* 100–01).

In the five years since Random House had published *Singin' and Swingin' and Gettin' Merry Like Christmas*, Angelou had received innumerable accolades. She had been nominated for a Tony Award after her Broadway debut in the play *Look Away*, and a second Tony

Maya with sister writers Rosa Guy and Louise Merriwether on one of their sojourns together in North Carolina. Photo © by poet Eugene Redmond. Used by permission of Eugene B. Redmond.

Award nomination for best supporting actress for the television film *Roots*. She had been appointed by President Gerald Ford to the American Revolution Bicentennial Council. She had served on the National Commission for the Observance of International Women's Year. She was chosen a member of the board of trustees of the American Film Institute. She had served as interviewer, narrator, and host for African American specials and theater series on television. She had appeared in *Ajax*, the adapted Sophocles play at the Mark Taper Forum, as well as directing her own play, *And Still I Rise* (both produced and published), and also directing the film *All Day Long*. She had been given honorary degrees from Smith College, Mills College, and Lawrence University. She had been named "Woman of the Year in Communications." She had been named distinguished visiting professor at Wake Forest University, Wichita State University, and

California State University. In 1975 her second collection of poems, *Oh Pray My Wings Are Gonna Fit Me Well*, appeared from Random house, again to excellent reviews.

Few women writers had been more visible during the 1970s than Maya Angelou. Her autobiographies and poem collections sold by the hundreds of thousands, in both English and other languages. Millions of viewers had watched her in the television production of *Roots*, and her distinctive name appeared in news items both artistic and political. Readers welcomed the appearance of *The Heart of a Woman*, perhaps partly because it had been five years since her last memoir was published. But as David Levering Lewis noted, the excellence of this autobiography was unquestionable—it was the best of her books since *I Know Why the Caged Bird Sings*. Lewis called it "uproarious, passionate and beautifully written." He further defined "excellence" as stemming from "a melding of unconcerned honesty, consummate craft, and perfect descriptive pitch, yielding a rare compound of great emotional force and authenticity, undiluted by polemic" (Lewis 133). (Although reviewers did not mention the effectiveness of this title, it compared in poignancy and the reach of its metaphor with *I Know Why the Caged Bird Sings*—and the Georgia Douglas Johnson poem also included the comparison of a woman and a "lone bird.")

Himself a scholar of comparative literature, Lewis linked Angelou to both the French writer Colette, famous for her outspoken autobiographies, and to the American anthropologist, fiction writer, and memoirist Zora Neale Hurston, an African American whose work was being rediscovered during the 1970s. In his words, Angelou "has achieved a kind of literary breakthrough which few writers of any time, place, or race achieve" (Lewis 132).

Good reviews of *The Heart of a Woman* were the rule. Carol E. Neubauer sees this autobiography as resting at the heart of Angelou's writing strategy, as well as her personal life (Neubauer

Black 123). Stephanie Stokes Oliver writes in *Essence* about Angelou's use of the roles of both personal romantic love and the important African continent, while Barbara Omolade emphasizes the writer's recognition of a woman's sexuality. Sondra O'Neale reads not only the Maya Angelou character but numerous other women in the autobiographies, placing Angelou's work in the wider context of African American women's writing. Critic Opal Moore points out that, like *I Know Why the Caged Bird Sings*, this book illustrates the "deep talk" Angelou aimed to create. Moore lists various moral choices in this book that readers must confront: "choosing life over death; choosing courage over safety; choosing discipline over chaos; choosing voice over silence; choosing compassion over pity, over hatred, over habit; choosing work and planning and hope over useless recrimination and slovenly despair" (Moore 51).

Angelou does not make *The Heart of a Woman* quite so exclusively about womanliness. In fact, she begins the text proper with lines from a beloved spiritual, rather than the Georgia Douglas Johnson poem.

The ole ark's a-moverin', a-moverin', a-moverin',

    the ole ark's a-moverin' along (*Heart* 623).

She uses this trope to establish the spirit of 1957 in the restless postwar United States. She does not detail the way she has established herself on the Pacific coast, after her return from Europe. Financially solvent, Angelou moves, with Guy, across the Golden Gate Bridge and into what she terms "a houseboat commune in Sausalito where I went barefoot, wore jeans, and both of us wore rough-dried clothes." Maya and Guy "joined the beatnik brigade" (*Heart* 623).

Her description of 1957 is wide-ranging and accurate: "We created a maze of contradictions. Black and white Americans danced a fancy and often dangerous do-si-do. In our steps forward, abrupt turns, sharp spins and reverses, we became our own befuddlement. The country hailed Althea Gibson, the rangy tennis player who was the first black female to win the U.S. Women's Singles. President Dwight Eisenhower sent U.S. paratroopers to protect black school children in Little Rock, Arkansas, and South Carolina's Senator Strom Thurmond harangued for 24 hours and 18 minutes to prevent the passage in Congress of the Civil Rights Commissions' Voting Rights Bill. Sugar Ray Robinson, everybody's dandy, lost his middleweight title, won it back, then lost it again, all in a matter of months. The year's popular book was Jack Kerouac's *On the Road*, and its title was an apt description of our national psyche. We were indeed traveling, but no one knew our destination nor our arrival date" (*Heart* 623).

Months of houseboat living reminded Angelou that she was *not* a hippie: she loved "privacy, wall-to-wall carpets and manicures." She rented a house (after she was turned down for the rental, white friends of hers secured the lease) in Laurel Canyon. She knew that her neighbors considered her a poor black woman living above her means and driving an old car, but she liked having Guy in school with largely white friends, and she could maintain enough musical work to support the household.

More episodic than any of her autobiographies except *Gather Together in My Name*, *The Heart of a Woman* begins in effect with a loop back to Angelou's musical career. From the teenaged mother educating herself by listening to the records she sold, Angelou has become a singer and dancer well enough known to keep an agent employed. Of the records she had valued a decade before, those by Harry Belafonte, who brought calypso music to the States, and jazz singer Billie Holiday, remained her lifelines. Accordingly, this fourth memoir begins with the account of the famous Billie Holiday's visiting Angelou. She is initially brought for a visit by Angelou's voice coach. Exhausted from her recent tour, Holiday likes her hostess' cooking; she comes back to Angelou's home day after day, and when Angelou leaves for her nightclub job, she drives Holiday back to her hotel. The singer also generally respects the fact that Guy, at 12, is very young. Each night she sings a song for him after he goes to bed. She is careful not to use her club talk or the street talk that occasionally slips into her hours with Angelou. But on her last night in town, Holiday sings the rough anti-lynching protest song, "Strange Fruit." Angelou recalls, "Her rasping voice and phrasing literally enchanted me. I saw the black bodies hanging from Southern trees. I saw the lynch victims' blood glide from the leaves down the trunks and onto the roots.

Guy interrupted, "How can there be blood at the root?" I made a hard face and warned him, "Shut up, Guy, just listen." Billie had continued under the interruption, her voice vibrating over harsh edges.

She painted a picture of a lovely land, pastoral and bucolic, then added eyes bulged and mouths twisted, onto the Southern landscape.

Guy broke into her song. "What's a pastoral scene, Miss Holiday?" Billie looked up slowly and studied Guy for a second. Her face became cruel, and when she spoke her voice was scornful. "It means when the crackers are killing the niggers. It means when they take a little nigger like you and snatch off his nuts and shove them down his goddam throat. That's what it means."

The thrust of rage repelled Guy and stunned me.

Billie continued, "That's what they do. That's a goddam pastoral scene."

Guy gave us both a frozen look and said, "Excuse me, I'm going to bed." He turned and walked away.

I lied and said it was time for me to go to work. Billie didn't hear either statement (*Heart* 633).

Gracious as always though deeply troubled at Holiday's behavior, Angelou allowed Holiday to come along to her club. After her first number, she introduced the famous singer to the audience. She gave homage where she knew it was due—but the pathos of the condition of the thin and sorrowful singer was not wasted on the crowd. Billie Holiday died in an Eastern hospital a few months later.

The anger Guy felt at being exposed to the lynching song—for which he somehow blamed his mother even more than he did Billie Holiday—lasted months, despite Angelou's efforts to show him she was the same mother, the same mother/friend she had always tried to be. By opening *The Heart of a Woman* with this story, using what Carol Neubauer calls a technique that suggests "folk history" (Neubauer Heart 28), Angelou exposes herself to the complaint that some readers made about all her autobiographies—that her language was sometimes too crude for youngsters to read (some of the banning of her later autobiographies was based on this response). One wonders how else the lyrics of "Strange Fruit," and Billie Holiday's purposefully shocking comments about those lyrics, could have been conveyed. For instance, in *I Know Why the Caged Bird Sings*, Angelou describes how painful the handsome members of her family are for her to observe: "Where I was big, elbowy and grating, he [Bailey, her brother] was small, graceful and smooth. When I was described by our playmates as being shit color, he was lauded for his velvet-black skin" (*Caged* 21).

When Angelou describes the frightening events that could have led to Uncle Willie's death at the hands of the Ku Klux Klan, she uses language both acerbic and vivid:

The "boys"? Those cement faces and eyes of hate that burned the clothes off you if they happened to see you lounging on the main street downtown on Saturday. Boys? It seemed that youth had never happened to them. Boys? No, rather men who were covered with graves' dust and age without beauty or learning. The ugliness and rottenness of old abominations.

Uncle Willie lies in the potato bin, covered with potatoes and onions like a casserole.

If the boys had come and had insisted that Momma open the Store, they would surely have found him, and just as surely lynched him.

Grandmother knelt praying in the darkened store.

He moaned the whole night through as if he had, in fact, been guilty of some heinous crime. The heavy sounds pushed their way up out of the blanket of vegetables and I pictured his mouth pulling down on the right side and his saliva flowing into the eyes of the new potatoes and waiting there like dew drops for the warmth of morning (*Caged* 19).

Angelou's description of the physically deformed (but beloved) uncle, wrenched by his fear, adds to the protest rhetoric.

The "unsuitability" of her language occurs throughout these autobiographies, sometimes without warning. When she describes the African American women having to carry home the laundry of their white employers (which they will wash, starch, iron, and return), she mentions "that white men wore shorts . . . and that they had an opening for taking out their 'things' and peeing, and that white women's breasts weren't built into their dresses . . . because I saw their brassiers in the baskets" (*Caged* 24).

Intentionally strident as in the Billie Holiday narrative, or intentionally crude as if to awaken readers to realities that are indisputably harsh and even life-threatening, Angelou's language and phrasing varies with the story she is choosing to tell. In *The Heart of a Woman*, for instance, she moves quickly past the scene where

Guy is shamed by the school principal because he has used what the white teachers consider inappropriate language with his classmates— Angelou, in turn, looks for a house to rent in a neighborhood that is more mixed than it is white. (Blame for *difference* is a weight she does not want her young son to experience—or at least not regularly.)

Angelou has resumed writing; she works on scripts, songs, stories. John Killens comes to Hollywood to help write the screenplay for his novel *Youngblood*: they meet and become friends and he encourages her writing. She considers moving to New York, a scene of much more political activity as well as the site of the Harlem Writers' Group. While she is there, looking for housing and work, she finds the evenings she spends with the Killenses depressing because of what she calls their "unrelenting diatribe" about the behavior of mainstream white culture: "We discussed the treatment of Reverend Martin Luther King, Jr., the murder of Emmett Till in Mississippi, the large humiliations and the petty snubs we all knew were meant to maim our spirits. I had heard white folks ridiculed, cursed and envied, but I had never heard them dominate the entire intimate conversation of a black family" (*Heart* 651). Killens points out that— years before—when Angelou had come to New York to study dance, she did only that. He advised her to "look at New York with a writer's eyes, ears and nose; then you will really see New York."

She immerses herself in the city, but she thinks Guy will be able to survive along with her. Once he arrives, Angelou admits, "The black mother perceives destruction at every door, ruination at each window" (*Heart* 655). Understanding the politics of race has become crucial for her.

Angelou finds a job singing in a small Lower East side club, one so undistinguished that it embarrasses her, but her real energy is going into her writing attempts. She is, however, envious of the success her friends are having: "Abbey and Max Roach were performing jazz concerts on liberation themes. Lorraine Hansberry had a play on Broadway which told some old truths about the black American Negro family to a new white audience [*Raisin in the Sun*]. James Baldwin had the country in his balled fist with *The Fire Next Time*. Killens's *And Then We Heard the Thunder* told the uncomfortable facts about black soldiers in a white army. Belafonte included the South African singer Miriam Makeba in his concerts, enlarging his art and increasing his protest against racial abuse . . . I made the decision to quit show business. Give up the skintight dresses and manicured smiles" (*Heart* 662). Weeks later, when she is invited to appear at the Apollo Theater in Harlem, however, she forgot that resolution.

It was 1959. Then it was 1960. The fervor that would bring the freedoms of civil rights protests during the 1960s was building. When Angelou sang her program of Southern blues and calypso at the Apollo, she got some response from her audiences. But when she did "Baba Fururu," a Cuban religious song she had learned a year earlier, syllable by syllable—which was the song of black Cuban religious ritual, imploring the gods for freedom—the audience wanted to join in with her singing. The grapevine brought new listeners. She told them all, "If you believe you deserve freedom, if you really want it, if you believe it should be yours, you must sing:

U bu uburu oh yea freedom
U bu uburu oh yea freedom
Uh huh Uh hum" (*Heart* 666).

She recalled that: "The audience sang passionately. They were under my voice, before my voice. Understanding beyond my own understanding. I was the singer, the entertainer, and they were the people who were enduring. They accepted me because I was singing the anthem and carrying the flag" (*Heart* 667). As Eleanor Traylor noted years later, Angelou taught the audience "call-and-response" and they participated enthusiastically: common to both African singing and the American black church, even if the Apollo Theater did not allow audience participation, some deep level of voiced response was comforting to people in her audience. Angelou was always ready to "switch the code" (Traylor 92).

Angelou's associations in New York led to introductions for other kinds of work. Eventually, with the help of comedian Godfrey Cambridge, she organizes a stage show that will raise money for political action—specifically, for the work of Martin Luther King and the Southern Christian Leadership Conference. With the keen success of performances of "Cabaret for Freedom," both she and Cambridge become well-known in activist circles. When, later, Bayard Rustin takes a different position (with A. Phillip Randolph in the Brotherhood of Sleeping Car Porters), Angelou is asked to take Rustin's place and coordinate the New York office of the SCLC. Fund-raising is also a large part of her job.

Earning a living is still a difficult chore for her—and as Guy matures and needs more of the trappings of teenagers the world over, Angelou feels a kind of financial desperation. The reader remembers her pleased statement about Tosh Angelos from early in *Singin' and Swingin' and Gettin' Merry Like Christmas*, when she wrote, "I had a son, a father for him, a husband and a pretty home for us to live in" (*Singin'* 416). Months after she takes over the SCLC, Angelou becomes engaged to a man about whom she says little—Thomas Allen is a bail bondsman, and she sometimes wonders if the gifts he gives her are purchased or stolen. She and Thomas are to be married in three months time when her activism brings her into the company of a relatively famous South African freedom fighter, Vusumzi Make (Vus). After several meetings, he invites her and Guy to come with him to Cairo, Egypt—to marry and set up a household. Were it not for her 1950s idealization of the suburban life she has witnessed around her, Angelou would no doubt have looked harder at her choices. As it is, taking on a truly activist role, and having what will surely be glorious travel and living experiences, seems preferable to continuing life in New York. (She has written some stories, one of which has seen print; some songs; some scripts, but she still earns her living from coordinating the Conference office. In Guy's case, decisions will soon have to be made about college. Cairo, Egypt, seems to be a choice that solves problems that await both mother and son.)

After she has dissolved the relationship with Thomas and settled in to help Vus Make create sympathy for the African situation in New York—before they begin their Egyptian life—she plays the role of The White Queen in Jean Genet's *The Blacks*. Just as Angelou was already well known in the musical world, having done the *Porgy and Bess* European and African tour, so now she worked in a substantial way with Broadway and off-Broadway's leading African American actors. For a time, her friends Abbey Lincoln and Max Roach were a part of the troupe, but they later resigned over an argument with the producers; the often satirical characters drawn by Genet were played by such luminaries as James Earl Jones, Louis Gossett, Cicely Tyson, Roscoe Lee Browne, Charles Gordone, Ethel Ayler, Cynthia Belgrave, Helen Martin, Lex Monson, Jay J. Riley, Raymond St. Jacques, Godfrey Cambridge, and Maya Angelou Make (using her pseudo-married name in the program).

During 1961 *The Blacks* was a long-running hit at the St. Marks Playhouse. Reviews were good and it was nominated for a plethora of awards. The fomenting racial strife to come, as well as the superb acting, created appreciative audiences. Angelou remembers with pleasure her good reviews; she writes, "I started enjoying my role. I used the White Queen to ridicule mean white women and brutal white men who had too often injured me and mine. Every inane posture and haughty attitude I had ever seen found its place in my White Queen.

> I dressed myself in the hated gestures and made the White Queen gaze down in loathing at the rotten stinking stupid blacks, who, although innocent, like beasts were loathsome nonetheless.

> It was obvious that the other actors also found effective motivation. The play became such a cruel parody of white society that I was certain it would flop. Whites were not so masochistic as to favor a play which ridiculed and insulted them, and black playgoers were scarce.

> James Baldwin was a friend of Gene Frankel's and he attended rehearsals frequently. He laughed loudly and approvingly at our performances and I talked with him often. When I introduced him to Vus they took to each other with enthusiasm" (*Heart* 791).

Angelou stayed in the cast for most of its run. Because Max Roach had pulled his music when he resigned, Angelou and Ethel Ayler had quickly (within a day) written two songs that were used in the production. Unfortunately, the producers never paid for that work, or for the use of the music. Angelou resigned, with Vus's support, when the payment did not come as promised.

Among the African American elite that filled the theater was one of Angelou's idols, Langston Hughes. He left before the play ended, and his biographer Arnold Rampersad reported that (although he had enjoyed Genet's *The Balcony*) he called *The Blacks* "a 33rd degree bore, . . . more outrageous than Samuel Beckett's *Waiting for Godot* and even less amusing." He decided that the production needed "lightness and a humorous approach to its fantasy—which is extreme, grotesque and long-winded." Hughes subsequently promised himself, "NO MORE ART SHOWS" (Rampersad II, 330).

After she and Guy had become part of Vus's household in New York, Angelou began receiving threatening phone calls from "agents of South Africa's apartheid regime, who considered her husband an enemy of the state." Macabre and frightening threats, reports of Guy's being injured, whatever horrors could come across the phone line, did (Gillespie 65). Angelou remembers those months, saying "I had opposed the racist regime on principle, because it was ugly, violent, debasing and murderous. But . . . to break a mother's heart for no gain was the most squalid act I could imagine. My defiance from now on would be personal" (*Heart* 805).

Still living together in New York, with Vus taking trips for world conferences that included South Africa, Angelou realized that infidelity was going to be the rule within their relationship. "The lipstick smudge was not mine, nor did the perfume come from my bottles" (*Heart* 796). Angelou's staying with Make became as much a political choice as a personal one, but unfortunately Angelou knew that his reassurances were as false as was his behavior—that he was the man in control. Make bought new furniture, even if he could never pay the rent; he assumed the pose of African statesman, but he allowed his senses to drive his actions. Yet Guy admired him and all he had been through in his choice to fight for black freedom in Africa, his choice to ignore apartheid. Angelou reflects, "Now Vus was teaching him [Guy] to be an African male, and he was an apt student. Ambiguity stretched me like elastic. I yearned for our old closeness, and his dependence, but I knew he needed a father, a male image, a man in his life" (*Heart* 799).

The Heart of a Woman shifts focus slightly. Long considered the memoir of Angelou's romance with the South African freedom fighter, it comes again and again to be instead the narrative of *Angelou as mother*. The structure of the entire memoir feeds into this emphasis. As will be summarized in the next chapter ("Africa"), dedicated to the remarkable effect the continent of Africa had on Angelou's consciousness and psyche, her thorough immersion in Africa and the people who have chosen to live there—including many African Americans from the United States—irretrievably marks the author's development. But the immediate narrative structure of *The Heart of a Woman* is itself somewhat truncated so that the reader understands that the great romance between Vus Make and Maya Angelou, and its disillusion, is less the pivotal story than is the serious auto accident that Guy experiences a few days after he and Angelou arrive in Ghana. With his neck broken in three places, along with other broken bones and injuries, the teenager undergoes extensive physical therapy during the first month of his convalescence in the hospital. He then requires another three months of healing and therapy at home, where his mother is his full-time nurse. As *The Heart of a Woman* closes with the boy's recuperation, Angelou always at his side, the fact that Vus Make is no longer a part of their household seems immaterial.

It is partly this narrative structure that led critics to compare *The Heart of a Woman*, Angelou's fourth autobiography, with *I Know Why the Caged Bird Sings*.

As in her first memoir, the later book reflects on women's roles; in the case of *I Know Why the Caged Bird Sings*, even though the character of Marguerite is abused, forced in childhood to become a sexual object, the strongly drawn character of her grandmother Annie Henderson becomes the image of the caregiver mother. By the time of *The Heart of a Woman*, Angelou has herself become that woman. Critic Siphokazi Koyana notes that in Angelou's writing, "self-reliance and motherhood are integrated" (Koyana 69).

Neither Annie Henderson nor Vivian Baxter will take government help, and Angelou prides herself on following their lead. Annie ran her store, Vivian rented out rooms in her fourteen-room house. This critic points out however, that the family arrangements described here are more relevant to African American culture than to white: she describes "a socio-cultural context in which self-reliance means sometimes relying on other people of the community. For Maya, family is neither nuclear, nor restricted by household" (Koyana 71).

The Heart of a Woman shows Angelou's leaving Guy with close friends, as she does when Grace and John Killens care for him while she takes a several-week singing engagement. In this memoir's narrative structure, her absence has unpredictable results; she had hired a neighbor woman to come over to cook his evening meal. That woman brought with her a teenaged grandchild, whose gang-member boyfriend was jealous of Guy. At that point, the Killenses moved Guy from his own house into their home. When Angelou returns from Chicago and hears the story, she borrows a gun from her musician lover and goes to the grandmother's house early in the day, ostensibly to pay her. Asking to speak to the granddaughter, suspecting that the boyfriend will also be there, Angelou delivers her own substantial threat to the boy:

> "I understand that you are the head of the Savages and you have an arrangement with my son. I also understand that the police are afraid of you. Well, I came 'round to make you aware of something. If my son comes home with a black eye or a torn shirt, I won't call the police."

> His attention followed my hand to my purse. "I will come over here and shoot Susie's grandmother first, then her mother, then I'll blow away that sweet little baby. You understand what I'm saying? If the Savages so much as touch my son, I will then find your house and kill everything that moves, including the rats and cockroaches."

> I showed the borrowed pistol, then slid it back into my purse.

For a second, none of the family moved and my plans had not gone beyond the speech, so I just kept my hand in the purse, fondling my security.

Jerry spoke, "O.K. I understand. But for a mother, I must say you're a mean motherfucker" (*Heart* 699–700).

Evocative of a tough persona which is nothing like the real Angelou, her language here—the steady pace of the vengeance ("shoot Susie's grandmother first, then her mother, then I'll blow away that sweet little baby," with the overly sentimental phrase "sweet little baby" acting as a cap to the unbelievably horrific scenario) comes across as almost humorous.

Angelou reports subsequently that there is no more trouble.

Koyana points out that this community-based family structure is a more African model than it is a United States pattern. In Africa, "Lineages, rather than married couples, are the core around which the typical African extended family is built . . . Marital and family stability are not the same thing." While Angelou was attracted to Make in part because his homeland was *Africa*, she also was not so involved with the romance of a couple's relationship that she put up with misbehavior on any man's part. She had divorced Tosh Angelos for his overly possessive and anti-religious control. She would leave Make for his incorrigible womanizing as well as for his irresponsible spending.

There is a further point to the tendency to elevate the role of mothering. Koyana writes that Angelou's autobiographies "show the tensions inherent in belonging to a group that values these notions of family while living in a larger society that devalues them. (She lists among the "black values," "respect for the working mother, the extended family, and for othermothers." Contrastingly, white culture values the "non-working mother in the nuclear family")

(Koyana 72). She also points out that Angelou's own life has been spent—so long as Annie Henderson is alive—coming and going, taking leave of one family to live on her own, but then returning. This cyclic pattern is reflected in Angelou's "double-consciousness, her oscillation between her intrinsic Afro-American and her imposed Euro-American cultural identities, in literary terms, by contrasting reality with fantasy" (Koyana 73).

Moving the centrality of what this critic calls the *mothering pattern* to the traditional organization of autobiography, Koyana sees the "unsurpassed" originality of what Angelou creates. "Her books bring sexuality, childbearing, and child rearing practices into the domains of politics . . . and attempt to reveal the multiple and dynamic interconnections between households—home and family—and the larger political community" (Koyana 68).

Angelou herself, in the 1983 Claudia Tate interview, had discussed the cultural roles of African American women. She explained, "In the social gatherings of black people, black women have always been predominant . . . In the church it's always Sister Hudson, Sister Thomas, and Sister Witheringay who keep the church alive. In lay gatherings it's always Lottie who cooks, and Mary who's going over to Bonita's . . . Also, black women are the nurturers of children in our community. White women have historically been cast in different roles" (in Braxton 150–1). She then connects this social fact with her writing: "Image making is very important for every human being. It is especially important for black American women in that we are, by being black, a minority in the United States, and by being female, the less powerful of the genders. So we have two areas we must address . . . we see whites and males in dominant roles. We need to see our mothers, aunts, our sisters, and grandmothers. We need to see Frances Harper, Sojourner Truth, Fannie Lou Hamer, women of our heritage. We need to have these women preserved. We need them all: . . . Constance Motley, Etta Motten . . . All of these women are important as role models. Depending on our profession, some may be even more important. Zora Neale Hurston means a great deal to me as a writer. So does Josephine Baker. I would imagine that Bessie Smith and Mammie Smith, though they are important to me, would be even more so to Aretha Franklin" (ibid. 149).

Angelou becomes even more specific as she defends the fiction of African American *women* writers when they are continuously compared—often unfavorably—to the fiction written by African American *men*. "If we look at works by Toni Morrison or Toni Bambara, if we look at Alice Walker's work or Hurston's, Rosa Guy's, Louise Meriwether's, or Paule Marshall's, we must say that these works are meant as general statements, universal statements . . . If *Daddy Was a Numbers* [sic] *Runner* [by Louise Meriwether] is not a microcosm of a macrocosm, I don't know what it is. If Paule Marshall's *Chosen Place and Timeless People* is not a microcosm, I don't know what it is. I don't know what *Ruby* [by Rosa Guy] is if it is not a microcosm of a larger world. I see everybody's work as an example of the particular . . . I don't see any difference really, whether it's Claude Brown's or Gayl Jones's. I can look at *Manchild in the Promised Land* and at *Corregidora* and see that these writers are talking about particular situations and yet about the general human condition. They are instructive for the generalities of our lives" (ibid. 153).

In the Tate interview, Angelou said with a bit more humor: "I'm impressed by Toni Morrison a great deal. I long for her new works. I'm impressed by the growth of Rosa Guy. I'm impressed by Ann Petry. I'm impressed by the work of Joan Didion. Her first collection, *Slouching Toward Jerusalem* [sic] contains short pieces, which are absolutely stunning. I would walk fifty blocks in high heels to buy the works of any of these writers. I'm a country girl, so that means a lot" (Tate in Braxton 158).

Rita Dove, Toni Morrison, and Maya Angelou at the latter's party celebrating Toni Morrison's being awarded the Nobel Prize for Literature, 1993. Winter, 1994. Photo © by Eugene Redmond. Used by permission of Eugene B. Redmond.

It goes without saying that Angelou is an accurate and appreciative reader. It also goes without saying that she must draw from her own particular life events, since that is the natural tradition of the *autobiography* as a literary form. She does not use the term "autobiographical novel." She consistently calls her nonfiction works "autobiographies." Yet she makes an important distinction when she qualifies: "When I wrote *Caged*, I wasn't thinking so much about my own life or identity. I was thinking about a particular time in which I lived and the influences of that time on a number of people . . . I used the central figure—myself—as a focus to show how one person can make it through those times" (ibid.).

From the childhood of Marguerite to the birth of her baby, *I Know Why the Caged Bird Sings* recounts the despair of the segregated South, as Annie Henderson not only copes with it but outsmarts it.

It outlines the community as a surrogate parent, headed by the same Annie Henderson, "mother of the church" as well as "Momma" to Marguerite, Bailey, and Uncle Willie. It is an odyssey of personal and group survival, but even with the birth of Marguerite's baby son, it is in no way triumphant.

Angelou's subsequent autobiographies describe successive decades of life in both the United States and the world at large; sadly, the problems are not so different from those revealed in *I Know Why the Caged Bird Sings* as the reader might have hoped.

8

Africa

Maya Angelou's fourth and fifth autobiographies (*The Heart of a Woman*, published in 1981, and *All God's Children Need Traveling Shoes*, published in 1986) are about her experiences trying to live as an African on the continent of Africa itself. The mature Angelou purposefully takes her college-age son into these areas, knowing that his inheritance from living only in the United States is slim. Part of her accepting Vus Make as a partner stems from her aim to allow Guy to experience a rich, African-based existence so that he can fully understand the various currents that comprise his own life.

In *The Heart of a Woman*, readers have experienced her initial sojourn to Cairo, Egypt, a city where the company of *Porgy and Bess* had earlier performed. Enthralled as she had been to visit Egypt, it held few attractions comparable to those of Accra in West Africa. As Angelou and Guy walk through the Accra airport, en route to enrolling Guy in the University of Ghana, Angelou is ecstatic: "The sight of so many black people stirred my deepest emotions . . . Three black men walked past us wearing airline uniforms, visored caps, white pants and jackets whose shoulders bristled with epaulettes. Black pilots? Black captains? It was 1962. In our country, the cradle of democracy, whose anthem boasted 'the land of the free, the home of the brave,' the only black men in our airports fueled planes, cleaned cabins, loaded food or were skycaps, racing the pavement for tips" (*Heart* 865).

Their hegira continues. "We passed through customs, delighted to have our bags examined by black people. Our taxi driver was black. The dark night seemed friendly to me, and when the cab's lights illuminated a pedestrian, I saw a black face. By the time we reached the address Vus had given me, a knot in my stomach, which had bunched all my remembered life, had unfurled. I realized I hadn't seen a white face for over an hour. The feeling was light and extremely strange" (*Heart* 866).

Living in Cairo had familiarized Angelou and Guy with the international community of blacks who wanted to return to the African continent. As Marcia Ann Gillespie described the "sub-Saharan African diplomatic community, it was comprised of Black American artists and intellectuals who were choosing to make Africa their home" (Gillespie 69). Angelou admitted that, "Africa had always been with her. It was imprinted in the fabric of Black Stamps, in the games she played as a child, the folktales elders shared. It influenced sensibilities and behavior, the grave formality of elders in Ghana so like her Grandmother Henderson's demeanor." She later advised that a person who wanted to learn about Africa—particularly its emphasis on "deep thinking"—must understand African folktales (Con 172).

Perhaps the fullest explanation for what Angelou and Guy found in Ghana comes from critic Dolly McPherson: "Ghana is the center of an African cultural renaissance. Unlike Liberia, which was founded by former American slaves, Ghana is culturally African. The early 1960s is a period of cultural rebirth—a time of pride in old values and new freedom, a time of promise and growth. The attraction to Ghana is both symbolic and cultural for, like many blacks, Angelou perceives it to be a lost homeland" (McPherson 107).

The exotic sights and sounds of Ghana, like the colorful crowded streets of Cairo, also drew substance from the political base that unites Angelou's fourth and fifth autobiography, the author's "unrelenting protest against racial injustice." Koyana continues assessing the memoirs, "By recognizing the centrality of remembering and rewriting the history of black mothers while underscoring the intricate connection between maternal concerns and the racial or economic politics of her country, Angelou radicalizes autobiography and acknowledges its contribution to the struggle for racial equality" (Koyana 70, 78). As critic Teresa Washington notes, Africa was formed by matriarchal families. It is not unusual that male figures are sometimes omitted: "the male principal is deemed irrelevant to the mother-daughter Aje relationships . . . fathers are dead, are not mentioned, or have been moved out of the sphere of interaction" (Washington 218). Throughout Angelou's writing career, she chooses to write about her grandmothers and her mother; even though her only child is male, she fills in that gender difference with her 2008 book, *Letter to My Daughter*.

Guy's automobile accident and his months of recovery dominate the last segment of *The Heart of a Woman*, but before Angelou's fifth memoir, *All God's Children Need Traveling Shoes*, he has managed to enroll himself as a regular student at the University of Ghana. Then, Angelou admits, "Accra became a wondrous city as Guy's health improved. The sprawling Makola market drew me into its heaving perfumed bosom, and held me there for hours. Black women, sitting before stalls, offered for sale peanuts, peanut butter, wax-printed cloth, cutlery, Pond's face cream, tinned milk, sandals, men's pants, hot pepper, pepper sauce, tomatoes, plates, palm oil, palm butter and palm wine. The open-air shopping center, alive with shouted language and blaring music, its odors and runny children, its haggling customers and adamant saleswoman, made America's great department stores seem colorless and vacant by contrast" (*Heart* 874).

Even though Angelou lived cheaply in a room at the Y, she was in need of income. She approached the head of Ghana's theater, Efuah

Sutherland, a woman who was also a poet, a playwright, and a mother. Because Angelou had no formal degrees, she could not teach but J. H. Nketia, head of African Studies, found a secretarial job for her. Efuah sweetened the deal by giving Angelou the house of a professor who was on leave: Guy had a home to come to as he grew healthy again. And once he leaves for the university, living in a dormitory where he will be without his mother for the first time in his life, Angelou is surprised at the relief she feels. This is the closing of *The Heart of a Woman*:

> I closed the door and held my breath. Waiting for the wave of emotion to surge over me, knock me down, take my breath away. Nothing happened. I didn't feel bereft or desolate. I didn't feel lonely or abandoned.
>
> I sat down, still waiting. The first thought that came to me, perfectly formed and promising, was "At last, I'll be able to eat the whole breast of a roast chicken by myself" (*Heart* 878–9).

The opening of *All God's Children Need Traveling Shoes* places Angelou and Guy in Ghana for the first time: "Guy was seventeen and quick. I was thirty-three and determined. We were Black Americans in West Africa, where for the first time in our lives the color of our skin was accepted as correct and normal . . . For two days Guy and I laughed. We looked at the Ghanaian streets and laughed. We listened to the melodious languages and laughed. We looked at each other and laughed out loud" (*All* 889).

The sense of welcoming that they drew from the African faces, the African voices, is crushed beneath the weight of the accident that nearly kills Guy. But after some months, they are ready to resume their explorations of what they assume will be their beloved continent. "We had come home, and if home was not what we had expected, never mind, our need for belonging allowed us to ignore the obvious and to create real places or even illusory places, befitting our imagination . . . The community of Black immigrants opened and fitted me into their lives as if they had been saving my place" (*All* 900–01).

As Angelou flourishes in Ghana, she admits, "I was soon swept into an adoration for Ghana as a young girl falls in love, heedless and with slight chance of finding the emotion requited. There was an obvious justification for my amorous feelings. Our people had always longed for home. For centuries we had sung about a place not built with hands, where the streets were paved with gold, and were washed with honey and milk. There the saints would march around wearing white robes and jeweled crowns. There, at last, we would study war no more and, more important, no one would wage war against us again. The old Black deacons, ushers, mothers of the church and junior choirs only partially meant heaven as that desired destination. In the yearning, heaven and Africa were inextricably combined" (*All* 902).

McPherson says, correctly, that in the late 1950s "Africa was for many Black Americans their first opportunity to identify in a positive way with their ancestral home. Instead of looking *away* from Africa, numerous Black American men and women began to look *at* it. Familiar feelings of indifference, rejection and shame began to be replaced by feelings of interest, acceptance and pride. This change began to manifest itself with the approach of independence in Ghana and the emergence of Kwame Nkrumah as the first new African world leader, followed by other new African states and the appearance of other African Black men and women in places of power . . . through newspapers, radios and televisions [the world's people] were introduced to a succession of African dignitaries: Lumumba, Kenyatta, Mboya, Toure, Nyerere, Balewa, Senghor, Houphouet-Boigny. From the late fifties through much of the sixties,

Africa, as symbolized by these distinguished African visitors who were achieving national and international visibility, offered Black Americans a new place in history" (McPherson 104–05). Conscious of the political ramifications of her going to Ghana—doubly conscious because of her involvement with Vus's efforts, Angelou yet wrote in *All God's Children Need Traveling Shoes*, that she was more interested in the Ghanaian people than in their politics:

> Their skins were the colors of my childhood cravings: peanut butter, licorice, chocolate and caramel. Theirs was the laughter of home, quick and without artifice. The erect and graceful walk of the women reminded me of my Arkansas grandmother, Sunday-hatted, on her way to church. I listened to men talk, and whether or not I understood their meaning, there was a melody as familiar as sweet potato pie, reminding me of my Uncle Tommy Baxter, in Santa Monica, California. So I had finally come home" (*All* 903).

Of the approximately two hundred American visitors to Ghana— coming from St. Louis, New York City, Washington, DC, Los Angeles, Atlanta, and Dallas—it was clear that many of them, including Angelou, "hoped to live out the Biblical story" (*All* 903).

Angelou had written as a journalist for the *Arab Observer* in Cairo—even though Vus Make had objected strenuously to her working. Now she was hired to cover African news at *The Ghanaian Times*, a new weekly magazine. She learned to use the politically correct designation for Kwame Nkrumah, "man who surpassed man, iron which cuts iron" (*All* 902). She wore a Ghanaian hair style, took on Kojo as her "small boy"—a position that pleased his family, and became active in The National Council of Ghana Women. For one of the first times in her mature life, Maya Angelou was not the appendage of a male partner; her pseudo-marriage to Make had been dissolved in a group conversation, with friends surrounding the couple in question, she referred to as a "palaver."

Angelou's best women friends in Ghana were well-established university employees, as well as expatriates from the United States. Her early housemates, Alice Windom from St. Louis and Vicki Garvin from New York, were happily settled in Accra (and dissuaded Angelou from traveling to Liberia, where a good position awaited her). Other academics such as sociologist Sylvia Boone and graduate student Leslie Lacy were part of the social group—meeting regularly at the home of Julius and Ana Livia Mayfield—as well as Efuah Sutherland, head of the Ghanaian National Theater, and Grace Nuamah, a dance professor, along with Jim and Annette Lacy and the T. D. Bafoos. These and others comprised an easy collective group, often meeting over a meal, itself an important African spiritual ritual (Zauditu-Selassie 74).

Africans also value friendship and community. The Kongo idea that human beings are representations, bringing radiance in the form of light from the spirit world, plays out in a saying attributed to the Bantu: "A person is a person because of people." Critic Kokahvah Zauditu-Selassie explains, "The African communal psyche is demonstrated by intersubjectivity, mutuality, and interdependence." This sense of personhood is also a component of spirituality, which links the ancestors with people living today (Zauditu-Selassie 8, 11, 90).

Even as Angelou's sense of excitement at moving to Ghana had been stymied by her son's auto accident and long recovery, she still recalled her initial mood flying into the Accra airport: "I was on my way to *another adventure*. The future was plump with promise" (*All* 889). When she later saw that Guy was at home in his dormitory, surrounding himself with friends of his own choice, she felt free to find people she liked and form her own circles of friends. Julian

Mayfield and his physician wife Ana Livia were friends from her New York past; it is Julian who scolds Angelou (for not caring for herself) during the depression she experiences as she watches over Guy during his hospitalization.

Soon Angelou was back at her customarily intense slate of activities—learning to do good journalistic work, continuing her office management job at the University (that provided a small car, which she enjoyed driving), and learning to speak and interpret Fanti so that she might get "behind the modern face of Ghana, and get a glimpse of Africa's ancient soul" (*All* 923). At the university, she played the lead role in Bertolt Brecht's *Mother Courage* in a production directed by the visiting Abbey Theatre's Bryd Lynch *(All* 909*)*.

Travel money appears: theaters in both Berlin and Venice have requested that the original cast of Jean Genet's *The Blacks* reprise the New York performance. (Angelou arranges a stop-over in Cairo to see her Egyptian friends.) Pleased at the opportunity for more travel, and a reunion with the fabulous cast, Angelou takes on her difficult role as the White Queen, feeling somewhat rusty since—except for "Mother Courage"—she has not been on stage for years.

Living separately from Guy also teaches Angelou that he exists successfully on his own (except for the gossip that his current girlfriend is an employee in the American Embassy who is as old as his mother. When Angelou questions him about this relationship, he politely tells her that he will choose his own friends.) (*All* 1004).

All God's Children Need Traveling Shoes is written as a more subdued autobiography, with fewer scenes filled with dialogue, fewer comic episodes, and fewer digressions. It stands as a clear testament to the four years Angelou and Guy spent in Cairo and Ghana, and to the inherent (and highly publicized) relationship between Africa as an essential personal, religious, and traditional source, whether or not the African Americans from the United States chose to make

Ghana their permanent home. As the important African American writer Ishmael Reed noted, in his theoretical study *Writin' Is Fightin',* readers understand that "much African American writing [today] comes from 'an ancient Afro-American oral literature,' modernized by current authors to reach today's readers." The efficacy of this returning to roots is clear in that "millions of people in North, South, and Central America, the Caribbean, and Africa are acquainted with the structures" (*Writin'* 137). Reed also discusses what he calls this "blurring of cultural styles," evident in daily life in the United States, creating a kind of "cultural bouillabaisse" (*Writin'* 53).

Without understanding how tightly focused most of Angelou's autobiographical writing is, readers might assume that this was a woman persona who traveled for the sake of traveling. The title of this fifth memoir, in fact, suggests that need for movement: the comic effect of *All God's Children Need Traveling Shoes* is less visible than the location of Angelou and her son in, first, Cairo, Egypt, and then Accra, Ghana. As the author often did, here her reliance on spirituals and on the Bible *per se* creates a nostalgic "old church" mood: we can hear the minister intoning about what is good for "all God's children." And at one point in this fifth memoir Angelou halts the narrative in order to tell the B'rer Rabbit story. Its position as she repeats it with dialogue has relevance for both her emphasis on folk wisdom and in relation to Angelou's personal circumstances as she realizes (with a kind of panic) that she is the only woman in the Cairo newsroom. Just as the rabbit had asked to be punished by being thrown into the briar patch, so she had asked for the job in journalism.

She had said clearly in both *Letter to My Daughter* and her *Paris Review* interview, "I never agreed, even as a young person, with the Thomas Wolfe title *You Can't Go Home Again.* Instinctively I didn't. But the truth is, you can never *leave* home. You take it with you—it's under your fingernails; it's in the hair follicles; it's in the way you

smile; it's in the ride of your hips, in the passage of your breasts; it's
all there, no matter where you go. You can take on the affectations
and the postures of other places and even learn to speak their ways.
But the truth is, home is between your teeth. Everybody is always
looking for it: Jews go to Israel; black Americans and Africans in the
Diaspora go to Africa; Europeans, Anglo-Saxons go to England and
Ireland; people of Germanic background go to Germany. It's a very
queer quest . . . This book [referring to *All God's Children*] is about
trying to go home" (Paris 254–5). In *Letter to My Daughter*, Angelou
makes some of the same points but also says, "I believe that one can
never leave home. I believe that one carries the shadows, the dreams,
the fears and dragons of home under one's skin, at the extreme corners
of one's eyes and possibly in the gristle of the ear lobe . . . Geography,
as such, has little meaning to the child observer. If one grows up
in the Southwest, the desert and open skies are natural. New York,
with the elevators and subway rumble and millions of people, and
Southeast Florida with its palm trees and sun and beaches are to the
children of these regions the way the outer world is, has been, and
will always be. Since the child cannot control the environment, she
has to find her own place, a region where only she lives and no one
else can enter" (*Letter* 6).

Much of the second half of *All God's Children Need Traveling
Shoes* relates to United States and African politics, with a substantial
segment of the memoir relating to Malcolm X's visit to Ghana. Much
beloved already, Malcolm Little had met Angelou several years earlier
in New York. His teachings were considered divisive, but most of the
expatriate Americans in Ghana admired and respected him and his
work. There are several days of colloquies, receptions, lectures, and
parties. He explained in informal conversations that he had visited
Mecca and then "stopped in Cairo and met Egyptian government

officials and David Du Bois, and had gone to Nigeria to confer with other African politicians. He needed as many governmental contacts as possible so that when he took the case of the Black American before the General Assembly of the United Nations, he could be sure at least of some African and maybe other nationals' support." (The year is 1963; the Civil Rights Act will be passed in 1964, but Malcolm X will soon be assassinated. *The Autobiography of Malcolm X* will be published in 1965.)

Angelou fills several pages summarizing conflicting responses to Malcolm X. At the Press Club dance, he somewhat tactlessly reprimanded people for enjoying themselves ("I think of our brothers and sisters in Southern Africa squirming under the heel of apartheid, and I do not care to dance," *All* 992). Giving longer talks, he is more impressive. "Immediately his oratorical skill captured the audience. The years in prison, in mosques, on street corners, at college lecterns and before television cameras had produced a charismatic speaker who could play an audience as great musicians play instruments. He spoke moderately loud, then thundered, whispered, then roared. He used the imagery of Black American Baptist preachers and the logic of university intellectuals. He spoke of America, White and Black Americans, racism, hate and the awful need to be treated as humans." He answered every question. One faculty member asked him why he encouraged violence. "He said, 'I am *responding* to violence. If your house is on fire and I come to warn you, why should you accuse me of setting the fire? You should thank me for my concern. Maybe you can put out the fire before it is too late'" (*All* 994). He defines himself as being "a Black Muslim man of African heritage," not ducking the importance of Islam. He spoke seldom about that set of beliefs, however, instead repeating, "We have much work to do at home [in the United States]. Even as you have your work here in Africa. We are lambs in a den of wolves. We will need your help. Only with the help of Africa and Africans can we succeed in freeing ourselves" (*All* 997).

Angelou recalled the synergy when Malcolm X met with Nana Nketsia, noting that "the two men acted magnetized. I had not heard Nana speak so quietly nor seen Malcolm listen so deeply. Each man grew in the other's presence and when I took Malcolm to his hotel, he said, 'Now I have met African royalty. A chief. True, true. He knows his people and he loves them, and they love him.' Malcolm's face wore a mask of wistfulness so telling I had to look away" (*All* 993).

Angelou accepted Malcolm X's suggestion that she, and some of the other United States expatriates, return home to carry out the serious political work which needed to be done there. Guy agreed that it was probably time for her to return. He apologized that she had needed to leave an account for his university expenses and his living, and thought ahead to when he might repay her. Despite Angelou's comfort in being identified as African (mistaken at one time as a Bambara, at another as an Ahanta), she was equally proud to be an African American survivor: "The middle passage and the auction block had not erased us. Not humiliations nor lynchings, individual cruelties nor collective oppression had been able to eradicate us from the earth. We had come through despite our own ignorance and gullibility, and the ignorance and rapacious greed of our assailants . . . Through the centuries of despair and dislocation, we had been creative, because we faced down death by daring to hope" (*All* 1050–1).

Remembering specific, though collective, sorrows was another practice valued by Africans. In Teresa Washington's words, the person descended from slaves has probably "ignored the genetic scars of slavery in order to survive but must re-member every fragmented affliction to fully heal and evolve" (Washington 233). Critic Justine

Tally adds "it is the nature of 'collective' memory to recall what has long been forgotten of a primal, mythic past, even though the 'signifiers' have long since been divorced from their 'signifieds'" (Tally 86).

It should be emphasized here as well that one of the primary goals of African philosophy was to help its citizens achieve balance. "Balance, the goal of life, is achieved by the recognition of the elements of bad, which complement the elements of good" (Zauditu-Selassie 35).

Angelou brings *All God's Children Need Traveling Shoes* to its close with an echo of the memoir's opening, her flying into the Accra airport with Guy. This time she is leaving that same airport, without her son, but many friends have gathered for a celebratory send-off. She notes to her reader, "I was not sad departing Ghana . . . now I knew my people had never completely left Africa. We had sung it in our blues, shouted it in our gospel and danced the continent in our breakdowns. As we carried it to Philadelphia, Boston and Birmingham we had changed its color, modified its rhythms, yet it was Africa which rode in the bulges of our high calves, shook in our protruding behinds and crackled in our wide open laughter" (*All* 1051).

9

A Song Flung Up to Heaven

Angelou clearly shapes her fifth memoir, *All God's Children Need Traveling Shoes*, around her experiences trying to live as an African in Ghana—building to her accepting a role in the new African American political organization which Malcolm X was planning to form. When she returned to the United States in February 1965, he is the first person she phones from the airport. He is eager to come and pick her up there, but she tells him that she is flying directly to San Francisco where she will spend time with her mother and brother, Bailey, who has traveled from his home in Hawaii to their mother's house in order to see her when she arrives.

A Song Flung Up to Heaven opens with this information. Within pages, Angelou is in San Francisco and Malcolm X has been assassinated. The memoir describes how sorrow changes Angelou's expectations, how her grief over the loss of Malcolm X disorients her. In fact, she becomes as close to dysfunctional as the reader has ever seen her. In the words of critic Eleanor Traylor, the magnificence of Angelou's six volumes of autobiography is that they collectively do not pause: the work continually "dislocates received concepts of self and liberates an antecedent life-writing genre." In it, Angelou insists that "the self is a process" (Traylor 102).

*Holograph sheet of Maya Angelou's hand-
writing from* A Song Flung Up to Heaven,
*reflecting on her troubled state of mind after
the assassination of her friend Malcom X.
(She had returned from Ghana to open a
New York office for Malcom X's fund-raising
efforts just a few days before his death.)*

As Angelou often achieves structural balance, autobiography
by autobiography, *A Song Flung Up to Heaven* closes with the
assassination of Martin Luther King, Jr. It essentially opens with the
killing of Malcolm X and closes with the death of King.

Again, Angelou's immersion in overpowering grief—her
personal sorrow—is the emotional keynote. By the time this sixth

autobiography is published, the American 1960s and the plethora of assassinations—of John F. Kennedy, Robert Kennedy, Malcolm X, the Civil Rights workers (James Chaney, Andrew Goodman, Mickey Schwerner), Medgar Evers, and—finally—Martin Luther King, Jr.—is little more than history. It is for Angelou's success in bringing this history back into reader's minds that reviews of *A Song Flung Up to Heaven* praise the comparatively short memoir. When Traylor summarizes the importance of the series of Angelou's autobiographies, this is her focus: Angelou's memoir series

> highlights American and global response to the lurid murder of Patrice Lumumba in the Congo; the catastrophe at New York's Audubon Theatre, the murder of Malcolm; the horror at Memphis, the murder of Martin Luther King, Jr.; and the relentless sacrifice in South Africa before the walls came rumbling down at Robbins Island (Traylor 92).

In an accompanying analysis of Angelou's poetry, Traylor links the thematic emphases of these last two autobiographies with the fact that "The word *remember*, the predominant signifying word in the poetic production of Maya Angelou, also names her project of contemporary African American poetics *not* restricted to verse. Of the 20,000 words that comprise the four volumes of the Angelou poetic canon so far, 10,050 ring the word *remember* or its cognates" (Traylor 94).

One might insist that by the time Angelou wrote *All God's Children Need Traveling Shoes*, she had come to see herself as a *memorialist* (in addition to continuing to be a *memoirist*). It may well be, however, that she was not sure what she had accomplished until Random House suggested that the six autobiographies—including the most recent, *A Song Flung Up to Heaven*—be published as one collection. In 2004, the omnibus book, *The Collected Autobiographies of Maya Angelou*, appears to rave reviews. Reading the books sequentially makes clear the author's consistent honesty, her ability to compress ranges of events so as to give readers clear scenes, complete with natural-sounding dialogue, that illustrate the whole—and her excellence in achieving the effects she wants. These qualities all mark her ability as a life-writer. (The tendency to use this phrase, "life-writing," rather than the more formal "autobiography" is fairly recent. Angelou knew instinctively that to be a serious, even great, autobiographer called for both technical skill, the use of a fine writer's command, and the ability to reveal both the conscience and, to use her phrase, "the heart of a woman.")

In the case of Maya Angelou's aims in writing the autobiographies that cover her life from the mid-1930s, when she is 7, through 1970 (the books themselves published from 1970 through 2002), her focus was clear: self-revelation, no matter how conflicted the character's responses to events, was the foundation for any writer's accuracy. Of great importance too was the narrator's awareness of nonlocal events—the wide political and social contexts, which eventually become global contexts. Angelou also knew that the pressured effect she could achieve with word choices, as well as the level of diction and her honoring the peculiarity of each person's individual speech, was as important in writing memoir as it was in writing poetry. In the African tradition, Angelou the autobiographer could be considered "a memory keeper and an historian" (Zauditu-Selassie 4).

Angelou's dedication to the omnibus volume was itself like a poem: Dedicated to Angelou's great-grandchildren, Caylin Nicole Johnson and Brandon Bailey Johnson, with the first part of the text giving "grateful acknowledgment" for "the gifts of all my ancestors." Rooted in the African belief of a living spiritual ancestry, of the need to recognize and respect the wisdom of "the ancients," Angelou's work has stemmed in part from her years on the African continent. Yet just as she returned to the United States in 1965, intent on making a useful contribution to African American lives and destinies in this country, she found peace with the understanding that her immediate bloodline was continuing. Random House, in bringing out this collected autobiographies volume, created the bridge that loomed so important to Angelou—between her sometimes lost African heritage and her United States life of writing, inspiring, and leading her readers to both praise God and to go on adventures themselves. Angelou never relinquished her tendency to seek for both excitement and self-fulfillment of all sorts, just as she never gave up on her faith in God. As one poem in *Rainbow in the Cloud* reads:

> Let gratitude be the pillow upon which you kneel to say your nightly prayer. And let faith be the bridge you build to overcome evil and welcome good (*Rainbow* 64).

A Song Flung Up to Heaven does not announce itself as the last—a kind of culminating, abstract apogee—of her autobiographies. Angelou uses her customary deft structural arrangement to slip into the reader's consciousness without pomp or fanfare. The first page of *A Song Flung Up to Heaven* instead describes Angelou's sudden personal fear as she boards the Pan Am jet in Accra and sees all those white (read *hostile*) faces.

> I boarded, wearing traditional West African dress, and sensed myself immediately, and for the first time in years, out of place. A presentiment of unease enveloped me before I could find my seat at the rear of the plane [the flight had originated in Johannesburg; most seats were taken]. For the first few minutes I busied myself arranging bags, souvenirs, presents. When I finally settled into my narrow seat, I looked around and became aware of the source of my discomfort. I was among more white people than I had seen in four years. During that period I had not once thought of not seeing white people; there were European, Canadian and white American faculty at the university where I worked . . . So my upset

did not come from seeing the white complexion, but rather, from seeing so much of it at one time (*Song* 1059–60).

Angelou admits that the white faces on the plane had looked at her and the other blacks boarding in Accra "with distaste, if not outright disgust." She knew that Ghana's adored president, Kwame Nkrumah, was about to be deposed; if that occurred, then Ghana might not be any better off than the United States. Yet, race made a difference: she admitted "at least all the visible participants in that crowded ambience [in Ghana] were black, in contrast to the population in the environment to which I was returning. I knew that the air in the United States was no less turbulent than that in Ghana. If my mail and the world newspapers were to be believed, the country was clamoring with riots and pandemonium. The cry of 'burn, baby, burn' was loud in the land, and black people had gone from the earlier mode of 'sit-in' to 'set fire,' and from 'march-in' to 'break-in'" (*Song* 1060).

Part of Angelou's great sorrow over the killing of Malcolm X was the loss of what she had believed would be an alternate path for angry African Americans, his Organization of African-American Unity. She was returning home to help him work with that group; she thought that troubled Africa could also learn from the efforts of black Americans. Much of the first half of this last memoir recounts her personal devastation at the loss of both the man and the promise inherent in the Organization of African-American Unity.

Angelou had never minced words about racism in the United States. She recalled as she grew up in Stamps, Arkansas: "My real growing up world was a continual struggle against a condition of surrender. Surrender first to the grown-up human beings who I saw every day, all black and all very, very large. Then submission to the idea that black people were inferior to white people, who I saw rarely . . . The South, in general, and Stamps, Arkansas, in particular had had hundreds of years' experience in demoting even large adult blacks to psychological dwarfs. Poor white children had the license to address lauded and older blacks by their first names or by any names they could create" (*Letter* 5). In the Kabir Suman interview, Angelou explains, "There is still, and there has always been, a qualitative difference between being an American and being a *black* American. Let's look at the differences: all white Americans arriving on this soil, before America was the United States or after, came here willingly. Only a very small percentage of white Americans, that is Europeans, came here under bondage . . . less than 2%. Europeans (English or Anglo-Saxons or whatever) came here willingly, escaping conditions which they found untenable. No *African* paid his or her way on a slave ship, paid passage—other than in blood and tears and sweat and agony and fear."

> "If everything had worked out back in 1650 so that there were no slaves and no bondsmen, even that would already make a difference. But 1650 was one of the peak years, because slaving had not by that time so crystallized, it was not "big business" at that time. It only became big business by the end of the seventeenth century. Early in the eighteenth. The majority of the Africans brought to this country were brought from that period until 1850. These people, my ancestors, . . . lived under a condition called "Chattel Slavery." That made quite different psychological complexions—first for the slave and for the slave-holder, and for the white who didn't hold slaves. We bring the baggage of our inheritance, whether we like it or not . . . the intangible invisible baggage with us. And it weighs upon us to varying degrees, but it *does* weigh, and it makes for a different carriage . . . a different stance" (Suman 108).

Angelou continued in her conversation with the Indian interviewer who was also her friend, discussing the differences in her being a *black* American woman writer. "I cannot write esoterically. My pen owes its every movement to the struggle . . . I am who I am because of who I am. I am all these people who have been oppressed, who have been enslaved and murdered, and who have been discriminated against. And so, *that's* who I am. So, when I write, I am obliged to write *because* of *who* I am. And that means then that I am obliged to talk about it. So, the white writer sometimes feels that he or she can tell about the clouds, the sky, the waving of the first green, and I write about that too. But when I am really on my job—Black Americans say 'when I am on my J'—I have to get to my axe. My axe is always hewing on the same stone, and that is: how can we make this country more than what it is today?" (Suman 108).

Asked to write the Introduction to Brian Lanker's magnificent collection of photographs of African American women, Angelou rehearsed this version of history. She begins this introduction by quoting Mari Evans's famous poem "I Am a Black Woman," a key touchstone for African American women's writing in the later twentieth century. Its opening lines, "I/am a black woman/tall as a cypress/strong/beyond all definition still/defying place/and time/ and circumstance" seem to relate directly to the body and history of Angelou. The poem closes with a series of one-word lines—"assailed/ impervious/indestructible"—leading to Evans's apologia:

> Look
>   on me and be
> renewed.

Without any other preamble, Angelou takes readers back to the early 1600s, describing "conditions of cruelty so horrible, so bizarre, the women had to re-invent themselves. They had to find safety and sanctity inside themselves or they would not have been able to tolerate those tortuous lives. They had to learn to be self-forgiving quickly, for often their exterior exploits were at odds with their interior beliefs."

She incorporates the following lines into her text:

"Lives lived in such cauldrons are either obliterated or forged into impenetrable alloys."

"They knew the burden of feminine sensibilities suffocated by masculine responsibilities."

"They wrestled with the inescapable horror of bearing pregnancies which could only result in issuing more chattels into the rapacious maw of slavery."

"They knew the grief of enforced separations from mates who were not theirs to claim" (Lanker 10).

Acknowledging the abuses of the mainstream white culture, which demonized these strong African American women by tarring them with sexual wrongdoings, or drawing them as "acquiescent, submissive Aunt Jemimas," Angelou closes her introduction with a kind of benediction: "The heartbreaking tenderness of Black women and their majestic strength speak of the heroic survival of a people who were stolen into subjugation, denied chastity, and refused innocence" (Lanker 11).

The solemnity of Angelou's Introduction sets the tone for the entire book, a collection in which each woman who has been photographed then adds her own essay to her section. When Angelou writes *this* essay (in contrast to her essay that becomes the book's introduction), she speaks more acerbically, more vehemently. That essay opens, "Can you imagine if this country were not so afflicted with racism? Can you imagine what it would be like if the vitality, humor, and resilience of the black Americans were infused throughout this country?"

She makes several important points in this brief commentary. At one point she notes, "one cannot legislate love," and then continues, "the larger society said that I belonged to an unwelcome tribe. My feeling was, 'Unwelcome to you, but my people don't say that.' Which is one of the reasons black women have survived, and done better than that, thrived." In a characteristic shift of tone, Angelou asserts about herself, "I have no modesty, none. It's a waste of time. It's a learned affectation stuck on from without. If life slams the modest person against the wall, he or she will drop that modesty quicker than a stripper will drop her G-string. What I hope I have and what I pray for is humility. Humility comes from within" (Lanker 166).

Moving to a pervasive concern with younger generations, Angelou notes that she fears cynicism. (She worries that a young person "has gone from knowing nothing to believing in nothing.") "Young people must not get to the point of saying 'You mean to tell me we had Malcolm X, Martin Luther King, Medgar Evers? You mean to tell me we had the Kennedys, we had Fannie Lou Hamer and Mary McLeod Bethune? You mean to tell me we had all these men and women and we have made no progress? Then what the hell—there is no progress to be made."

As Angelou does in the lengthy Sumar interview, she closes this essay with her testimonial: "I'm convinced that I'm a child of God. That's wonderful, exhilarating, liberating, full of promise. But the burden which goes along with that is, I'm convinced that everybody is a child of God. The brutes and bigots, the batterers and the bastards are also children of God. And that's where the onerous burden comes in for me as a practicing Christian, to try to keep that in mind and not grit my teeth until they break off into little stubs" (Lanker 166). She says a bit differently to Sumar that, "I keep my roots in the black church. Wherever I am, I am a part of that black community. And I serve them and I ask them to serve me. I never make any distinction. I work hard, I would love to live pretty, and I will do so as long as I can afford to do so. Malcolm had a wonderful story, you know in a lecture he gave at Yale. He asked: What is the difference between this black man who has these degrees and this black man who is a janitor? And he said: one is a doctor nigger and the other is just nigger. That's it. You know, there is no qualitative difference . . ."

"The white society sees a superficial difference," Angelou says wryly. "They think my achievements make me 'white'" (Sumar 111).

When she turns to expressing her belief in Christian living, as well as in God, she emphasizes, "One person standing on the Word of God is the majority." She notes in *Rainbow in the Cloud*:

Stand up straight and realize who you are, that you tower over your circumstances. You are a child of God. Stand up straight.

There is a place in you that you must keep inviolate, a place that you must keep clean. A place where you say to any intruder, "Back up, don't you know I'm a child of God."

In the silence we listen to ourselves. Then we ask questions of ourselves. We describe ourselves to ourselves, and in the quietude we may even hear the voice of God (*Rainbow* 58, 56).

A Song Flung Up to God distills many of these sentiments. Part of Angelou's great hopefulness about coming back to New York to work with Malcolm X stemmed from her belief that the African American promise which might be created in the United States would lead the world to achieve similar reforms, and abolish the curse of racism. In her words, she felt sympathy for the Africans in South Africa. The United States, with Malcolm X as its leader, would "rid our country of racism once and for all . . . We were going to give them [the South Africans] something new, something visionary, to look up to. After we had cleansed ourselves and our country of hate, they would be able to study our methods, take heart from our example and let freedom ring in their country as it would ring in ours" (*Song* 1061).

When Mary Jane Lupton writes about her visiting Angelou in 1997, urging her to write what would become the sixth autobiography—after over a decade of waiting for the book to be published, Angelou tells her that she has been troubled by not only her sorrow over the deaths of Malcolm X and Martin Luther King, Jr. but by the state of the world. Lupton notes that her visit to Angelou comes just before the author will be flying to New York to be at the bedside of Betty Shabazz, recently burned in a macabre accident (Shabazz is the wife of Malcolm X, the mother of his children; she will die only six days later on June 23, 1997). Lupton explains, "The deaths of Malcolm X and Martin Luther King, Jr., were much on Angelou's mind" (Lupton 85).

In reply to Lupton's questions about when she might undertake this sixth autobiography, Angelou said she would not be able to write the book until, or unless, "I want to be able to look at horror and not find a justification but a lesson. If I can find a lesson, I can live with it if I can put it in a place." The orderly mind of the writer, creating structure even when no structure exists, attempts to face what she rightly calls "horror." She describes that state of mind to Lupton as the result of the killings of "her friend and associate el-Hajj Malik el-Shabazz" (Lupton 86), as well as Martin Luther King, Jr. According to Lupton's unpublished interview with Angelou, Angelou then explained, "I will do it, I say, but when? I still have to live a little longer and learn how to extract. I have to learn it. And the only way I can learn it is living" (Lupton 86).

The time Angelou remembered was a period when days were marked by grief. Those days moved differently; she was not yet ready to even attempt to re-create those sorrowful events.

Although Malcolm X had dominated the latter chapters of *All God's Children Need Traveling Shoes*, Angelou felt that she had not yet told his important story. Innocent of the dangers of his trying to lead a race-divided country, Angelou seemed not to hear his frightening comment during their last telephone call. Malcolm X interrupted her to tell her that he had had to leave his car in the Holland Tunnel. He said bluntly, "Somebody was trying to get me. I jumped in a white man's car. He panicked. I told him who I was, and he said, 'Get down low, I'll get you out of this.' You believe that, Maya?" (*Song* 1064). Her calm reply, that she would call him next week from California, indicated that she had no way of interpreting what had happened— no way to find *meaning* in the heroic man's being literally hunted through the streets of New York. His story about this threat did not even register in her consciousness.

Before Angelou makes the phone call a part of Malcolm X's tragic narrative, she has quoted one of his last letters, sent to her in Accra.

Dear Maya,

I was shocked and surprised when your letter arrived but I was also pleased because I only had to wait two months for this one whereas previously I had to wait almost a year. You see I haven't lost my wit. (smile)

Your analysis of our people's tendency to talk over the head of the masses in a language that is too far above and beyond them is certainly true. You can communicate because you have plenty of (soul) and you always keep your feet firmly rooted on the ground.

I am enclosing some articles that will give you somewhat of an idea of my daily experiences here and you will then be better able to understand why it sometimes takes me a long time to write. I was most pleased to learn that you might be hitting [sic] in this direction this year. You are a beautiful writer and a beautiful woman. You know that I will always do my utmost to be helpful to you in any way possible so don't hesitate.

Signed

Your brother Malcolm (*Song* 1061).

Quoted in critic Dolly McPherson's book is an earlier letter from Malcolm X to Angelou, this one following up a still earlier letter in which he scolds her for being so critical of Shirley Du Bois because of her comparative isolation from her people in Africa. In that letter Malcolm says, "We need people on each level to fight our battle. Don't be in such a hurry to condemn a person because he doesn't do what you do, or think as you think or as fast. There was a time when you didn't know what you know today" (McPherson 116).

The next letter from Malcolm X, dated January 15, 1965, shows his trying to pave the way for a visitor: "I hope that you will get this letter before James Farmer arrives. The Afro-American community there [in Accra] should not shun him but should encircle him and make sure that he is exposed to the right kind of thinking . . . to the most undiluted African thinking" (McPherson 116, from the Angelou archive, Wake Forest University). It echoes the letter he had previously sent to Angelou (she called it a "directive"), "A young painter named Tom Feelings is coming to Ghana. Do everything you can for him. I am counting on you.

"The U. S. State Department is sending James Farmer to Ghana. The Ambassador will pick out special people for him to see and special places he should go. I want you all to collect him and show him around. Treat him as you treated me. I am counting on you" (*All* 1040).

When Malcolm X mentioned in other correspondence that: "Death threats were proliferating in his post box and he changed his telephone number frequently to protect his wife from vulgar and frightening callers," Angelou again failed to register what this level of anxiety meant in the orderly and "safe" United States (*All* 1039–40). Smug in her thinking that America offered more possibilities for change than did Africa, Angelou instead reflected on what she saw as the losing battle that Vus Make and Oliver Tambo waged. Malcolm X had created the "Organization of African-American Unity." Among its proposals was a meeting with the United Nations, "taking the plight of the African-Americans and asking the world council to intercede on the part of beleaguered blacks." The South Africans, in contrast, were attempting to change "the hearts and thereby the actions of the apartheid-loving Boers. In the early sixties," Angelou recounts, "I called them Nation Dreamers. When I thought of Robert Sobukwe, leader of the Pan-African Congress who had languished for years in prison, and Nelson Mandela, who had recently been arrested, I was sure that they would spend their lives sealed away from the world" (*Song* 1061).

It is only forty-eight hours after Angelou reached San Francisco that her friend Yvonne phoned to tell her she should never have come back to this "crazy" country. What her girlhood friend says is representative of the lack of intelligent information throughout the United States: "These Negroes are crazy here. I mean, really crazy. Otherwise, why would they have just killed that man in New York?"(*Song* 1071). Unnamed here, Malcolm X was the first assassinated black United States leader; there would be others.

What Angelou does with this death takes much of the entire autobiography: her grieving finally begins to lessen in 1967 when she visits the Audubon Ballroom in New York City so as to revision "the grisly scene." An African American landmark, the Audubon was clearly raced: "The dance hall and theater had been famous for decades. When I had gone visiting in the fifties, I often imagined Langston Hughes and Arna Bontemps and Zora Neale Hurston dancing the Charleston to the big-band music of Jimmy Lunceford, Count Basie and Duke Ellington" (*Song* 1125). In a poem-like meditation, Angelou re-creates the gala 1965 fund-raiser for the Organization of African-American Unity: Malcolm X is speaking. This is the closing six sentences of her meditation:

> Had I stayed in New York when I returned from Ghana, would I have been sitting with Betty Shabazz and her children?
>
> Would I have heard the final words of Malcolm X?
>
> Would I have heard the shots puncture the air?
>
> Would I have seen the killers' faces and had them etched in my mind eternally?
>
> I could see no shadow inside; no chimera arose and danced.
>
> I walked away (*Song* 1125).

Part of Angelou's grief about the killing of Malcolm X resisted common sense: her mother, for instance, preferred that Maya would work for Martin Luther King, Jr. She felt that Malcolm X was too abrasive, that he wanted too much change (and she did not understand his Muslim enthusiasms). She obviously sympathized with her daughter after the assassination of her friend, but her own lack of information frightened Angelou. If even bright African American people did not understand what could be accomplished, what hope could she have for the betterment of the United States?

Even though Bailey had reassured her that within a few years, people would understand what Malcolm X would have done, his comforting did not help her crawl out of her deep despair.

In *Rainbow in the Cloud*, Angelou writes one of her last commentaries on her beloved friend: "Malcolm X was America's

Molotov cocktail, thrown upon the White hope that all Black Americans would follow the nonviolent tenets of Dr. Martin Luther King, Jr." (*Rainbow* 15). In the same collection, she wrote about King, "It is a great blessing to have lived in the time of Martin Luther King, Jr., when forgiveness and generosity of spirit encouraged our citizenry to work for a better world for everybody" (*Rainbow* 63). (In 1964 Martin Luther King, Jr., had been honored by receiving the Nobel Peace Prize.)

Before *A Song Flung Up to Heaven* gains momentum to encompass the difficult last years of the life of Martin Luther King, Jr., Angelou moves into the pattern of describing the travel that had underlay *All God's Children Need Traveling Shoes*. There she had created the flavors of the foreign, and many of those

Coretta Scott King and Maya Angelou. Because Martin Luther King, Jr., had been assassinated on the morning of Angelou's birthday, she renounced any personal celebration. Every year, she and the widow Coretta King communicated on the day of his assassination. Photo © by Eugene Redmond. Used by permission of Eugene B. Redmond.

struck her as pleasurably exotic. In entering "everyday" Cairo, for instance, Angelou wrote:

> The shiny European cars, large horned cows, careening taxis and the throngs of pedestrians, goats, mules, camels, the occasional limousine and the incredible scatter of children made the streets a visual and a tonal symphony of chaos.
>
> When we entered the center of Cairo, the avenues burst wide open with such a force of color, people, action and smells I was stripped of cool composure.
>
> Emaciated men in long tattered robes flailed, ranted at heavily burdened mules. Sleek limousines rode through the droppings of camels that waved their wide behinds casually as they sashayed in the shadow of skyscrapers. Well-dressed women in pairs, or accompanied by men, took no notice of their sisters, covered from head to toe in voluminous heavy black wraps . . . Scents of spices, manure, gasoline exhaust, flowers, and body sweat made the air in the car nearly visible (*All* 822–3).

Exotic as Egypt was, sometimes in the midst of their native and expatriate friends, Angelou and David Du Bois would break into a spiritual or two. They found themselves intent on reminding others that those melodies were "dearly known," and that they were the epitome of "the sounds of black America" (*All* 829).

For Angelou, the vestiges of her Southern childhood translated into her life on the African continent. She compares the comforting sheltering of the black American women to the strength of the African women: both groups are compassionate, as well as strong. Angelou writes, "This is the way the African thinks and the way Southern blacks where I grew up think. So that's why it continues in the South . . . there are so many Africanisms . . . that gave me another sense of continuity" (Con 17). Further, "In Africa, I saw many customs that were the same as here" (Con 4).

During the 1970s, Angelou maintained her love of, and her loyalty to, Ghana, "I consider that [Ghana] home. Whenever I'm away from Ghana, I feel that I am traveling. While the rest of the world has been developing technology, Ghana has been improving the quality of man's humanity to man" (Con 4).

Besides charting and describing geography, Angelou links daily travel with the African-United States nexus. She says in an interview, "The story of the Black Americans trying to return home is the central story. It is central in that all human beings look for home. It is given to us. And maybe all living things for all I know. For as soon as the flower, vegetable or tree grows it gives forth so that it can return home to the sources of life. That African at home who has never been sent abroad is a story in that book . . . So there are many" (Con 169). Later, about herself, she writes, "I had to come home to America to write about coming home to Africa" (Con 158).

When asked specifically about *All God's Children Need Traveling Shoes*, she was sometimes more candid than at others. One answer that recurs is this: "There is the story of a single mother raising a male child and trying to learn when to let go and how not to smother, how not to abandon either . . . bring him to [*sic*] close or push him away" (Con 169). As she makes clear throughout the six volumes of her autobiographies, Angelou relies on her friends—friends of both genders—to help her rear Guy. His adulthood becomes a living example of the *community's* best efforts, whether those efforts are seen as manifestations of African thought or of African American benevolence.

Over-riding Angelou's sense of satisfaction in the life of her son is the daily anxiety of her paramount question: what will become of the United States of America? She concludes *A Song Flung Up to Heaven* with narratives that make the reader revisit both the accomplishments of Martin Luther King, Jr., and the vision of her son Guy, once again hospitalized after a car accident upon his return from Ghana. His neck is again broken, but he will survive. King, however, assassinated in Memphis on the morning of Angelou's fortieth birthday, becomes another visible and indelible warning to the millions of African Americans around the world: even the most kindly, even the best-hearted, are not safe.

As Charron Barnwell points out, *A Song Flung Up to Heaven* memorializes more deaths than those of Malcolm X and Martin Luther King, Jr. Angelou starts recounting the tragedies that relate to United States (and global) politics in *All God's Children Need Traveling Shoes*. On August 27, 1963, when the Ghanaian women (and Angelou) march on the American Embassy with their written statement, they are joining in solidarity with the Washington, DC, march at which King will speak: that is the day of W. E. B. DuBois's death. (Patrice Lumumba has been killed in a previous volume.) Angelou uses this occasion at least partly to describe the naïve behavior of the protesting women ("brave revolutionaries . . . of course, none of us, save Julian, had ever been close to bloody violence, and not one of us had spent an hour in jail for our political beliefs") (*All* 982, Barnwell 145).

Much of *A Song Flung Up to Heaven* describes not only Angelou in sorrowful despair after Malcolm X's assassination, but also the chaos Angelou finds once she returns to Los Angeles—including some self-dramatising days when she prowls Watts in the midst of that ongoing riot, thinking she is doing investigative reporting as she talks with residents. The author seems to be repeating her earlier pattern of putting herself at risk when she thinks life has disappointed her beyond any positive realization.

Angelou tells a more pleasant financial story, when her old New York friend Jerry Purcell becomes her patron. The wealthy man believes in her talent and insists she take his support so that she can write, whether it be scripts or songs or life-narratives. In seemingly quick succession, she is hired to create and film a series of television programs about the black experience; and then Robert Loomis phones her—again—about the possibility of her writing an autobiography, using the ploy of emphasizing the difficulty of such an undertaking: this time she accepts the invitation. The last book of her memoirs, in fact, ends with her starting what will become *I Know Why the Caged Bird Sings.*

What you looking at me for. I didn't come to stay (*Song* 1167).

When Barnwell says that Angelou's six-book cycle created "a canon of life-sustaining songs," she is reading through the miasma of death that centers the last two autobiographies. Like many of Angelou's readers, this critic, too, interleaves the author's editorial sections where they can usefully change the tone of the memoir. A few paragraphs before Angelou "closes" the book—and the series of autobiographies entire—she gives her reader an ebullient Maya Angelou, musing about African American progress in relation to that of Angelou herself:

"We had come so far from where we started, and weren't nearly approaching where we had to be, but we were on the road to becoming better. I thought if I wrote a book, I would have to examine the quality in the human spirit that continues to rise despite the slings and arrows of outrageous fortune."

"Rise out of physical pain and the psychological cruelties."

"Rise from being victims of rape and abuse and abandonment to the determination to be no victim of any kind."

"Rise and be prepared to move on and ever on" (*Song* 1166).

10

Poems and the public spotlight

If readers were responding to Angelou's autobiographies, poems, and essays only on the basis of their *content*—that is, what she was writing about, the wide appeal of her work would have been considerably less than it was. Random House, her publisher, found it hard to believe the sales figures: every book Maya Angelou published with them sold hundreds of thousands of copies. Nearly every book was translated into thirty or more languages. Beginning with the 1970 appearance of *I Know Why the Caged Bird Sings*, Angelou's writing had such an extensive following that observers sometimes mentioned her "cult" of admiring readers.

This book has discussed Angelou's autobiographies in the sequence in which they appeared. Perhaps it is a misleading choice, to trace her life as writer from *I Know Why the Caged Bird Sings* to *Gather Together in My Name* in 1974, *Singin' and Swingin' and Gettin' Merry Like Christmas* in 1976, *The Heart of a Woman* in 1981, and *All God's Children Need Traveling Shoes* in 1986—leaving the last of her autobiographies (*A Song Flung Up to Heaven* in 2002) and *The Collected Autobiographies* in 2004 to represent her work in the twenty-first century. We have seen that the fifth and sixth memoirs are dominated by Civil Rights activities as well as the sense of overwhelming loss after the assassinations of both Malcolm X and Martin Luther King, Jr. The first four books of Angelou's autobiography do not share that emphasis.

These autobiographies, rather, have as focus the author's life—her family (or lack of family), her brother's crucial role throughout her childhood and adolescence, her several geographic locations, her sexual abuse and the resulting voluntary mutism, her religious belief, her academic excellences, her early yen for adventure, the birth of her son, her talents as dancer and singer, her struggle as single mother to earn a living, the death of Annie Henderson, and—not least—her heterosexual relationships with Tosh Angelos, Vus Make, Paul Du Feu, and others (one man named only "the African").

Had Angelou conceived of herself as a "celebrity" when she began writing her first autobiography in the late 1960s, she would probably have felt compelled to write more fully about her marriages and liaisons. Her treatment of these male partners in her memoirs, however, suggests that she was motivated less, and less often, by her partners than she was by her son. Her worries about Guy as he grows and matures dominate nearly all the autobiographies. Even without much description, Angelou as she considers her love relationships suggests their existence during the years covered by her collective memoirs—from her marriage to Tosh Angelos in 1950 through her time in New York and Egypt with Vus Make in the early 1960s, through her marriage to the British architect and cartoonist Paul De Feu (1973–81), and beyond.

Somewhat unexpectedly, it is Angelou's poems rather than her autobiographies that give readers information about her loves. In 1975, her second collection of poems is published. *Oh Pray My Wings Are Gonna Fit Me Well* is dedicated to "Paul," her husband during much of the 1970s: it includes many of her best love poems. (Angelou's first poem collection, *Just Give Me a Cool Drink of Water 'Fore I Diiie*, appeared in 1971 and was nominated for the Pulitzer Prize in Poetry.)

In 1978 *And Still I Rise* is published (following Angelou's stage play of
the same title) and in 1981, *Shaker, Why Don't you Sing?* Alternating
within the ongoing volumes of Angelou's autobiographies, the poem
collections were well-reviewed. Considering that the United States
was not a country in which people avidly bought books of poems,
Angelou's poetry interested a wide readership. The longer and
often woman-centered poems that appeared in *And Still I Rise* were
becoming the new best-loved works of this African American writer.
That she drew heavily from blues, jazz, and folk music in creating the
paced rhythms of her 1980s poems surprised no one.

Maya Angelou sometimes borrowed from a very different context
of poems when she sat down to write her poetry. She privileged the
works of Langston Hughes, but she also read John Milton. (Because
Annie Henderson avoided the works of white writers, Marguerite and
Bailey recited from James Weldon Johnson, Melvin B. Tolson, Claude
McKay, Anne Spencer, Frances Harper, and Paul Laurence Dunbar.
Later, words by Jean Toomer, Lucille Clifton, and Gwendolyn Brooks
would come into their lives. Marguerite sometimes crawled under
the house to read quietly, a practice her grandmother respected.) As
Angelou told George Plimpton, "I want to hear how English sounds,
how Edna St. Vincent Millay[1] heard English. I want to hear it so I
read it aloud. It is not so that I can imitate it. It is to remind me what
a glorious language it is. Then I try to be particular and even a little
original. It's like reading Gerard Manley Hopkins or Paul Laurence
Dunbar or James Weldon Johnson" (Paris 239). Also to Plimpton,
Angelou explained why she spent hours reading the Bible, often
aloud. "The language of all the interpretations, the translations, of
the Judaic Bible and the Christian Bible, is musical, just wonderful.
I read the Bible to myself. I'll take any translation, any edition, and
read it aloud, just to hear the language, hear the rhythm, and remind
myself how beautiful English is . . . English remains the most beautiful
of languages. It will do anything" (Paris 238). By the time Angelou

is successfully writing her own poems, some of them starting as
songs, she knows most of Hughes's work, that of Aime Cesaire, all the
Harlem Renaissance writers, and African American women writers
(Mari Evans, Gwendolyn Brooks, Sonia Sanchez, June Jordan, Toni
Morrison, Alice Walker, Rita Dove, and others). As she said in the
Claudia Tate interview, "I love them. I love the rhythm and sweetness
of Dunbar's dialect verse. I love 'Candle Lighting Time' and 'Little
Brown Baby.' I love James Weldon Johnson's 'Creation.' I'm impressed
with James Baldwin—his craftsmanship and his courage. That means
a lot" (Tate in Braxton 158).

Like many of Angelou's book titles, *Oh Pray My Wings Are
Gonna Fit Me Well* is taken from a spiritual (this one dating from
the nineteenth century). Less exuberant than some, this song has a
mournful second and fourth line:

I'm a lay down this heavy load . . .

Because of the line's pace and repetition, there is little sense of peace
conveyed to the reader.

Angelou's second collection is divided into five sections rather
than the two-part arrangement of her first book. It is more varied but
the divisions don't necessarily correlate with the poems' themes. (It
should be noted that *The Complete Collected Poems of Maya Angelou*
[1994] is the standard edition today, but Angelou included only some
poems from each separate collection in *The Complete Collected*. For
instance, she chooses only 36 poems from the separate book *Oh Pray
My Wings Are Gonna Fit Me Well* (Wedin 173). As Lyman B. Hagen
noted years ago, forty percent of Angelou's poems are short, as are
many of the lines within those poems. He also suggests that while
she may be creating what he calls "black rhythms" through her poetic
voice, she also works with "counter rhythms" (Hagen 119).

Of the five sections of this second poem collection, three replicate
the strengths of Angelou's first book. The heavily accented refrain of

For several years Maya maintained a home in Atlanta, Georgia. At one of the many parties she hosted while living there she paused for this photo with Amina Baraka at the side, Val Gray Ward, and the writers Sonia Sanchez and Mari Evans. Photo © by poet Eugene Redmond. Used by permission of Eugene B. Redmond.

"Pickin Em Up and Layin Em Down," like the effects Angelou achieves in "Come. And Be My Baby," "The Pusher," and "Prisoner," are playful. More often, however, the poems work as if they were laments. Tone conveys more than stanza shape. In the midst of a cluster of love poems, for example, Angelou places "Alone," which opens:

Lying, thinking
Last night
How to find my soul a home . . .

a poem that becomes a convincing religious statement. The three-line refrain that closes the poem's three long stanzas is also used as a "response" triad between each stanza:

—That nobody,
But nobody
Can make it out here alone.

ends the first stanza. Repeated as a stand-alone tercet, it then reads:

Alone, all alone
Nobody, but nobody
Can make it out here alone.

There are four other repetitions, all variants of the basic pattern.

Far different in effect is "Poor Girl," another spoken and refrain-centered poem. In these ten-line stanzas, Angelou works toward the uniform concluding couplet of each verse: "Poor girl/Just like me." The relinquishing of love fights against an implied angry resolution. (Such other love poems as the evocative "Passing Time," "A Conceit," and "I Almost Remember" use fewer rhythmic tricks and rely on the arrangements of single words.) "Song for the Old Ones," placed in section five, is an effective ballad, less a love poem than it is the poet's defense for the often-criticized "Uncle Tomming" necessary to keep blacks alive during harsh times. Similarly, "Elegy," dedicated to Harriet Tubman and Frederick Douglass, images the African American power to endure. The sonority of its closing speaks of promise rather than of defeat:

I lie down in my grave
and watch my children
grow.

The single poem from this collection that foreshadows work to come that will enhance Angelou's name as poet is a mid-length poem titled "Woman Me." The poem opens, "Your smile, delicate/rumor of peace," and it evokes "A bride of hurricanes. A swarm of summer wind." What the reader hears is "Your laughter, pealing tall/above the bells of ruined cathedrals." In her use of synaesthesia, Angelou creates momentum for the reader's reaction. Here, the body of a beloved woman may be lush, even over-ripe, but the premise—that the woman's body is filled with glory that could change the existing world—sets the tone for such of Angelou's poems to come as "Remembrance," "Woman Work," "Phenomenal Woman," and "And Still I Rise." Triumphant and energetic, lines arranged to force the reader to take deeper and deeper breaths, these are the poems I earlier referred to as "anthems." They demand full voices, and they have less empty space on the page than do Angelou's shorter poems. They are in many different respects all-encompassing.

In her Claudia Tate interview, Angelou explained that the titles for both her first and second poem collections were meant to be inspirational. *Just Give Me a Cool Drink of Water* "refers to my belief in our innocence as a species. Innocence is 'lonely.'" *Oh Pray My Wings* "originally comes from a slave holler, and the words from a nineteenth century spiritual . . . I planned to put all the things bothering me—my heavy load—in that book, and let them pass." Of *And Still I Rise*, Angelou said, the title (and the title poem) "refers to the indomitable spirit of black people." To illustrate, she quotes:

You may write me down in history
With your bitter, twisted lies.
You may trod me in the very dirt
But still, like dust, I'll rise (Tate in Braxton 157).

Angelou's third collection of poems to be included in *The Complete Collected* is *And Still I Rise*. Perhaps more positive, and certainly more sexual, than the work in her first two books, these poems are scattered among characters and speakers, taking on a kind of fictional movement: read one, associate its title and its dedication, process the words, move on to the next. For example, the reader moves from "Kin," dedicated to Angelou's brother Bailey, back to the two-quatrain poem "The Traveler," in which the speaker is described as "Manless and friendless," and then back through "Kin," with its poignant early stanza:

> You left me to force strangers
>
> Into brother molds, exacting
>
> Taxations they never
>
> Owed or could ever pay.

And ahead to "The Memory," which closes (and replays the poet's memories of Arkansas):

> Sugar cane reach up to God
>
> And every baby crying.

Strategies for reading poems are not usually printed along with the poems in poetry collections. Such an omission is unfortunate because reading the work of Maya Angelou presents several genuine difficulties. One of these is that Angelou is a woman writer, and readers have been troubled for centuries by the work of "lady poets." Another difficulty is that Angelou is African American so readers unfamiliar with black American speech might be somewhat put off by the poet's use of idiomatic language (as well as in writing about experiences that might be seen as race-specific). From the history and traditions of African American literature may come important qualities that an observant poet such as Angelou would practice. A third difficulty that readers might deduce in reading Angelou's poetry is her political bent, her tendency to draw from African American life and law (and the abuses of that law) in the twentieth and the twenty-first centuries. As critic Zofia Burr commented in linking the work of

Angelou to that of Emily Dickinson, Josephine Miles, Audre Lorde, and Gwendolyn Brooks, readers may have a "tendency to devalue the poetry as prosaic, propagandistic, or journalistic and to interpret it as narrowly autobiographical, expressive of personal experience and sensibility, rather than engaged with the poet's—and the reader's—world" (Burr 180). What could the novice reader expect from reading "women's poetry?" As Burr points out, most of these women writers "have regularly been misunderstood and marginalized as poets." She accurately summarizes that none of these writers figure in "any of the larger narratives about twentieth century American poetry."

By this statement, Burr refers to the issues of canonized versus uncanonized writers as determined and grouped by literary theorists. Certain writers always appear in books about the development of American poetry in the twentieth century: Robert Lowell will be included though Anne Sexton may not be, and Maya Angelou and Audre Lorde most certainly will not be. Yet both Lowell and Sexton are considered "confessional" poets—and the work of both Angelou and Lord has confessional elements. In Burr's assessment, writing by Brooks, Miles, Lorde, and Angelou may be considered somewhat defiant. These poets do not care to copy mainstream poetic traditions. In fact, their poems are, most likely, "widely and variously addressed . . . deeply engaged in public issues . . . and interested in moving their audiences to action" (Burr 2–3).

Within this group, Burr places Maya Angelou in a still more specialized category. Because of the wide readership for her autobiographies, Angelou had become "the most widely recognized poet in contemporary United States culture. She is found on television, in the movies, on the radio, in print, on the lecture circuit, on the internet, at the 1993 Presidential inauguration, and at the Million Man March" (Burr 181). Her fame, Burr points out accurately, and her "success with a larger public audience," has made poetry critics suspicious of Angelou's poetry as a *written* genre.

In Burr's apt discussion, she calls attention to the fact that poems by women may not necessarily lead to unsympathetic readings. The difference between poems by women and poems by men may not be one of gender so much as it is one of performance versus reading. Years ago, critic Robert Stepto had urged African American writers to consider the fact that their writing needed to accommodate "the performative aesthetic of oral storytelling by fashioning characters (voices) who pose as tellers and hearers and occasion thereby certain types of narrative structuring" (Stepto 200). A decade later, Gayl Jones echoes this mandate. (Although poets have been giving readings since the 1950s, using the mode drawn from the performances by British writer Dylan Thomas, most established American poets read formally, even stiffly, and evenings with them reading from their works are hardly enjoyable. In contrast, Maya Angelou had worked out a model in which she combined lecture with readings, and as she moved smoothly from one segment of discussion into a poem—perhaps without announcing the poem by its title—listeners sometimes did not know that she was speaking a poem at all. Her "talks" were filled with cajoling, pleading, reaching out to audience members to urge them to live morally, push themselves to achieve, as well as to find inner satisfactions and [perhaps] peace, creating narratives that served to illustrate significant principles for upright living. Angelou said in an interview that she was no "goody-two shoes," but part of her appeal as a lecturer was that she was not afraid to be just that [Paris 250]. As Burr points out, even Angelou's model for "reading" her poems was unique.)

Critic Eleanor Traylor makes the point that Angelou in an occasional poem is drawing from a number of famous African American poems, earlier poems that manage to stand like revered ghosts in the wings of the readers' conscious minds. She calls these "undersong" poems and suggests that among those models are some by Sterling Brown ("Willie"), Countee Cullen, James Baldwin, Julian

Mayfield, and particularly Langston Hughes's "Son to Mother" and his "Madam" poems (in his "Madam to You").

Traylor compares Hughes's "My name is Johnson/Madam Alberta K." with Angelou's "Weekend Glory," which closes:

> My life ain't heaven
> but it sure ain't hell.
> I'm not on top
> but I call it swell
> If I'm able to work
> and get paid right
> and have the luck to be Black
> on a Saturday night.

Heavily reliant on the cocky speaker's vernacular, "Weekend Glory" opens with a particularly black-language introduction, "Some dichty folks/ don't know the facts,/ posin' and preenin'/ and puttin' on acts,/ stretchin' their necks/ and strainin' their backs." Traylor's point here is what she calls "the do-op, the swing, the beat, not exact but close enough to hear the play and bring the smile. It is the discursive banter going on between 'weekend' speaker and Madam—the textual play— that is the wink of a salute to the antecedent poet Langston Hughes" (Traylor 97 and see also Jasmin Y. DeGout 130).

For critic Cherron A. Barnwell, who reads Angelou's work as a whole, whatever she writes (and/or performs) becomes a means of *sustaining* the African American community. Without using the word "spiritual," Barnwell lists a number of ways Angelou accomplishes this aim, and she includes a long paragraph from the writer's *A Song Flung Up to Heaven* as illustration:

> We put surviving into our poems and into our songs. We put it into our folk tales. We danced surviving in Congo Square in New Orleans and put it in our pots when we cooked pinto beans. We wore surviving on our backs when we clothed ourselves in the

colors of the rainbow. We were pulled down so low we could hardly lift our eyes, so we knew, if we wanted to survive, we had better lift our own spirits (Barnwell 145).

The resonance of these accurate critical comments stems in large part from the effect of Angelou's longer, less formally crafted, and thematically relevant poems. She achieved some of this power as early as "Woman Me" in the second collection, *Oh Pray My Wings Are Gonna Fit Me Well*. Angelou's third book, *And Still I Rise* includes a quantity of poems seemingly written about what DeGout refers to as her "woman-centered space" (DeGout 123). The title poem, "Still I Rise," is representative of the indomitable African American spirit.

> You may write me down in history
> With your bitter, twisted lies, . . .
> Does my sassiness upset you?
> Why are you beset with gloom?
> 'Cause I walk like I've got oil wells
> Pumping in my living room.

As the poem continues—with a kind of unusually ironic humor—the seven quatrains lead to two longer stanzas comprised of more frequent repetitions. The closing lines, which are repeated seven times in the last two stanzas, create a triumphal pace; the poem closes:

> Bringing the gifts that my ancestors gave,
> I am the dream and the hope of the slave.
> I rise
> I rise
> I rise.

Angelou here does not create a speaker different from the implied "you" persona of the writer. Her reader/listener must accept the dogmatism of these words. As critic Jasmin DeGout points out, this kind of poem aims to create "a community of listeners or witnesses, those who share in the pain or trauma of the speaker. Such pieces undertake the healing process by creating a community of healers . . . part of the blues mode in the Angelou canon" (DeGout 128).

An even better-known poem from this collection is "Phenomenal Woman," a poem that has been published separately, in collections of Angelou's most beloved works, and as a chapbook (Random House using the brilliant colors and shapes of Paul Gauguin's stately, flamboyant women as illustration). Eleanor Traylor points out that in this poem Angelou has adapted the formal structure of the traditional ode, lending dignity and weight to this suite of words. Traylor writes, "It is a praise song practicing the beat, the rhythm, the slide, the cadence, the be-bop, the assonance and dissonance, the jam session, that embodies the poetics of identity. It triggers memory if you can hear in it the laughter and appeal of a ring-game poem or a hip-hop rap" (Traylor 95). Some phrases and lines from this particular poem appear as borrowings in works by other poets. It opens:

> Pretty women wonder where my secret lies.
> I'm not cute or built to suit a fashion model's size
> But when I start to tell them,
> They think I'm telling lies.
> I say,
> It's in the reach of my arms,
> The span of my hips,
> The stride of my step,
> The curl of my lips.
> I'm a woman

Phenomenally.
Phenomenal woman,
That's me.

Each of the four sections (rhythms maintained in the thirteen- or fourteen-lined stanzas) concludes with this same couplet: "Phenomenal woman,/ That's me." With drumming regularity, the woman poet's voice insists that *she* understands her sometimes inscrutable charms, and she evinces genuine sisterhood in teaching other women about her various attractions. Critic Jacqueline Thursby points out that the poem first appeared in *Cosmopolitan* in 1978; in 1993 it was featured in John Singleton's film *Poetic Justice*. After it appeared in *And Still I Rise*, often paired with another of Angelou's poems from that collection, "Men," it was regularly reprinted in collections of women's poetry, of southern literature, and of feminist-inspired literature. Angelou performed the work frequently in her readings and talks, doing so "with vigor and passion, creating a euphoric spell through her unwavering, coaxing voice" (Thursby 230; see also Cosgrove, Essick, Ramsay, and Stepto's essay).

Angelou published two more poem collections in the 1980s— after *And Still I Rise* appeared in 1978, she wrote the poems in one of her most successful books, *Shaker, Why Don't You Sing?* (1983). In 1987 that collection was followed by *Now Sheba Sings the Song* (which helped in her winning The North Carolina Award in Literature) and, in 1990, *I Shall Not Be Moved*. These five collections of Angelou's poems are included in *The Complete Collected Poems of Maya Angelou*.

Brilliant in its conception, *The Complete Collected* was somewhat premature; surely Angelou would be writing other poems during the remaining years of her life. But Random House was taking advantage of the fact that Angelou, at President Clinton's invitation, had written a poem for his January 1993 Inauguration. She read that poem—titled "On the Pulse of Morning"—at the inauguration ceremony, and immediately became the de facto poet laureate of the United States. *The Complete Collected Poems of Maya Angelou* ends with that poem. (It will be published in other of her collections as well, but in 1994, her *Collected Poems* was the way to get the poem as people had just heard it. The book sold even more copies than had *I Know Why the Caged Bird Sings*, and—after the inauguration—Random House saw sales of *all* Angelou's books reach toward a million.)

As critic Mary Jane Lupton remarked, not only was the long poem effective, "it was the vitality of her performance" that stayed in viewers' minds (see this book's cover). "The poem, like the incoming president, offered the dream of hope [President Clinton's home town was Hope, Arkansas, not far from Angelou's childhood town of Stamps, Arkansas]—for Native Americans, gays, homeless, Eskimos, Jews, West Africans, Muslims" (Lupton 17).

Lupton, Tinnie, and other critics point out that Angelou's theatrical but always reverent delivery of the poem was, in one way, "a return to African American oral tradition, when slaves like Frederick Douglass stood on platforms in abolitionists meeting halls to register their concerns about the slave system. The ode also echoes the rhetorical grace of the African American sermon, as practiced and modified by Martin Luther King, Jr., Malcolm X, Jesse Jackson, Louis Farrakkan . . . The oral traditions of such spirituals as 'Roll, Jordan, Roll' were also suggested" (Lupton 18; the flood of journalistic response to both her performance and the poem can be sampled in Cawley, Coulthard, T. Davis, Fulghum, Hinson, Manegold, Molotsky, O'Connell et al., Schmich, Streitfeld, and Terry, among others). Without realizing what Angelou's words reminded them of, the millions who watched the inauguration ceremonies on satellite television, viewed electronically throughout the world, were collectively moved.

One of the most accurate readings of this poem occurs in Wallis Tinnie's essay, pointing out that Angelou uses three "familiar hymns to solidify her message" ["No Hiding Place Down Here," "I Shall Not Be Moved," and "I Will Study War No More"]. In Tinnie's words, "This sacred music of black Americans, which served both spiritual and political ends in the antebellum South, becomes a source of transcendence as the poet intones the sacred lines. Angelou converts this music into a wellspring from which all people can drink and be fulfilled. This is what the cultural griot/shaman does; she turns the violence and mayhem into healing medicine through the power of natural rhythms and word magic" (Tinnie 523).

The opening metaphor of the poem, "A Rock, A River, A Tree/ Hosts to species long since departed," brings readers to the important international concerns with ecology. The United States had just participated in the 1992 United Nations Conference in Environment and Development; serious attention to such problems as toxic waste and pollution was just beginning to draw the world's powerful countries into a kind of harmony that was rare. "[T]oday, the Rock cries out to us, early, forcefully,/ Come, you may stand upon my/ Back and face your distant destiny." In Angelou's enumeration of the forces of the natural world, her audience could find a means of entering this wide-reaching poem.

> Across the wall of the world,
> A River sings a beautiful song. It says,
> Come, rest here by my side.
>
> Each of you, a bordered country,
> Delicate and strangely made proud,
> Yet thrusting perpetually under siege,

Your armed struggles for profit
Have left collars of waste upon
My shore, currents of debris upon my breast.
Yet today I call you to my riverside,
If you will study war no more.

As Angelou draws visibly upon the phrasing of her heritage—in spirituals, sermons, and hymns as well as print sources—she echoes the earlier experiences of millions of her viewers. The world's religions, as well as those common to the United States, find representation in her choices of words. In effect, when the poem says, "There is a true yearning to respond to/ The singing River and the wise Rock," the viewers of her reading probably nodded their heads in agreement. To take people back to a simpler time, a more religiously based time, was one part of her poetic strategy.

Another was the inclusion of all the countries of the world. Peace was on people's minds, it had been part of Clinton's strategy for being elected. Angelou's gift of speaking for all peoples of the world—using the information she had found as she had lived in Egypt and Ghana as well as disparate parts of the United States—gave her words an authenticity that was undeniable. Her phrasing, as well, gave women listeners and readers a sense of inclusion, and critic Eleanor Traylor uses this poem in particular to move Angelou into the feminist camp, an affiliation the poet often played down.[2] Speaking specifically of Angelou's references to achieving the American dream, Traylor reads a feminist turn in:

Lift up your eyes
Before this day breaking for you.
Give birth again
To the dream.
Women, children, men,

Take it into the palms of your hands,
Mold it into the shape of your most
Private need. Sculpt it into
The image of your most public self.

By beginning the stanza with "women" and following that noun with, first, "children" and then "men," Angelou directs listeners' attention to this feminization. In the following lines she gives these women the power to "shape" events, just as she acknowledges the necessary division between any woman's private self and her public self. The stanza continues with lines that are less obviously gendered:

Lift up your hearts.
Each new hour holds new chances
For a new beginning.

Yet the stanza concludes with metaphors that suggest heterosexual marriage, taking the reader back to women's consciousness:

Do not be wedded forever
To fear, yoked eternally
To brutishness.

The horizon leans forward,
Offering you space
To place new steps of change.
Here, on the pulse of this fine day,
You may have the courage
To look up and out and upon me,
The Rock, the River, the Tree, your country.

Leaving issues that might be read as gendered, Angelou takes the reader into the ending stanza of the hundred-line poem without any rhetorical flourish: she associates the act of looking up with "grace," with acceptance, and with a humility that underscores the kind of persona she has been creating throughout the poem, a character who has the personal power to say "simply/ Very simply/ With hope—/ Good morning." Here she manages to emphasize the commonness of the real person, as she repeats the "hope" of Clinton's taking the reins and stresses the "Good" of the start of his administration. "On the Pulse of Morning," accordingly, ends with that same promising "morning" and yet seems to speak for the diverse group of Americans who had just elected him. Angelou's poem speaks again and again for not only the President but for the common person, finding a route to the United States, "Sold, stolen, arriving on a nightmare/ Praying for a dream."

The poem succeeds in creating what Jasmin DeGout terms "a community of healing," perhaps more so than had her shorter poems in the earlier collections. Collectively, DeGout says that Angelou's poems reveal "the strains of liberation, survival, self-acceptance, and transcendence" (DeGout 127, 122).

After giving this poem at President Clinton's Inauguration, Angelou then found herself receiving invitations to give public readings (hopefully, of new poems written for these occasions) at other ceremonial events. In 1995 the most important of these invitations were the September 1995 commemoration of the Fiftieth Anniversary of the founding of the United Nations. Staged in San Francisco, this ceremony gave Angelou another widely televised venue as she read the poem she had written for the celebration. "A Brave and Startling Truth" repeated the somber tones of "On the Pulse of Morning," but widened its reference points to seem to include a world audience. Lupton calls it "a majestic, yet sad poem" (Lupton 18) but it is also redolent of a tragic international history that might still be redeemed with more humane contemporary policies. In this poem—available now in an important book titled *Celebrations,*

Rituals of Peace and Prayer, published in 2006 and including all these ceremonial works as well as such more recent poems as "Sons and Daughters," "Amazing Peace," "Mother: A Cradle to Hold Me," "Vigil," and others—the dedication gives readers an insightful path. "Dedicated to the hope for peace, which lies, sometimes hidden, in every heart," becomes an intrinsic part of the poem. The work proper opens:

> We, this people, on a small and lonely planet
> Traveling through casual space
> Past aloof stars, across the way of indifferent suns
> To a destination where all signs tell us
> It is possible and imperative that we learn
> A brave and startling truth.

Moving immediately to what the truth should be, Angelou laments the "fists of hostility" that now exist. She has linked herself as speaker to the billions of the world's citizens in that artful opening, she being just one of "*this* people" (rather than the public body of archaic political documents, in which the phrase would have been "*the* people") and all such people populating "a small and lonely planet." Taking her readers out into the universe of galaxies is a move calculated to put any self-important political figures in a place that creates some humility.

Angelou uses the effective "*this* people" designation in a third of the stanzas that comprise this 77-line poem. Later, for example, an important stanza opens:

> We, this people, on this miniscule globe
> Who reach daily for the bomb, the blade, and the dagger.

Another refrain the poet uses for continuity is even more crucial. Rhythmically incremental, her long lines here add weight to the poem's message. The stanza quoted here closes with even more vivid imagery:

> When religious ritual is not perfumed
> By the incense of burning flesh
> And childhood dreams are not kicked awake
> By nightmares of sexual abuse

Angelou avoids bringing the reader to a dead end in the futility of abstract language; she here brings the Marguerite of *I Know Why the Caged Bird Sings* into this stately poem. (Beyond the personal, of course, rape and abuse dominate the lives of women and children—as well as men—around the globe.)

Voiced passionately, Angelou's repetitions of not only the refrain phrases but the single words—*earth, fear, the possible, miraculous, wonder*—bring the readers, the listeners, in the chanting unity for which she aims. Spiritual-like (but not heavily marked by African American language, in this case), "A Brave and Startling Truth" is a poem that borders on song. Less familiar than "On the Pulse of Morning," it still has immense reach.

The third of Angelou's public poems—what a century ago might have been called "occasional poems," in that they were requested for a definite occasion and so they needed to match the circumstances of that occasion[3]—is "A Black Woman Speaks to Black Manhood." She read this poem at the October 16, 1995 "Million Man March" in Washington, DC. Lupton notes that this poem is less stately than "On the Pulse of Morning"—that it is, in fact, "fairly boisterous" (Lupton 18). Signaling a different kind of familiarity in her choice of title, the poet emphasizes here that she is, like most of the marchers, a black person. Her blackness as woman speaker should relate quickly to their blackness as men, struggling as black people of both genders are against the power of whiteness in the United States.

Angelou begins her poem, however, directly addressing the black men she sees before her:

> Our souls look back
> In wondrous surprise
> At how we have made it
> So far from where we started. . . .

The opening ten quatrains—short-lined and somewhat predictable—draw the images of slave people, men powerless to save either themselves or their women and children. The tenth stanza reads, in true direct address:

> Please my many million men
> Let us lay that image aside
> See how our people today
> Walk in strength and in pride. . . .

Her maternal opening, "*my* many million men," is privileged and it also announces that her comments about present-day black life are ready to change. Then the poem becomes a song, one complete with spaces for hands clapping, people dancing. This is the eleventh stanza:

> Celebrate, stand up, clap hands for ourselves
>   and those who went before
> Stand up, clap hands, let us welcome kind
>   words back into our vocabulary
> Stand up, clap hands, let us welcome
>   courtesies back into our bedrooms. . . .

The reader can envision the listeners responding to Angelou's voice and manner as she changes tempo, breaks out herself into these appealing rhythms . . . suddenly, the fact that she has used no punctuation through the poem makes sense. This is less a written poem than it is a song. The very end of "A Black Woman Speaks to Black Manhood" does feature a punctuation mark—the exclamation point. It follows the poet's moving back into the solemn quatrains of the beginning, and then ending with the final three lines, lines that once again convey the excitement of sheer promise:

Clap hands, celebrate
We deserve it
Jubilate!

With the major poems of 1993 and 1995, Angelou shows—in these poems and in many others she wrote far past the publication date of *The Complete Collected Poems of Maya Angelou*—that in poetry as well as in autobiography, she was able to *craft* a consummate voice, a voice that would not be confused with the writing style or the thematic emphases of any other United States literary person. Drawing effectively as she did from a range of sources and knowledge, Maya Angelou deserved to be better-known as a poet than she was: she gave readers what she called "art for the sake of the soul," not mere language pyrotechnics (*Stars* 119). Just as her radical changes to the form of autobiography sometimes brought her criticism, so too did her experimentation in the art of poetry, especially as she infused the poem with elements of song (and insisted on performative art). Russian theorist Tzvetan Todorov explained decades ago that "The fact that a work 'disobeys' its genre does not mean that the genre does not exist because 'the transgression' requires a law—precisely the one to be violated. We might go even further and observe that the norm becomes visible—comes into existence—owing only to its transgressions" (Todorov 14). Or, in Angelou's nontheoretical words, "I believe the most important single thing, beyond discipline and creativity, in any artistic work, is daring to dare" (*Stars* 67).

Notes

1   Throughout her life, Angelou read Millay, Emily Dickinson, Joan Didion, Lillian Hellman, Dorothy Parker, and many other mainstream (white) women poets, playwrights, and novelists.

2   In Jeffrey M. Elliot's introduction to his *Conversations with Maya Angelou*, he quotes her comment that "she believes black women to be more self reliant than white women." She also believes strongly in "equal pay, equal respect, equal responsibility" for everyone (Con 93). Lupton points out that Angelou herself worked with pro-African women's groups such as the Cultural Association for Women of African Heritage (CAWAH) (Lupton 71).

3   Critic Jacqueline Thursby notes that Angelou was not pleased to be giving such poems, though she made exceptions for causes and people that she supported. Thursby quotes from Lyman B. Hagen who repeats that Angelou had said that "'public' and 'poem' go together like buttermilk and champagne" (Thursby 182, Hagen 135).

11

From autobiography to the essay

Once Angelou had satisfied critics' requests that she finish her memoir cycle, she was still a writer in great demand from numerous anthologists, critics, and readers: in terms of her books' appeal in the market, it seemed as if people wanted to read more, and more, Angelou. In 1993 (well before her autobiographical project was finished in 2002), Random House published her first essay collection, *Wouldn't Take Nothing for My Journey Now*. Twenty-three years after the publication of *I Know Why the Caged Bird Sings*, Angelou was devising ways to speak in the same approachable voice, telling the same forthright stories about characters that readers recognized from Stamps, Arkansas, as well as from other locations in Angelou's travels.

As critic Clara Junker pointed out, like her memoirs, in many of these essays Angelou brings her stories to the reader using the "I" and "we" voice of familiarity. Such an approach may "disrupt essayistic objectivity . . . The essay's intersection of public and private space corresponds ideally to feminine experience and expression" (Junker 236). In *Wouldn't Take Nothing for My Journey Now*, this critic says, "texts slide between the personal and the public, the individual and the representative, even between lines of color and gender." In effect, the essay form as Angelou practices it creates "a hybrid form . . . Her shifts from quasifictional techniques to expository prose and back express the complexity of (African American) woman/ism" (Juncker 237).

In Juncker's assessment, Angelou's essays illustrate the principles Hélène Cixous was developing in "The Laugh of the Medusa." When this critic claims that "Angelou reinvents the essay," she intends high praise for the fact that Angelou "stresses and complicates the writing subject, which alternates between dominant presence and sudden absence" (Juncker 237–8).

She especially likes the author's emphasis on women's bodies and skin colors, quoting Angelou's words:

> If I feel good inside my skin and clothes, I am thus free to allow my body its sway, its natural grace, its natural gesture (*Wouldn't* 56).

Juncker also points to Angelou's use of other African American women in writing these essays, commenting on the "powerful physical presence" of Angelou's characters: "her big-boned cinnamon-colored Annie Henderson, Angelou's grandmother; Aunt Tee, who is sinewy, strong, and the color of old lemons" (*Wouldn't* 61; Juncker 232).

Not all Angelou's critics found her essays, and her deviations from the essay form, palatable, but most understood why the author made her choices. In a theoretical discussion, Ruth-Ellen Boetcher Joeres notes that from the beginning of the essay form, it "has been considered a *boundary* form, that is, a genre that does not comfortably fit into the traditional classical lyric-epic-drama pattern. One need only examine the theoretical and methodological treatments of the essay to see the defensiveness with which most scholars of the genre approach the form, the immense difficulties they encounter even when they are trying to define it. Its elusiveness, but more important its *fringe* nature, might well make the essay appeal to those who are themselves on the fringe" (Joeres 152). Given how rarely serious writers worked in autobiography even during the twentieth century, Angelou's publishing first *I Know Why the Caged Bird Sings* and then *Gather Together in My Name* had already signaled readers that she was not trying to write as if she were a white male formalist. As she told an interviewer, "We must remember that we are created creative and can invent new scenarios as frequently as they are needed" (Con 66). Happily located on the publishing "fringe," as both a woman writer and a writer of color, Angelou watched as the royalty and permissions-to-translate checks rolled in. While she never mentioned the income her writing brought to her (and to Random House), she used the success of her books to encourage others to write what they wanted to write, in the manner they chose.

The inclusiveness of Angelou's essays, evident here in *Wouldn't Take Nothing for My Journey Now* as well as in her second collection, *Even the Stars Look Lonesome*, published several years later in 1997, led to critic Karla Holloway's strong defense of Angelou's writing methods. Holloway privileges the author's inclusiveness, noting that "her history over-whelmingly [encourages] her to hold in tandem all of the components of her identity." For this critic, Angelou's blurring of the personal and the political into one fluid narrative makes sense in the essays, as it always had in the autobiographies (Holloway Codes 10–11).

Critic Annis Pratt formulated patterns within women's writing, drawing from works by British writers as well as American, by mainstream writers as well as those of color, in her study of the *bildungsroman* as literary form. Her assessment of women's writing that attempted to tell the stories of a character's growth into adulthood (the pattern of abandonment by parents, education, first sexual love, and then wise resolution) is that women characters cannot survive society unless they grow "down," rather than up. Angelou's narratives would, obviously, differ from that remarked pattern—her characters usually make progress toward some goal or other, even if society might frown at the goal itself. (For example, critics claimed that the ending of *I Know Why the Caged Bird Sings* is *triumphant*—with Marguerite's giving birth to Guy, knowing he is hers alone to raise, care for, and support; that opinion, however, was controversial.) More relevant to this consideration of Angelou's work is Pratt's observation that literature provides for the reader very few "equal marriage [narratives] novels." Supported here by the marriages of her own, which Angelou describes in her autobiographies as well as in select essays, this premise fits alongside Pratt's observation that the strong woman character finds herself at odds with her social group, which is largely controlled by patriarchal power. Of the women placed in the category of "strong woman," those of African American origin usually fare better in life's circumstances (Pratt 33, 41).

Relating specifically to Angelou, critic Valerie Baisnee groups her essays with her autobiographies to conclude that this writer is motivated by "her desire for justice as well as from a desire to record personal growth." Throughout her writing, states Baisnee, Angelou confronts "racial discrimination" by using "a strategy of valorization and confrontation" (Baisnee 55). A decade after Angelou's essay collections saw print, theorist Nancy Miller defined twenty-first-century autobiography (and all life narratives) as "cultural criticism," marked by its being "confessional, narrative, political, and anecdotal" (Miller 3). She does not mention Angelou's works specifically, but because of the prominence of the autobiographies (as well as the sales figures for the essays), Maya Angelou's writing had a role in changing critical perspectives about what the possibilities of the genre were. As Cheryl Wall had explained in 2005, much writing by African American women intends to "challenge the structures of patriarchy" (Wall 13). She sees Angelou's tailoring all the genres she writes in as characteristic of African American writers collectively. "Writing in and across genres, contemporary black women writers revise and subvert the conventions of the genres they appropriate." They no doubt know and understand the conventions, but they choose to "rewrite canonized texts in order to give voice to stories those texts did not imagine. Their revisions are often signaled by the recurrence of metaphor and structures drawn from African American oral forms, such as folktales, sermons, spirituals, and blues . . . They also draw on the Bible, political rhetoric, classical myth and popular fiction" (Wall 13).

At the time Angelou was being hounded for essays, poems, and stories to appear in edited collections of writing—writing by women, writing by African Americans—readers were not very sophisticated about the genre of the essay. Angelou wrote essays that read like stories, or essays that read like her colloquial talks; therefore, editors wanted Maya Angelou in their books because people responded well to her narratives. The demand for her essays was so large, in fact, that at Random House's suggestion, in her first cookbook, *Hallelujah! The Welcome Table*, she used essays within the recipes, for context relating to, for example, Annie Henderson's caramel cake.

She also published many highly informative essays—"Africa," for instance, and "The Art of Africa"—that read like traditional, informative pieces, written economically and factually. She opens "Africa" with Countee Cullen's poem "Heritage," and mentions as well Ernest Hemingway's "depiction of the romantic Dark Continent populated with wild animals, white hunters and black bearers" (*Stars* 13).

What Angelou does in this long essay is to explain the relationship between Africa as the source of slaves and the negative image that white cultures world-wide had formed of the continent. "Slavery's profiteers had to convince themselves and their clients that the persons they enslaved were little better than beasts. They could not admit that the Africans lived in communities based upon sociopolitical structures no better or worse than their European counterparts of the time. The slave sellers had to persuade slave buyers that the African was a primitive, a cannibal, and richly deserved oppression. How else could the Christian voice be silent—how soothe the Christian conscience?"

In clear and accurate prose, Angelou expands this information: "African history and culture have been shrouded in centuries of guilt and ignorance and shame. The African slaves themselves, separated from their tribesmen and languages, forced by the lash to speak another tongue immediately, were unable to convey the stories of their own people, their deeds, rituals, religion, and beliefs. In the United States the slaves were even exiled from the drums, instruments of instruction, ceremony, and entertainment of their homeland. Within a few generations details of the kingdoms of Ghana and Mali and of the Songhai Empire became hazy in their minds. The Mende concept of beauty and the Ashanti idea of justice all but faded with the old family names and intricate tribal laws. The slave, too, soon began to believe what their masters believed: Africa was a continent of savages" (*Stars* 15–16).

As Angelou traces the ways in which the Africans were made to relinquish their culture and their homeland, she notes, "Even in religious matters, the African was called a mere fetishist, trusting in sticks and bones. Most failed to see the correlation between the African and his gris-gris (religious amulets) and the Moslem with his beads or the Catholic with his rosary." She also discusses her years living in Ghana, and her earlier year in New York studying dance with Pearl Primus, "a social anthropologist, a famous concert dancer of African dance," in order to give credibility to her rendering of African history. The essay, then, benefits from Angelou as persona, but most of it tells straightforward history. The essay concludes, "Although millions of Africans were taken from the continent from the sixteenth until the middle of the nineteenth century, many Africans on the continent display no concern over the descendants of their lost ancestors. Many have no knowledge that their culture has been spread around the world by those same hapless and sometimes hopeless descendants. African culture is alive and well. An African proverb spells out the truth: 'The ax forgets. The tree remembers'" (*Stars* 17).

Closely associated with this essay is "Art in Africa," placed somewhat later in the collection. Angelou's enthusiasm for the collectivity of African art—sometimes being created by groups rather than by an isolated artist—spreads throughout this informational piece. Filled with unusual information, the essay focuses on African women as artists. "In Africa, as in other places of the world, women created their own portraits—distinctive portraits of themselves and their universe. They used cloth, beads, leather . . . to express their views of the real and abstract worlds. Beliefs, spirits, omens, djinns, disappointments, fears and accomplishments were named, confessed, called, admitted and explained in the women's designs . . . Their art, like all art, means to delight the eye, console the troubled mind, appease the highest authority and educate the children in the ways of the world. The aim also, whether or not articulated, is to infuse and sustain the family in an appreciation for life and the expectation of beauty" (*Stars* 66).

Because of her years in Ghana, Angelou differentiates between the art of East Africa and West, pointing out that women of West Africa avoid bright primary colors; rather, they "allow themselves black, white, ocher, yellow and beige earth tones. They do employ blue, but it is the blue-black, electric indigo or the soft, subtle blue of West African mornings." The story Angelou includes here is about the Yoruba and that tribe's weaving, privileging the work women have done. The visible art reflects what Angelou notes as foundational design: "outer beauty is believed to be the result of good inner moral character."

Commenting on the expert designs of West African weavers, Angelou praises them as setting the standard for modern modes. "Most of the ancient designs, whether on cloth, walls or houses or on earthenware, were inspired by proverbs and sayings. She uses as illustration, 'If you do not appreciate the things you have, other people will treat them with contempt.' A second saying is 'Art made by all can be enjoyed by all. The African saying is proved true: "Sea never dry"'" (*Stars* 69–70).

The inclusion of these two essays in particular illustrates what Wall notes as one rationale for African American essays: she states that these writers are trying to expand what readers know about United States history by adding what has been missing—"Narratives of the enslaved and exploited, stories of black workers (cooks, cobblers, factory workers, and maids), and of residents of rural backwaters and inner cities" (Wall 13).

In Angelou's organization of her essays within the two collections lies the same kind of rationale she shows in her various autobiographies. When Sandi Russell had criticized the first book, *Wouldn't Take Nothing for My Journey Now*, by calling it "a series of sermonettes," Angelou realized that some part of a thought-provoking essay collection was missing. Reviewing the second collection, Russell was more complimentary, terming *Even the Stars Look Lonesome* "the work of a spirited and spiritual woman" (Russell 157).

What readers more often remember from Angelou's essays are the deft character sketches, almost fully realized in a few short pages. Here is a vignette about Annie Henderson:

When I was very young, my grandmother raised me. She was everything to me. And if I acted startled about something that had happened, I'd ask her to explain and she would say, "Sister, that isn't even on my littlest mind."

Somehow I decided that there was a small mind and a large mind. Now, when I'm trying to get back, I use the cards to occupy my small mind. In the course of writing a book I will use maybe two or three decks of Bicycle cards before I'm finished. Just playing solitaire. I don't really get down. I don't play the cards. I'm playing at playing. But that's fine (Epel 28).

The child's misunderstanding of literal language, and then Angelou's reversing her use of careful language as she turns to street talk at the end—the essay becomes a tour de force of not only character but characters' language (Annie's and Angelou's).

A longer excerpt from an essay by Angelou describes how she learned to explore courage, and to take what she here called "exceptional risks." "Years ago, I deduced that it costs everything to win, and that it costs everything to lose. So, if I didn't take a risk, if I didn't take a dare, then I would lose everything. And if I did take the dare, if I lost—I'd lose the same thing. But I might win. So since everything is always at stake, I may as well risk everything for the good thing."

So when I was asked if I could conduct the Boston Pops, I said, "Yes, of course." Now it's true I've gone to a few concerts at one time in my life, and I've been conducted, and I've put together choirs. But the Boston Pops with Keith Lockhart as the Maestro? I said "Yes" because ten more years might pass before another woman might be invited, and twenty years might pass before another African American woman might be invited. I said "Yes," and I got a book and I read, and I found out what music they were planning to play. I put that on my tape recorder, and I played it all around our house. I played it in my bus. I played it in my car. And on that day in Massachusetts, I stepped up and conducted the Boston Pops.

I sent a message that I enjoyed it so much that I'd be glad to do it a second time. But I was told they'd never invited anyone a second time. They had Ted Kennedy there that evening. So I said, "Well, that's alright then, but I'd be glad to do it." And I was invited the next year to do it again. So, had I not risked, I could always say, "Well, you know I was invited," but not what it *felt* like. Would I have opened the door for someone else who's coming behind me? No, I wouldn't have. As it is now, I've opened the door and had fun doing it too (*Stars* 67–8).

By 2008, Angelou worked on a book of essays, poems and anecdotes that were aimed at women readers. One of the essays was a long and substantial meditation on poetry, excerpting from poems she loved (including some of her own recent work) and those from her background as an African American reader. Titled *Letter to My Daughter*, the book carefully explained that its author had one child, a beloved son, but that she loved—and felt loved by—many women the world over. As she had written earlier, "I have so many daughters. So many . . . of every race you can imagine. You think only God could have brought those women together! And I'm Mom to a lot of people: Asian, Latino, White, African, and African-American, Jewish. Mostly I wish each one had the vision to see themselves FREE.

I was married . . . to a builder. It was my best marriage. And he taught me to build. He said, "Building has nothing to do with strength or with sex, or with gender. It has to do with insight. If you can see it, you can build it. But you must see it."

So I wish women could see themselves FREE. Just see and imagine what they could do if they were free. The national and international history of diminishment. Just imagine, if we could have a Madame Curie in the nineteenth century, suppose that twenty other women had been liberated at the same time? Is it possible that we would have gotten small pox and chicken pox and other un-social diseases obliterated? Just imagine, try to envision if, in this country, African Americans were not in a holding position because of racism. Imagine if all that energy and intelligence and enthusiasm could be put to the use of the school system, to the economy . . .

So that's what I wish for women: SEE IT. TRY TO SEE yourself Free. What would you do? One thing, you'd be kinder (*Stars* 70–1).

Angelou repeats a good bit of this in the letter that opens *Letter to My Daughter*. She emphasizes there that few people mature, that most people are "children inside . . . still innocent and shy as magnolias. We may act sophisticated and worldly but I believe we feel safest when we go inside ourselves and find home, a place where we belong, and maybe the only place we really do" (*Letter* 7).

Repeating the idea of *home*, Angelou traces a child's concept in relation to an adult's definition of the word: "Home is that youthful region where a child is the only real living inhabitant. Parents, siblings, and neighbors are mysterious apparitions who come, go, and do strange unfathomable things in and around the child." Isolated, as lonely as one can imagine, the child yearns for some adult who might understand her. Angelou draws a scene in Stamps, Arkansas, when her brother Bailey buys movie tickets, "trying to brave the hostile stares of white adults." The children are then "rudely thumbed toward a rickety outdoor staircase which led to the balcony (called a buzzard's roost) restricted to black customers. There we sat, knees to chin, in the cramped space, our feet crunching discarded candy wrappers and other debris. We perched there and studied how to act when we grew up and became beautiful and rich and white" (*Letter* 96).

Angelou begins the book with a lengthy dedication page, thanking "some women who mothered me/ through dark and bright days." The names listed include Annie Henderson, Vivian Baxter, her long-time friend Frances Williams, and others, with special emphasis on "one woman who allows me to be a daughter to her, even today, Dr. Dorothy Height." The lower part of the listing reads like this: "My thanks to women not born to me but who allow me to 'mother' them." Among those names is Lydia Stuckey, Valerie Simpson, and Oprah Winfrey. The dominant dedication emphasis is, "Try to be a rainbow in someone's cloud."

The essays that comprise *Letter to My Daughter* are the most varied, and the most personal, of those in the three books. Sometimes they are short and pithy, reminiscent of work in *Wouldn't Take Nothing for My Journey Now*. Sometimes Angelou reminisces about her last marriage, about her having decided to "give San Francisco" to the British husband who had loved the West coast (*Letter* 119). She, accordingly, had to find a different living space. With their divorce final in 1981, and Wake Forest University offering her a lifetime professorship in American Studies that same year, she chose to move back to the South—something she never planned to do. Several of the essays are about North Carolina. In one she focuses on the personal and the spiritual, telling her readers that "I began healing when I settled in Winston-Salem. The undulating landscape is replete with flowering dogwood, redbud, crepe myrtle trees, and six-foot-tall rhododendron. Multicolored four-foot-wide azaleas grow wild and wonderful throughout the area.

> Winston-Salem is in the Piedmont, it is literally at the foot of the mountains. The mountains that lean over us are the Great Smokies and the Blue Ridge. I like the humor in North Carolina. The natives say that our state is the valley of humility towered over by two towers of conceit, Virginia and South Carolina (*Letter* 120).

Another emphasis Angelou gives to her new Southern locale is the language she hears. "I fell for the soft singing accents of the natives and their creative ways with English. In the supermarket the checker asked me how did I like Winston-Salem? I replied, 'I like it, but it gets so hot. I don't know if I can bear it.'"

> The checker, not breaking her stride in totaling my items said to me, "Yes, Dr. Angelou, but it gone get gone" (*Letter* 121).

Angelou's praise for her happiness at Mr. Zion Baptist Church and its excellent choir, for the museums and schools at all levels, including the North Carolina School for the Arts, for her students at the university, and for a general kindliness marks this essay. A second one, "Reclaiming Southern Roots," brings a wider focus to spiritualism in the United States, as she remarks that some African Americans who had been eager to move north were now returning to the South. Angelou states, "in the North unskilled and undereducated black workers were spit out by the system like so many undigestible watermelon seeds . . . They began to find their lives minimalized, and their selves as persons trivialized" (*Letter* 130).

The more personal essays in this collection usually include several anecdotes, and more humor than usual. In "Vulgarity," for example, Angelou scolds women for not criticizing people who make mean jokes (about obesity, bad behavior, sarcasm), returning to an earlier caveat when she told readers to speak up against injustice of whatever kinds. She includes in this essay a paragraph, perfect in its timing and reference, that takes the sting from her lecturing:

> If the emperor is standing in my living room stripped to the buff, nothing should prevent me from saying that since he has no clothes on, he is not ready for public congress. At any rate, not lounging on my sofa and munching on my trail mix (*Letter* 42).

Singer-song-writers Nick Ashford and Valerie Simpson collaborating with Maya Angelou on one of the songs for their album Been Found. *Photo © by poet Eugene Redmond. Used by permission of Eugene B. Redmond.*

Angelou includes several essays that attack the social contexts of rape, and of excusing people who rape because of their own limited backgrounds. In "Violence," she says, "We must call the ravening act of rape, the bloody, heart-stopping, breath-snatching, bone-crushing act of violence, which it is . . . Let us call it a violent unredeemable sexual act" (*Letter* 46).

She repeats stories that readers may already know about Annie Henderson's bravery and her wit, and about Vivian Baxter's praise for Angelou as young mother. There are also retrospective essays about Angelou's visiting Senegal and Morocco, and another essay about her friendship with the British writer Jessica Mitford (author of *The American* Way *of Death*) and her husband Bob Treuhaft. The book ends with both a selection of Angelou's recent poems—among them "Survival," "Salute to Older Lovers," and "Commencement Address"—and a long and engrossing essay about poetry. In that essay, she rehearses a number of African American poems that give credence to her point—that great writing stems from true feeling. She prints in full works by Langston Hughes, Melvin B. Tolson, Claude McKay, Aime Cesaire, Mari Evans, and Sterling A. Brown—poems giving encouragement to the kinds of difficulties many African Americans have experienced during Angelou's lifetime. The opening to her own poem, "Surviving," reifies this purpose:

When the winds of disappointment
dash my dream house to the ground
and anger, octopus-like, wraps its tentacles around my soul
I just stop myself. I stop in my tracks
and look for one thing that can
heal me.
I find in my memory
one child's face
any child's face . . .
with hopeful expectation in his eyes (*Letter* 135).

This poem continues for another thirty-seven lines, in which the poet pretends to choose love that is not erotic. By the end, she casts doubt on her relinquishing romance. The heart of the poem is, however, this opening. Like Blake, Angelou privileges innocence, no matter where she finds it.

Letter to My Daughter also includes lines that take the reader, and the writer herself, back to her childhood experiences and her childhood surroundings. As she wrote, "I am remembering what Arkansas gave me. I came to understand that I can never forget where I came from. My soul should always look back and wonder at the mountains I had climbed and the rivers I had forged and the challenges which still await down the road. I am strengthened by that knowledge" (*Letter* 97).

It was as if the last debt that Maya Angelou needed to pay was her recurring thankfulness for both her grandmother Henderson and her mother, Vivian Baxter. When *Mom & Me & Mom* was published in 2013, reviewers seemed to find it something of an anachronism: many of these narratives had been told in the autobiographies (especially the Annie Henderson stories), and some of the Vivian Baxter stories had occurred in the essays and sketches. It may be, as theorist Sven Birkerts claimed, that all writers are driven by "the push to reconciliation . . . With the memoirist it often proves to be both the instigating impulse and the sustaining force . . . The writing is propelled by the need to find closure in the self, to make patterns for contingency, and to enact the drama of claiming a self from the chaos of possibility. For this reason, inescapably, memoir requires that a balance be struck between then and now, event and understanding" (Birkerts 187). It may also be that, according to Joanne Braxton's summary of all Angelou's memoirs, that the author had throughout used "selective remembering," as well as a "self-censoring strategy of recollection" (Braxton 7).

Much of *Mom & Me & Mom* revolves around Vivian Baxter. Factoring in Birkerts's contention may explain Angelou's emphasis: all readers of Angelou's autobiographies know that, as children, both Marguerite and Bailey resented the fact that their mother seemed not to want to care for them. Angelou seems to blame Vivian for her inaccessibility, laying Bailey's use of drugs squarely at the foot of his childhood situation, which included his deep love for Vivian. No matter how fond Angelou became of her mother, she could not forget that her being raped, which caused her to be hospitalized, to testify in court, and most importantly to stop speaking for five years, was the responsibility of her mother (it was her boyfriend who raped her child).

Mom & Me & Mom, however, presents a nearly sanguine portrait of the vivacious, hard-driving, and usually admirable Vivian Baxter. The reader hears her direct and lively speech, and admires her lying to make herself fifteen years younger, so that she can join the military. Although Angelou in a few places draws the obvious distinctions between Annie Henderson in her stolid, careful social behavior—rooted in her all-encompassing faith in God and His convictions—and Vivian, who judges much less often and appears to think whatever Marguerite decides is wise (when Marguerite herself has given the reader evidence to the contrary in her six autobiographies), the book is almost entirely her mother's. It is her mother who finds and saves her from the beatings Two Fingers Mark has given her—and yet once Angelou has recovered (at Vivian's house) and they have a plot to lure Mark out of his hiding place so that Angelou can shoot him, she does not. Instead, with the help of her mother's bail bondsmen friends, he is warned to get out of town. Vivian then tells her, "You didn't get that from me. That came from your Grandmother Henderson. I'd have shot him like a dog in the street. You are good, honey. You're a better woman than I am" (*Mom* 91).

Vivian Baxter was truly self-reliant. She seems to have paid little attention to her own family, and she was never visibly religious. She did, however, put herself at Maya Angelou's call throughout her later life, and Random House uses several dramatic photographs of the two now-mature African American women posed strikingly together. For the reader who has read the series of autobiographies, however, one of the interesting things about this late book is how much it narrates from those early years, the years that have already been discussed in Angelou's earlier memoirs. The events we learn about in *Mom & Me & Mom* show how much more difficult the years of Angelou's existing during her son's childhood were. Perhaps these missing episodes shape a more painful recollection. Perhaps that is one reason for her dedicating the book to Guy, with thanks to her mother "who generously taught me how to be a mother." Of her son, with more enthusiasm, she says that Guy is "the most courageous and generous man I know."

Most readers would see *Mom & Me & Mom* as the seventh autobiography in Maya Angelou's series: it treats Angelou's experiences in Sweden, when her mother's visit there reclaims her persona from the derogation she was experiencing; it treats Vivian Baxter and Angelou enjoying smoking cigarettes together—even as it shows the reader that Vivian dies from lung cancer. Taking her mother from the West coast to live with her in Winston-Salem, Angelou is able to partially repay the mother she has come to cherish. Vivian Baxter's death may be one logical conclusion for the story of Marguerite and Bailey Johnson. It occurs in this book without sentimentalism, but with ample sorrow.

When editor J. Bill Berry analyzes Angelou's *I Know Why the Caged Bird Sings* from the perspective of being a marker for the great memoir writing done in the South, he notes that telling an autobiographical story may be a "matter (and often a means) of survival." Maya Angelou re-created what Berry calls the heart of any autobiography: "the pattern of parents and children, children and parents, marks the cycle of our lives. It is intrinsic in and essential to whatever poetry there is in whatever lives we have. We move forward and backward through time—passing, being passed, finally we recognize that at each point we pass ourselves" (Berry 8–9).

As Frances Smith Foster wrote about that first memoir, Angelou creates the classic American hero, the child who must learn to live independently without family or parents. Such circumstances, hopefully, lead to "the development of a very essential 'I,' an 'I' that grows more egotistic as it progresses through a traditional quest pattern." By creating this character, Angelou gives her journey the legitimacy of becoming a heroic quest (Foster 99, 101). Critic Wallis Tinnie privileges what Angelou learned from the South but points out too that she "appropriates a deceptively guileless rhetoric to mask the syncopated rhythms of Europe, the American South, and Africa, stylistics germinating through quiet years of hearing and reading and internalizing the singsong melodies of Victorian couplets, the iambic pentameter of Shakespeare's sonnets, the biblical cadences and blues lyrics of African American poetry, the agony and transcendence of spiritual and gospel, and the coded, hieroglyphic messages of communal black southern language. Angelou's literary genius is firmly rooted in her southern heritage and crisscrosses several genres as she champions peace, redemption, and the sanctity of each human being" (Tinnie 523).

Eleanor Traylor also said, "the daughter's respect for and recognition of the text of woman-wisdom is a central point of moral authority by which the daughter's story may be corrected, revised, and protected from delusional and destructive forces" (Traylor 100).

Such comments send the reader of *Mom & Me & Mom* to the last page of the book, where a set of "Acknowledgments" can be found. There Angelou had written, "To all parents who have dared to raise daughters and sons/ with love, laughter, and prayers./ Who have stumbled and fallen, and yet arisen/ and gone on to be successful mothers and fathers./ And to all whom I have kept/ under a mother's watchful eye: [names listed]/ I thank God, and I thank you" (*Mom* 201). Angelou's words of both praise and generosity resonate with her customary readers: the fact about Maya Angelou's use of words, no matter their placement or their intent, is that they are believed.

12

Maya Angelou as spirit leader

In her book *Healing Narratives, Women Writers Curing Cultural Disease*, critic Gay Wilentz describes the African *spirit leader*, a position of power usually held by an older community member, often a woman. Drawing from the cultural premise that individual health is less important than the health of any community, and that "the health of an individual person is *directly* linked to the health of the community and the culture," Wilentz says as well that really significant "birth" is social as well as biological; just existing does not give a human being the true power that life necessitates. Wilentz places this belief in its African context, the belief "linked to the relationship between past and future generations through the role of the ancestor, whose importance is evident in much of the Caribbean as well as the United States African American society" (Wilentz 30–1).

Whereas men may fill the roles of traditional healers and *obeah*men, the power of leading others into health and wisdom remains a female role. The force of matriarchal understanding throughout African lives is incontrovertible. Yet, the woman who listens, absorbs, relates, and gives wise counsel is a rarity: her role is linked with the attainment of spiritual health.

This critic connects what she calls "dis-ease," often stemming from a culture's being leaderless, with the inevitable conditions of enslavement or colonization. Wilentz notes that African historians have long said that the roots of illness are often hidden throughout such cultures, especially illnesses of the nerves or those related to fatigue and malaise[1] (Wilentz 27).

Africanist Zauditu-Selassie explains that in Yoruba spiritual tradition, the Aje or *awon lya we* (our mothers) are also referred to as *Iyami Osoroga*, wise women with extraordinary powers. Such figures, though beneficent, "made people both revere and fear them because of their dense concentration of Ase." She defines this latter quality as "the divine power . . . the spiritual essence of God . . . All things are accomplished through Ase." Women so identified as the power mothers are named "Ma Dear, Other Mother, or Big Momma" in the African American tradition (Zauditu-Selassie 201–02). (The use of these names is seldom apparent in Angelou's writings, but the fiction of Toni Cade Bambara, Alice Walker, and particularly Toni Morrison often includes these designations.)

In Angelou's books of her closing years (beginning in 2013, with *Mom & Me & Mom*, followed in 2014 by *His Day Is Done, A Nelson Mandela Tribute*, and, posthumously, *Rainbow in the Cloud, The Wisdom and Spirit of Maya Angelou*), the author speaks with forthright conviction about her role in life as well as her beliefs in both God and the spirit world. In her autobiographical book about both her grandmother Annie Henderson and her mother Vivian Baxter, she seems to be charting paths toward the idealized state of such powerful women. She writes in the "Preface":

Frequently, I have been asked how I got to be this way. How did I, born black in a white country, poor in a society where wealth is adored and sought after at all costs, female in an environment where only large ships and some engines are described favorably by using the female pronoun—how did I get to be Maya Angelou?

Her answer is that "I knew that I had become the woman I am because of the grandmother I loved and the mother I came to adore . . . Their love informed, educated, and liberated me" (*Mom* 1).

About Nelson Mandela, Angelou said much the same thing. Imprisoned as he would be for the next twenty-seven years at the approximate time Angelou was leaving Ghana to return to the States (planning to work with Malcolm X in his Civil Rights efforts), Mandela was—for Angelou and for much of the peace-loving universe—a special kind of sainted believer and activist. His death in December 2013 prompted this eulogistic poem, which opens with his quotation, "Education is the most powerful weapon you can use to change the world."

About herself, the people who compiled the posthumous *Rainbow in the Cloud* collection (under the guiding hand of her son, Guy Johnson) felt a similarly intense reverence. Among the quotations used in her thinking about God are these:

I knew that if God loved me, then I could do wonderful things, I could try great things, learn anything, achieve anything.

Faith and prayer are important elements of my belief in God. Faith is my rock but it is also the way I align my thoughts, my heart, and my actions to realize my goals. Prayer is the way I connect with the energy of God, it is also the way I clarify to myself what I am asking for . . .

Spirit is one and is everywhere present. It never leaves me. In my ignorance I may withdraw from it, but I can realize its presence the instant I return to my senses.

I believe that each of us comes from the Creator trailing wisps of glory.

I think we must surrender the despair of unexpected cruelties and extend the wonder of unexpected kindnesses to ourselves and to each other . . . We deserve each other and each other's generosity (*Rainbow* 54–63).

One can never know too many good people. One must be open to what life has to bring. I have learned that a friend may be waiting behind a stranger's smile (*Rainbow* 42).

The human heart is so delicate and sensitive that it always needs some tangible encouragement to prevent it from faltering in its labor (*Rainbow* 77).

Angelou's visionary comments about not only her religious beliefs but also her humanistic ones—her understanding of other people, their fragility, their need to be understood and loved—merge in this book's sections. A talismanic collection, *Rainbow in the Cloud* will join the long list of Angelou's best-selling works, not so much because the compendium of her words is new but more so because in the book her wisdom is newly presented.

This concluding chapter was once titled "Maya Angelou as Public Intellectual." Given her prominence throughout the world, and given the familiarity she attained through the media and her appearances on its various sites—as when she received a third Grammy Award for her talking book recording of *A Song Flung Up to Heaven*, or when she (along with George W. Bush, Warren Buffett, and others) received the 2011 Presidential Medal of Freedom from President Barack Obama, or when Ross Rossin's portrait of her was presented to the Smithsonian National Portrait Gallery in the spring of 2014—Maya Angelou might be described in that way. I have come to think, however, that the phrase I now use, "spirit leader," has a more appropriate resonance for the kind of work Angelou did throughout her mature life in shaping people and their endeavors during much of the twentieth and the twenty-first centuries.

Maya Angelou was not a minister of any kind, though her devotion to the acts of ministering to people—individual people rather than political groups—gave her that kind of presence. She was a spirit guide in many senses of the word; she was spiritual but she also cared about helping others find paths that would allow them their own kinds of spiritual comfort. She cared little whether they were Protestant, Catholic, or Muslim; she wanted to give them some larger belief they could understand, always in relation to themselves and their own families.

Angelou was never parochial. She did not privilege the United States over other countries or other political systems. She believed, as Ishmael Reed once said, that North America should be (and often is) "a place where the cultures of the world crisscross" (Reed 56). Her facility with languages grew, as did much of her personal motivation, from her need to talk with others, to truly communicate with all kinds and all classes and races of people.

Angelou was pleased to be able to speak through her art. After her appearance reading "On the Pulse of Morning" at the Inauguration of President William Clinton, she felt a sense of great accomplishment— not so much for the world's attention to Maya Angelou as poet, but rather to the world's attention to the fact of the *poem*.

The praise for her poetry thrilled her; winning another Grammy Award for the Spoken Word recording she had done of the poem added another level to some universal understanding of poetry. As *The New York Times* said, "when Maya Angelou rendered with unprecedented resonance, a magnificent poem," the world paid attention: people were not going to question that "History was in the making" (January 20, 1993).

In a recent interview with Angelou, historian Marianne Schnall called her "a global renaissance woman, one of the most renowned and influential voices of our time" (Schnall 93). Similarly, Darlene Clark Hine and Kathleen Thompson, African American historians, conclude that following Angelou's literary contributions during the 1970s, "The story of America was no longer white and it was no longer male." (These writers entitle one of their chapters about gender as "The Caged Bird Sings," in reference to Angelou's historically ground-breaking *I Know Why the Caged Bird Sings*. They also make clear that the poetry of Angelou, Gwendolyn Brooks and Rita Dove is universally significant because it collectively "shows the courage, strength, and resourcefulness" of black women through history.) (Hine 294, 4). As Sandi Russell said about Angelou's oeuvre, her books "resonate with the love, wit, energy and spirit of an indomitable woman" (Russell 150). As Wallis Tinnie had said, Angelou "has become the people's poet and world cultural griot (keeper of the story to be passed on)." She has also become "a national matriarch who speaks to the world with a depth of wisdom" that this critic equates with the powerful writing of Twain, Faulkner, and Hurston. There is a unifying spirit in Maya Angelou's writing: "For Angelou, everyone is 'We'" (Tinnie 524).

In the words of the Governor of North Carolina, in June 2014, "Maya Angelou was a poet, civil rights activist, dancer, film and television producer, playwright, actress and professor; she may be best known for her book *I Know Why the Caged Bird Sings* . . . [she was] a 'Phenomenal' woman who touched many individuals through her writing, performance and teaching: she leaves a legacy of hope, determination and belief in oneself and abilities despite circumstances" (Resolution, Pat McCrory, Governor).

The fact that editors throughout the twenty-first century have continued to clamor for Maya Angelou to write an essay, or a letter, or a poem that they might include in their books adds urgency to

Holograph copy of Maya Angelou's important, and often-circulated, statement, "A Pledge to Rescue Our Youth." Written for the Essence Music Festival in 2006, this document has been widely circulated by community and church groups ever since.

the writer's still-evolving reputation, a reputation that combines name recognition with unqualified respect in a fusion so superior to that of most living writers as to be of a different ilk. Maya Angelou appears, with a cadre of nonliterary figures, in *Voice of America, Interviews with Eight American Women of Achievement* (a substantial volume published by the United States Information Agency). And, regretfully, there is little chance that any bibliographer has collected all the books in which Angelou's work has appeared: in the task of record keeping, she is one of this century's most elusive writers.

This book has occasionally mentioned some of Maya Angelou's honors and awards. According to critic Jacqueline Thursby, many others should be listed: given the frequency and regularity of accolades for media, literature, teaching, and humanitarian efforts, few living Americans have been so visibly honored. (To this long list must be added, collectively, honorary degrees at the PhD level from more than forty universities; at most of these ceremonies, Angelou was invited to speak to large audiences assembled; there are also countless invitations to speak at college graduations.)

1990   Candace Award, National Coalition of 100 Black Women

1990   American Academy of Achievement

1990   Nancy Hanks Lecture, American Council of the Arts, Washington, DC

1991   Langston Hughes Medal, City College of New York

1992   Horatio Alger Award

1992   Distinguished Woman of North Carolina

1992   Women in Film Crystal Award

1993   Citizen Diplomat Award

1993   Grammy Award for Best Spoken Word Album ("On the Pulse of Morning")

1993   Arkansas Black Hall of Fame

1994   Rollins College Wall of Fame

1994   Spingarn Medal, NAACP

1994   Black History Makers Award

1995   Frank G. Wells Award

1995 Grammy Award for Best Spoken Word Album ("Phenomenal Woman")

1996 President's Award, Collegiate of Language Association

1996 Southern Christian Leadership Conference of Los Angeles and Martin Luther King, Jr., Legacy Association National Award

1996 Lifetime Membership, NAACP

1996 The New York Black 100

1996 UNICEF, American Ambassador

1997 National Conference of Christians and Jews, Distinguished Merit

1997 Humanitarian Contribution Award

1997 NAACP Image Award, Outstanding Literary Work, Nonfiction

1997 W. K. Kellogg Foundation, Expert-in-Residence Program

1997 North Carolina "Woman of the Year" Award

1997 Presidential and Lecture Series Award, University of North Florida

1997 Black Caucus of American Library Association, Cultural Keepers Award

1997 Homecoming Award, Oklahoma Center for Poets and Writers

1998 Board of Governors, Winston-Salem State University, Maya Angelou Institute for the Improvement of Child and Family Education

1998 Alston/Jones International Civil and Human Rights Award

1998 National Women's Hall of Fame, Inductee

1998 Christopher Award

1998 Chicago International Film Festival, Gold Plaque Choice Award for *Down in the Delta*

1998 City Proclamation, Winston-Salem, North Carolina

1999 Sheila Award, Tubman African American Museum

1999 Speaker, Special Olympics World Games, Raleigh, North Carolina

1999 Lifetime Achievement Award for Literature

1999 Named one of the "top 100 best writers of the 20th century"

2000 Presidential Medal of Arts (Presidential Award, The White House)

2001 Member, US Holocaust Memorial Museum Committee

2002 Ethnic Multicultural Media Awards (EMMAS), Lifetime Achievement Award

2002 Grammy Award for Best Spoken Word Album (*A Song Flung Up to Heaven*)

2002 American Geriatrics Society's Foundation for Health in Aging Award

2004 Charles Evans Hughes Award, National Conference for Community and Justice

2005 Honoree, Howard University Heart's Day

2006 John Hope Franklin Award

2006 Black Caucus of American Library Association, Librarians of Color Author Award

2006 Mother Teresa Award

2006 *New York Times* Best Seller Awards List

2007 Martha Parker Legacy Award

2008 International Civil Rights Walk of Fame, Martin Luther King, Jr., National Historic Site

2008 Lincoln Medal (Presidential Award, The White House)

2008 Cornell Medallion, Cornell University

2008 Voice of Peace Award (first recipient), Hope for Peace and Justice

2008 Gracie Allen Award (the "Gracie")

2008 Marian Anderson Award

2011 Presidential Medal of Freedom (Presidential Award, The White House)

2012 Angelou founded the Maya Angelou Center for Women's Health and Wellness (Winston-Salem, North Carolina).

(Thursby 412–13)

As in the case of Angelou's bibliographers, keepers of her chronology of honors consistently fall behind. Whereas her publications and some of her films and televisions works are included in the bibliography here, not all of them are yet recorded. Along with the three very distinguished Presidential Medals—the Medal of Arts in 2000, the Lincoln Medal in 2008, and the Medal of Freedom in 2011—Angelou has been honored for her nonliterary work through the awarding of the Christopher Award, the Charles Evans Hughes Award, the John Hope Franklin Award, the Mother Teresa Award, the Voice of Peace Award, UNICEF and NAACP awards, and others. She has been similarly honored by groups distinguished for their interest in the achievements of women, and by groups distinguished for their interest in the achievements of African Americans of both genders. Perhaps one of the most significant points to be made

*Maya Angelou receiving the National Arts and Humanities
Medal from President William J. Clinton in December 2000.
In 2011 she was the recipient of the Presidential Medal of
Freedom from President Barack Obama. Photographer:
Ralph Alswang. Credit: William J. Clinton Presidential
Library.*

about this list of accolades is its length: from the publication of
I Know Why the Caged Bird Sings and *Just Give Me a Cool Drink of
Water 'Fore I Diiie*, in 1970 and 1971, Angelou has been the recipient
of awards from institutes that commend literary work, film and
television work, work with women, work with African Americans,
work with the disadvantaged, work with religious beliefs—a truly
humanitarian range.

Such achieved honors also chart the consistency of Maya
Angelou's personal involvement in not only her work, but in the
lives of people around her (as well as people in the larger sense of
those human beings occupying the earth with her). For another
significant point to be made about the work and the character of
the central *spirit* of Maya Angelou is that it seems to be unchanging.

When Marianne Schnall asked her—just a year before her death—why the United States has not yet had a woman president, Angelou's answer was compatible with answers to similar questions she had asked thirty and forty years earlier. In her moral understandings, Angelou seemed to be the fount of consistency. She told Schnall, "I think we are more ready for it than we think we are . . . I supported Hillary Clinton in her bid for the White House. After a while, some of the top Democrats phoned me and asked me to ask Mrs. Clinton to step down because it seemed certain that Senator Obama was going to be the choice. So I said, 'I told her twenty years ago that if she ran for anything, I had her back and would support her. When she steps down, I will step down.' I think that she would make a wonderful president. But when she decided that Senator Obama was a likely candidate that she could support, she stepped down and I stepped down with her. And I went over to the Obama camp and said, 'If I can be of any use, please use me.'"

Less specifically, when Schnall asks about essential qualities in good people, to enable them to do the important spiritual work the world requires, Angelou answered, "Courage . . . without courage you can't practice any other virtue consistently . . . if you decide, 'I will not stay in rooms where women are belittled; I will not stay in company where races, no matter who they are, are belittled; I will not take it; I will not sit around and accept dehumanizing other human beings'—if you decide to do that in small ways, and you continue to do it—finally you realize you've got so much courage . . . people want to be around you. They get a feeling that they will be protected in your company" (Schnall 96).

In speaking about the hard lives that many African Americans have endured, Angelou repeats caveats she has discussed before: "I know that my people did [have hope], because they couldn't have survived slavery without having hope that it would get better. There are some songs from the eighteenth and nineteenth centuries that say 'By and by, by and by, I will lay down this heavy load.' I mean, so many songs that spoke of hope—amazing songs. The slaves knew that they did not have the right legally to walk within one inch away from where the slave owner dictated, and yet the same people wrote and sang with fervor, 'If the Lord wants somebody, here am I, send me.' It's amazing."

When Schnall asks Angelou to discuss the twenty-first-century attention to ecological issues, Angelou replied that "we are growing up out of the idiocies—racism and sexism and ageism and all those ignorances." She continued, the worst social sins today are "ignorance, of course, but mostly polarization . . . We have to undo. We can learn to see each other and see ourselves in each other and recognize that human beings are more alike than we are unalike." As Angelou often does, she privileges the human moral sense: "All of us know not what is expedient, not what is going to make us popular, not what the policy is—but in truth each of us knows what is the right thing to do. And that's how I am guided" (Schnall 97, 99).

Nearly twenty-five years before Angelou answered these questions, she discussed many of the same ideas in her 1990 *Paris Review* interview-performance. When interviewer and author George Plimpton asked her about how to judge people's maturity, she took him a round-about way to the heart of her answer:

Oh my God, I've lived a very simple life! You can say, Oh yes, at thirteen this happened to me and at fourteen . . . those are facts. But the facts can obscure the truth, what it really felt like. Every human being has paid the earth to grow up. Most people don't grow up. It's too damn difficult. What happens is most people get older . . . They honor their credit cards, they find parking spaces, they marry, they have the nerve to have children, but they don't grow up. Not really.

They grow older. But to grow up costs the earth, the *earth*. It means you take responsibility for the time you take up, for the space you occupy. It's serious business. And you find out what it costs us to love and to lose, to dare and to fail. And maybe even more, to succeed. What it costs, in truth. Not superficial costs . . . That's what I write. What it is really like. I'm just telling a very simple story" (Paris 247).

Plimpton had begun his questioning by asking Angelou about her great love for the Bible, assuming that he would then move into discussing morality. She tells him how valuable all language is to her, whether she is just reading and enjoying or looking for ways to model her own writing, but she comes to a different point as she moves through an answer. What she finally says after she talks about words as a "melody," is this:

> I'm working at trying to be a Christian and that's serious business. It's like trying to be a good Jew, a good Shintoist, a good Muslim, a good Buddhist, a good Zorastrian, a good friend, a good lover, a good mother, a good buddy—it's serious business. It's not something where you think, Oh, I've got it done. I did it all day, hotdiggety. The truth is, all day long you *try* to do it, try to *be* it, and then in the evening if you're honest and have a little courage you look at yourself and say, Hmm. I only blew it eighty-six times. Not bad. I'm trying to be a Christian and the Bible helps me to remind myself what I'm about (Paris 238).

She muses over the idea that perseverance in all things creates worth. "We may encounter many defeats, but we must not be defeated . . . we are all much stronger than we appear to be and maybe much better than we allow ourselves to be. Human beings are much more alike than unalike. There's no real mystique. Every human being, every

Jew, Christian, backslider, Muslim, Shintoist, Zen Buddhist, atheist, agnostic, every human being wants a nice place to live, a good place for the children to go to school, healthy children, somebody to love, the courage, the unmitigated gall to accept love in return, some place to party on Saturday or Sunday night, and someplace to perpetuate that God. There's no mystique. None, And if I'm right in my work, that's what my work says" (Paris 250–1).

Because Plimpton was a successful writer himself, he posed several questions to Angelou about the art of writing. She had often written elsewhere about her very systematic daily routine, enabling herself to focus on the project at hand. Accepting her conscientious application of her talents, day by day, the interviewer pushed for specifics. Getting up early each morning and having coffee, Angelou then goes to a hotel room which she has rented for the months she thinks the project will take: although she will be there for only parts of each day, she wants the walls completely bare. "I don't want anything in there. I go into the room and I feel as if all my beliefs are suspended. Nothing holds me to anything. No milkmaids, no flowers, nothing. I just want to *feel* and then when I start to work, I'll remember. I'll read something, maybe the Psalms, maybe, again, something from Mr. Dunbar, James Weldon Johnson. And I'll remember how beautiful, how pliable the language is, how it will lend itself. If you pull it, it says, OK. I remember that and I start to write. Nathanael West says, 'Easy reading is damn hard writing.' I try to pull the language into such a sharpness that it jumps off the page. It must look easy but it takes me forever to get it to look so easy" (Paris 240).

In the hotel room every day will be the Bible, a poem collection, a dictionary, a thesaurus, a deck of playing cards (sometimes solitaire starts the flow of language), a bottle of sherry, cigarettes, an ashtray, and not much else. Angelou has no phone, no computer; she writes on a yellow legal pad in ballpoint pen. "To write, I lie across the bed, so that this elbow is completely encrusted at the end, just rough with calluses. I never allow the hotel people to change the bed, because I never sleep there. I stay until twelve-thirty or one-thirty in the afternoon and then I go home and try to breathe; I look at the work around five; I have an orderly dinner—proper, quiet, lonely dinner, and then I go back to work the next morning" (Paris 239).

To a question about revising, she continues to describe her writing process: "I write in the morning and then go home about midday and take a shower, because writing, as you know, is very hard work, so you have to do a double ablution. I go out and shop—I'm a serious cook—and pretend to be normal. I play sane—Good morning! Fine, thank you. And you? And I go home and prepare dinner for myself and if I have houseguests, I do the candles and the pretty music and all that. Then after all the dishes are moved away, I read what I wrote that morning. And more often than not if I've done nine pages I may be able to save two and a half or three. That's the cruelest time, you know, to really admit that it doesn't work . . . when I finished maybe fifty pages and read them—fifty acceptable pages—it's not too bad" (Paris 241).

Satisfying as Angelou finds it, writing is incredibly hard work—and she says her discipline has sometimes been personally costly. "I have lost lovers, endangered friendships, and blundered into eccentricity" ("Shades" 3). She also repeats in many of her answers about how she writes that in some cases, she serves as a recorder: "I write for the Black voice and any ear which can hear it . . . I search for sound, tempos, and rhythm to ride through the vocal cord over the tongue, and out of the logic of Black people. I love the shades and slashes of light. Its rumblings and passages of magical lyricism . . ."

Having said that, I must now talk about content. I have noted most carefully from the past twenty years our speech patterns, the ambiguities, contradictions, the moans and laughter, and I am even more enchanted at this time than I was when I began eavesdropping.

After, and during pestilential assaults of frustration, hate, demeanings, and murders, our language continues to expand and mature. Other lives, made inadequate and estranged by the experience of malice, loathing, and hostility, are enriched by the words we use to, and with, each other.

In this interview, Angelou also describes the way her daily writing work starts:

wash, pray . . . and arrange my mind in writing order. That is, I tell myself how lucky I am that this morning is new, a day never seen before, that ideas will come to me which I have never consciously known . . . [I] allow the work of the day before to flood my mind. The characters and situations take over the chambers of my existence until they are all I see and hear. Then I go to my writing room . . .

When asked about her deck of cards, as she often is, Angelou notes about playing solitaire: "It seems to me that when my hands and small mind (a Southern Black phrase) are engaged in placing the reds on the blacks and the blacks on the reds, my working mind arranges and rearranges the characters and the plot. Finally when they are in a plausible order, I simply have to write down where they are and what they say" ("Shades" 4).

When she gave Walter Blum an earlier interview, Angelou had paused for a time to elaborate on why living in the United States was valuable to any artist. She talks about the country's "*spirit* . . . almost like Martin Buber's good and evil conflict. There is that lust for life, for immortality. And I don't know how that seed was planted in the American breast, but it is more virulent here . . . In Asian and African cultures, people are sure they will be continued through their children, through their tradition, through their culture, through their gods. But in America everybody wants to live it *all*! There is a kind of lust that's wonderful to me, that's exciting as hell. Now I agree that ambition is probably the mother of all vices, and if you're ambitious enough you'll kill your mother for it, but it's still exciting. It's the American ethos, which if one could phrase it in a few words, would be *Yes I can*. And all Americans believe in it. *Yes*, I can get a twenty-foot Cadillac. *Yes*, I can go to the White House. *Yes*, I can raise some children. *Yes*, I can enslave people. *Yes*, I can free them. *Yes*, I can fight for my freedom. *Yes*, I can fight for my freedom. *Yes*, I can be a great woman. *Yes*, I can" (Blum 48).

Angelou's sincere belief in the equality of all people ties in to this moving defense of US attitudes. In the Suman interview, somewhat surprisingly, she talks about economic classes ("class" is much less often scrutinized in America than is race—or even gender). Angelou defines herself as a part of the "working class": "I work very, very hard in a system which believes that money dictates and explains the value of the person." Trying to help Suman understand the real class system, she adds, "We cannot separate the artists from the workers. The role of the artist is to serve—no more or no less than the role of a school teacher .... We are to serve for the betterment of our society. And we have all been equally exploited, equally debased" (Suman 110).

Repeatedly, Angelou (here, in answer to a question by Marianne Schnall) talks about morality. She refers to lessons she learned from Annie Henderson: "And when I want to think about what would be the right thing to do, the fair thing to do, the wise thing to do, I can just think of my grandmother. I can always hear her say, 'Now, sister, *you* know what's right. Just do *right*!'" (Schnall 98). As if in tandem, Angelou's words to Claudia Tate repeat this insistence: "I try to live what I consider a 'poetic existence.' This means I take responsibility for the air I breathe and the space I take up. I try to be immediate, to be totally present for all my work. I try to be present. I try for concentrated consciousness which I miss by more than half, but I'm trying." After she finishes discussing her writing life, Angelou adds, "I'm always trying to be a better human being" (Tate in Braxton 151–2).

State of North Carolina

PAT McCRORY
GOVERNOR

IN MEMORY OF MAYA ANGELOU
2014
BY THE GOVERNOR OF THE STATE OF NORTH CAROLINA
A PROCLAMATION

WHEREAS, the State of North Carolina mourns the loss of one of its most distinguished residents, Dr. Maya Angelou, who passed away in Winston-Salem on May 28, 2014; and

WHEREAS, Marguerite Annie Johnson was born April 4, 1928, in St. Louis, Missouri; she spent most of her formative years in Arkansas, where she and her older brother were raised by their grandmother, but also spent time in California with her mother; she was nicknamed Maya by her brother; and

WHEREAS, at the age of eight, Angelou was sexually assaulted by a boyfriend of her mother, who was convicted, sentenced to one day in jail and killed four days after his release; this horrific experience silenced Angelou for five years; it was also the impetus for her finding her voice in literature, social action and performance; and

WHEREAS, Dr. Maya Angelou was a poet, civil rights activist, dancer, film and television producer, playwright, actress and professor; she may be best known for her book, *I Know Why the Caged Bird Sings*, an autobiography of her childhood; and

WHEREAS, Dr. Maya Angelou was a "Phenomenal" woman who touched many individuals through her writing, performance and teaching; she leaves a legacy of hope, determination and belief in oneself and abilities despite circumstance; and

WHEREAS, the State of North Carolina recognizes Dr. Maya Angelou as a great North Carolinian and leader of our state;

NOW, THEREFORE, I, PAT McCRORY, Governor of the State of North Carolina, do hereby proclaim June 7, 2014, in memory and in honor of "MAYA ANGELOU" in North Carolina, and commend its observance to all citizens.

IN WITNESS WHEREOF, I have hereunto set my hand and affixed the Great Seal of the State of North Carolina at the Capitol in Raleigh this third day of June in the year of our Lord two thousand and fourteen, and of the Independence of the United States of America the two hundred and thirty-eighth.

PAT McCRORY
Governor

The Proclamation given by Governor Pat McCrory of North Carolina in memory of Maya Angelou soon after her death in May 2014.

Perhaps one of the most visible, and impressive, characteristics that marked Maya Angelou's life as well as her writing, was her constancy. She was always the same, a striving and yet encouraging person. She never stopped working toward being "a better human being," a better person, a better writer. She told Marianne Schnall, when that interviewer asked her what kinds of messages she gave the women who came to her for advice, "I would say, 'Look what you've already come through . . . if you've been alive until you're thirty-five, you have gone through some pain. It cost you something . . . Have the sense to look at yourself and say, 'Well, wait a minute. I'm stronger than I thought I was.' So we need to not be in denial about what we've done, what we've come through. It will help us if we all do that" (Schnall 99).

Approachable. That word is one of the highest tributes paid frequently to Maya Angelou. Just as she spoke and wrote often about the realities of people's lives, she also spoke and wrote about their beliefs, their sacrifices as they tried to enable partners, parents, and children. *Selfless* might be another word that is useful in thinking about Maya Angelou, but one can almost sense her taking offense at the piety that word implies: Maya Angelou was a fighter; she was not always "selfless." I would draw from the work done by psychiatrist Kay Redfield Jamison, as she analyzes the indefatigable personalities so often seen in scientific worlds. She calls these people *exuberant*, and defines that term as "an abounding, ebullient, effervescent emotion." Exuberant people cannot wait to get up early, and start their work. "It is a kinetic and unrestrained, joyful, irrepressible" [state] . . . It spreads upward and outward, like pollen toted by dancing bees, and in this carrying ideas are moved and actions taken." According to Jamison, such personalities get things done. Exuberance is "ancient, material, and profound."

Yet the psychiatrist has found, through many case studies, that the genius of the exuberant is also vulnerable. "Bubbles burst: a wince of disapproval can cut dead a whistle or abort a cartwheel. The exuberant move above the horizon, exposed and vulnerable" (Jamison 4–5).

Maya Angelou convinced her millions of readers that she was herself a vulnerable human being. She was *not* unlike everyone else alive. In her writing, she carefully revealed those burst bubbles, and the fact that there were many of them. She created wisdom through words she chose with care, words that reached an audience who never owned dictionaries or thesauruses, an audience reared on hearing language, and listening to that language, with candor, and perhaps curiosity, and respect.

Maya Angelou used words that *could* reach such an audience because she understood all too readily that information shrouded in obfuscation or housed in ambivalence was useless. In her 2014 collection, *Rainbow in the Cloud*, she wrote:

The wise woman thinks twice and speaks once or, better yet, does not speak at all (*Rainbow* 104).

She also wrote there: "What I have always wanted is to be of use. I will not be abused. I will not be misused, not willingly. But I will be of use. Anybody who is not of use is useless" (*Rainbow* 86).

When all the accolades are in, and all the closing tributes assembled, there will be no question as to the *approachability*, the *constancy*, the *giftedness*, the *candor*, the *exuberance*, the *health*, the *spiritualism*, and the *vulnerability* of Marguerite Johnson—known to her millions of avid readers as Maya Angelou.

Note

1 Wilentz also notes, "West African writers, both male and female, have often returned to their still intact traditional cultures to heal the wounds caused by five hundred years of penetration by traders and, later, colonists. Although separated by time and space, Black women writers in the United States and the Caribbean are investigating aspects of their African past that remain within the culture to understand both the postslavery and postcolonial disorders that plague their communities" (Wilentz 27). Because of Angelou's years in Egypt and Ghana, and her identification with the beliefs and the arts of these countries, such new philosophical directions are relevant.

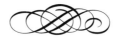

Bibliography

Primary

Autobiographies

Angelou, Maya. *All God's Children Need Traveling Shoes*. New York: Random, 1986. Print.

—. *Collected Autobiographies of Maya Angelou*. New York: Modern Library Edition by Random, 2004. Print.

—. *Gather Together in My Name*. New York: Random, 1974. Print.

—. *The Heart of a Woman*. New York: Random, 1981. Print.

—. *I Know Why the Caged Bird Sings*. New York: Random, 1970. Print.

—. *Mom & Me & Mom*. New York: Random, 2013. Print.

—. *Singin' and Swingin' and Gettin' Merry Like Christmas*. New York: Random, 1976. Print.

—. *A Song Flung Up to Heaven*. New York: Random, 2002. Print.

Essays and other non-fiction

Angelou, Maya. *Even the Stars Look Lonesome*. New York: Random, 1997. Print.

—. *Great Food, All Day Long: Cook Splendidly, Eat Smart*. New York: Random, 2010. Print.

—. *Hallelujah! The Welcome Table*. New York: Random, 2004. Print.

—. *Lessons in Living*. New York: Random, 1993. Print.

—. *Letter to My Daughter*. New York: Random, 2008. Print.

—. *Rainbow in the Cloud, The Wisdom and Spirit of Maya Angelou*. New York: Random, 2014. Print.

—. *Wouldn't Take Nothing for My Journey Now*. New York: Random, 1993. Print.

Poems

Angelou, Maya. *Amazing Peace: A Christmas Poem*. New York: Random, 2005. Print.

—. *And Still I Rise*. New York: Random, 1978. Print.

—. *A Brave and Startling Truth*. New York: Random, 1995. Print.

—. *Celebrations: Rituals of Peace and Prayer*. New York: Random, 2006. Print.

—. *The Complete Collected Poems of Maya Angelou*. New York: Random, 1994. Print.

—. *His Day Is Done, A Nelson Mandela Tribute*. New York: Random, 2014. Print.

—. *I Shall Not Be Moved*. New York: Random, 1990. Print.

—. *Just Give Me a Cool Drink of Water 'fore I Diiie*. New York: Random, 1971. Print.

—. *Mother: A Cradle to Hold Me*. New York: Random, 2006. Print.

—. *Now Sheba Sings the Song*. Illus. Tom Feelings. New York: Dutton, 1987. Print.

—. *Oh Pray My Wings Are Gonna Fit Me Well*. New York: Random, 1975. Print.

—. *On the Pulse of Morning*. New York: Random, 1993. Print.

—. *Phenomenal Woman: Four Poems Celebrating Women*. New York: Random, 1994. Print.

—. *Poems: Maya Angelou*. New York: Bantam, 1997. Print.

—. *Poetry for Young People: Maya Angelou*. Ed. Edwin Graves Wilson. New York: Sterling, 2007. Print.

—. *Shaker, Why Don't You Sing?* New York: Random, 1983. Print.

Spoken word albums

Angelou, Maya. *An Evening with Maya Angelou,* 1975.

—. *Been Found*. Music & Spoken Word album with Nicholas Ashford and Valerie Simpson, Record Label Ichiban/Ryko, 1996.

—. *Hallelujah! The Welcome Table*. Random House Audio Voices Unabridged, 2004.

—. *Maya Angelou,* 1979.

—. *Miss Calypso* (recorded songs), 1957.

—. *On the Pulse of Morning*. Ingram audio production, 1993.

—. *Phenomenal Woman*. Ingram audio production, 1995.

—. *The Poetry of Maya Angelou*, GWT Records, 1969.

—. *A Song Flung Up to Heaven*. Library Edition, 2002.

—. *Women in Business*. University of Wisconsin, 1981.

Children's books, screenplays, plays, essays, poems, interviews, and documentaries

Angelou, Maya. "A Brave and Startling Truth," Online. http://w3.arizona.edu/-amunl/unpoem.html

—. Academy of Achievement Induction remarks, Museum of Living History (January 20, 1997). Online. www.achievement.org/autodoc/printmember/angOint-1.

—. *Adjoa Amissah.* Two-act musical, 1967.

— (Producer). *Afro-Americans in the Arts.* Documentary, PBS, 1977.

—. *AJAX.* Two-act drama, adapted from Sophocles' play, 1974.

—. *All Day Long.* Screenplay, American Film Institute, 1974.

—. *Amazing Peace.* Illus. Steve Johnson and Lou Fancher. New York: Schartz & Wade, 2008.

—. *And Still I Rise.* One-act musical, 1976.

—. *Angelou on Burns.* Documentary. United Kingdom, 1996.

—, (Narrator). *As Seen through These Eyes.* Written and directed by Hilary Helstein. Menemsha Films, 2008.

—. *Assignment America*, series of six half-hour PBS programs, 1975.

—. *The Best of These.* Play, 1966.

—. *Black, Blues, Black.* TV series, National Educational Television, 1968.

—. "*The Black Scholar* Interviews Maya Angelou," by Robert Chrisman. *Black Scholar*, 8.4 (January/February 1977): 44–53. Print.

—. *Brewster Place.* TV series, coauthor, 1990.

—. *Cabaret for Freedom,* musical review (co-authored with Godfrey Cambridge), 1960.

—. *The Clawing Within.* Two-act play, 1966.

—. *Conversations with Maya Angelou.* Ed. Jeffrey M. Elliot. Jackson: UP of Mississippi, 1989. Print.

— (Director). *Down in the Delta.* Written by Myron Goble. Amen Rafilms and Chris/Rose Productions, 1998.

—. *Georgia, Georgia.* Screenplay, 1972.

—. *Getting Up Stayed on My Mind.* Play, 1967.

—. *How Do You Spell God?* Screenplay, TV movie, 1996.

— (Co-screenwriter with Leonora Thuna). *I Know Why the Caged Bird Sings.* Dir. Fielder Cook, Tomorrow Entertainment, Inc., 1979. 96 minutes.

—. "Interview with Amiri Baraka," *Conversations with Amiri Baraka.* Jackson: UP of Mississippi, 1994: 260–6. Print.

—. "Interview with Maya Angelou, The 'Paper Napkin' Interview," *Southern Living*, 46.12 (December 2011): 20. Print.

—. "Interview with Maya Angelou," with Kabir Suman. *Discovering the Other America, Radical Voices from the 1980s.* Kolkata, India: Thema, 2012: 107–18. Print.

—. "Interview with Maya Angelou, The Art of Fiction," with George Plimpton, 1990. *The Paris Review Interviews* IV. New York: Picador, 2009: 236–58. Print.

—. *Kofi and His Magic.* Photographs by Margaret Courtney-Clarke. New York: Clarkson Potter/Publishers, 1996. Print.

—. *Kwanzaa.* Cowritten with M. K. Asante, Jr., 2008.

—. *The Least of These.* Two-act play, 1966.

—. *The Legacy and the Inheritors.* Two-part program, the US Information Agency, 1976.

—. *Life Doesn't Frighten Me At All.* Ed. Sara Jane Boyers. Illus. Jean-Michel Basquiat. New York: Stewart, Tabori & Chang, 1993. Print.

—. *Love's Exquisite Freedom.* New York: Random, Print.

—. (Narrator). *Madagascar: A World Apart.* PBS Home Video, 1998. 60 Minutes.

— (Actress). *Madea's Family Reunion: The Movie.* Lionsgate and the Tyler Perry Company, 2006. 110 minutes.

—. "Maya Angelou," (essay), *I Dream a World: Portraits of Black Women Who Changed America.* Ed. Brian Lanker. New York: Stewart, Tabori, and Chang, 1999: 166. Print.

—. "Maya Angelou," *Writers Dreaming.* Ed. Naomi Epel. New York: Carol Southern Books: 1993, 25–30. Print.

—. *Maya Angelou's America: A Journey of the Heart.* Documentary; also host, 1988. Online.

—. "Maya Angelou's Million Man March Poem," October 16, 1995. Online. http://www.lgc.apc.org/africanam/hot/maaya.html

—. *Maya's World: Angelina of Italy.* Illus. Lizzy Rockwell. New York: Random, 2004. Print.

—. *Maya's World: Izak of Lapland.* New York: Random, 2004. Print.

—. *Maya's World: Mikale of Hawaii.* New York: Random, 2004. Print.

—. *Maya's World: Rene Marie of France.* New York: Random, 2004. Print.

— (Director). *Moon on a Rainbow Shawl,* play by Errol John. London, 1988.

—. *Mrs. Flowers: A Moment of Friendship.* Minneapolis: Redpath P, 1986. Print.

—. "My Grandson, Home at Last," *Woman's Day* (August 1986): 46–55. Print.

—. *My Painted House, My Friendly Chicken and Me.* Photographs by Margaret Courtney-Clarke. New York: Clarkson Potter/Publishers, 1994. Print.

—. "New Directions" (essay), *Black-Eyed Peas for the Soul.* Ed. Donna Marie Williams. New York: Simon & Schuster-Fireside, 1997: 206–08. Print.

—. *On a Southern Journey.* One-act play, 1983.

—. *Poetry for Young People*. Ed. Edwin Graves Wilson. Illus. Jerime Lagarrigue. New York: Sterling, 2007. Print.

—. "The Reunion," episode in *America's Dream*. TV miniseries, 1996.

— (Actress). *The Runaway*. Dir. Arthur Alan Seidelman. Hallmark Hall of Fame, 2001. 98 Minutes.

—. "Shades and Slashes of Light," *Black Women Writers (1950–1980)*. Ed. Mari Evans. Garden City, NY: Doubleday, 1984: 3–5. Print.

—. *Sister, Sister*. TV drama, also producer, 1982.

—. *Theatrical Vignette*. One-act play, 1983.

—. *Trying to Make It Home*. Byline, TV 1988.

— (Director) *Visions*, TV single episode, 1976.

—. "Why I Moved Back to the South," *Ebony* (February 1982): 130–4. Print.

—. "Why My Great Grandmother's Name Matters," *The Root* (February 6, 2008). Online. http://www.theroot.com/views/why-my-great-grandmothers-name-matters.

—. *Soul Looks Back in Wonder*. Illus. Tom Feelings. New York: Dial, 1993. Print.

Bleiler, David. *TLA Video and DVD Guide* . . . . . New York: Macmillan, 2005.

"*Down in the Delta*," *Ebony* (February 1, 1999). Paging refers to EBSCOhost online printout, 1–4. http://www.starpulse.com/Notables/Angelou,_Maya (links to current news items, biography, film credits, other links).

Archives

North Carolina Collection, Wilson Library, The University of North Carolina-Chapel Hill.

Rare Books and Manuscripts, Wilson Library, The University of North Carolina-Chapel Hill.

Schomburg Center for Research in Black Culture, New York ("Going Home, Coming Home: Remembering" exhibit, 2014–15).

Z. Reynolds Smith Library, Rare Books Collection, Wake Forest University, Maya Angelou Archive.

Secondary Bibliography

"About the Author: Maya Angelou," *Read* 55.13 (February 2006): 31. Print.

Abrahams, Roger D. *Talking Black*. Rowley, MA: Newbury House, 1976. Print.

Adams, Phoebe. "Review of *Gather Together in My Name*," *Atlantic* (June 1, 1974): 233. Print.

Adams, Timothy Dow. *Telling Lies in Modern American Autobiography*. Chapel
    Hill: U of North Carolina P, 1990. Print.
Adzei, Kwaku. "The Meaning of Names in Ghana," *Negro Digest* 12 (1962): 95–7.
    Print.
"The AFI-Aspen Conference," *American Film* 5 (July–August 1980): 57–64. Print.
Als, Hilton. "Songbird: Maya Angelou Takes Another Look at Herself," *New
    Yorker* (August 5, 2002): 72–6. Print.
Andrews, William L. "Autobiography: Secular Autobiography," *The Oxford
    Companion to African American Literature*. Ed. William L. Andrews,
    Frances Smith Foster, and Trudier Harris. New York: Oxford UP, 1997: 34–7.
    Print.
"Author Maya Angelou Honoured by *Glamour*," *Miami Times* (November 18,
    2009): 3C. Print.
Baisnee, Valerie. *Gendered Resistance: The Autobiographies of Simone de
    Beauvoir, Maya Angelou, Janet Frame and Marguerite Duras*. Amsterdam:
    Rodopi, 1997. Print.
Baker, Houston A. *Blues, Ideology, and Afro-American Literature. A Vernacular
    Theory*. Chicago: U of Chicago P, 1984. Print.
—. "Review of *All God's Children Need Traveling Shoes*," *New York Times Book
    Review* (May 11, 1986): 14. Print.
—. *Workings of the Spirit: The Poetics of Afro-American Women's Writing*.
    Chicago: U of Chicago P, 1991. Print.
Banfield, William C. *Representing Black Music Culture: Then, Now, and When
    Again?* Lanham, MD: Scarecrow, 2011. Print.
Baraka, Amiri (LeRoi Jones). *Blues People: Negro Music in White America*.
    New York: Perennial, 1963. Print.
Barnwell, Cherron A. "Singin' de Blues, Writing Black Female Survival in
    I Know Why the Caged Bird Sings," *Modern Critical Views: Maya Angelou—
    New Edition*. Ed. Harold Bloom. New York: Infobase, 2009: 133–46. Print.
Bell, Bernard W. *Bearing Witness to African American Literature*. Detroit, MI:
    Wayne State UP, 2012. Print.
Benson, Carol. "Out of the Cage and Still Singing," *Writer's Digest* (January
    1975): 18–20. Print.
Benston, Kimberly W. "I Yam What I Am: Topos of (Un)naming in Afro-
    American Literature," *Black Literature and Literary Theory*. Ed. Henry Louis
    Gates, Jr. New York: Methuen, 1984: 151–72. Print.
Berry, J. Bill. "Introduction," *Home Ground: Southern Autobiography*. Ed. J. Bill
    Berry. Columbia: U of Missouri P, 1991: 1–10. Print.
Bertolino, James. "Maya Angelou Is Three Writers: *I Know Why the Caged Bird
    Sings*," *Censored Books*. Ed. Nicholas J. Karolides, Lee Burress, and John M.
    Kean. Metuchen, NJ: Scarecrow, 1993: 299–305. Print.

Bethel, Lorraine. "Maya," *Equal Times* 20 (November 1978): 14–16. Print.

Billingslea-Brown, Alma Jean. *Crossing Borders through Folklore: African American Women's Fiction and Art.* Columbia: U of Missouri P, 1999. Print.

Birkerts, Sven. *The Art of Time in Memoir.* Saint Paul, Minnesota: Graywolf, 2008. Print.

Blair, Sara. *Harlem Crossroads: Black Writers and the Photograph in the Twentieth Century.* Princeton, New Jersey: Princeton UP, 2007. Print.

Bloom, Harold, ed. *Modern Critical Views, Maya Angelou.* Philadelphia: ChelseaHouse, 1998. Print.

—. *Modern Critical Views: Maya Angelou—New Edition.* New York: Bloom's Literary Criticism (Infobase), 2009. Print.

Bloom, Lynn Z. "Coming of Age in the Segregated South," *Home Ground: Southern Autobiography.* Ed. J. Bill Berry. Columbia: U of Missouri P, 1991: 110–22. Print.

—. "Heritages: Dimensions of Mother-Daughter Relationships in Women's Autobiographies," *The Lost Tradition: Mothers and Daughters in Literature.* Ed. Cathy N. Davidson, and E. M. Broner. New York: Ungar, 1980: 291–303. Print.

—. "Stories of Resilience in Childhood: The Narratives of Maya Angelou, Maxine Hong Kingston, Richard Rodriguez, John Edgar Wideman, and Tobias Wolff," *MELUS* 25.3 and 4 (October 2000): 311–21.

Bloom, Lynn Z., and Ning Yu, "American Autobiography: The Changing Critical Canon," *a/b: Auto/Biography Studies* 9.2 (Fall 1994): 167–80. Print.

Bluestein, Gene. *The Voice of the Folk: Folklore and American Literary Theory.* Amherst: U of Massachusetts P, 1972. Print.

Blum, Walter. "Listening to Maya Angelou," *San Francisco Examiner*, California Living (December 14, 1975): 12–23. Print.

Bolden, Tony. "Maya Angelou," *The Oxford Companion to Women's Writing in the United States.* Ed. Cathy N. Davidson and Linda Wagner-Martin. New York: Oxford UP, 1995: 51–2. Print.

Bononno, George A. *The Other Side of Sadness: What the New Science of Bereavement Tells Us about Life After Loss.* New York: Basic, 2009. Print.

Boyce Davies, Carol. *Black Women, Writing and Identity: Migrations of the Subject.* London: Routledge, 1994. Print.

Bracks, Lean'tin L. *Writings on Black Women of the Diaspora.* New York: Garland, 1998. Print.

Braxton, Joanne. "Ancestral Presence: The Outraged Mother Figure in Contemporary Afra-American Writing," *Wild Women in the Whirlwind: Afra-American Culture and the Contemporary Literary Renaissance.* Ed. Joanne M. Braxton and Andree Nicola McLaughlin. New Brunswick, New Jersey: Rutgers UP, 1990: 299–315. Print.

—. *Black Women Writing Autobiography: A Tradition within a Tradition.* Philadelphia: Temple UP, 1989. Print.

Braxton, Joanne M., ed. *Maya Angelou's I Know Why the Caged Bird Sings, A Casebook.* New York: Oxford UP, 1999. "Symbolic Geography and Psychic Landscapes: A Conversation with Maya Angelou," 3–20. Print.

Broeck, Sabina. *White Amnesia—Black Memory? American Women's Writing and History.* Frankfurt am Main: Peter Lang, 1999. Print.

Brooks, Tilford. "The Blues," *America's Black Musical Heritage.* Englewood Cliffs, NJ: Prentice-Hall, 1984: 51–60. Print.

Burgher, Mary. "Images of Self and Race in the Autobiographies of Black Women," *Sturdy Black Bridges.* Ed. Roseann P. Bell, Bettye J. Parker, and Beverly Guy-Sheftall. Garden City, NY: Doubleday, 1979: 107–22. Print.

Burr, Zofia A. *Of Women, Poetry, and Power: Strategies of Address in Dickinson, Miles, Brooks, Lorde, and Angelou.* Urbana: U of Illinois P, 2002. Print.

Bush, Vanessa. "*Great Food, All Day Long,*" *The Booklist* 107.3 (December 2010): 21. Print.

—. "*Mom & Me & Mom,*" *The Booklist* 109.12 (February 2013): 17. Print.

Buss, Helen M. "Reading for the Doubled Discourse of American Women's Autobiography," *a/b, Auto-biography Studies* 6.1 (Spring 1991): 95–108. Print.

Butterfield, Stephen. *Black Autobiography in America.* Amherst: U of Massachusetts P, 1974. Print.

Cameron, Dee Birch. "A Maya Angelou Bibliography," *Bulletin of Bibliography* 36 (1979): 50–2. Print.

Cawley, Janet. "Poet Aims to Capture Spirit of America," *Chicago Tribune* (January 19, 1993): 6. Print.

Christian, Barbara. *Black Feminist Criticism: Perspectives on Black Women Writers.* New York: Pergamon, 1985. Print.

—. "Maya Angelou's African Sojourn Links Two Worlds," *Chicago Tribune* (March 23, 1986): Sec. 14, 35. Print.

Cole-Leonard, Natasha. "Maya Angelou's *Hallelujah! The Welcome Table, A Lifetime of Memories with Recipes* as Evocative Text, or, 'Ain't' Jemima's Recipes," *Langston Hughes Review* 19 (Spring 2005): 66–9. Print.

Coleman, Wanda. "Black on Black: Fear & Reviewing in Los Angeles," *Ishmael Reed's KONCH Magazine* (October 21, 2002): 1–12. Print.

—. "Review of *A Song Flung Up to Heaven,*" *Los Angeles Times* (September 14, 2002). Print.

Collier, Eugenia. "Maya Angelou: From 'Caged Bird' to 'All God's Children,'" *New Directions* (Howard University) (October 1986): 22–7. Print.

Collins, Patricia Hill. *Black Feminist Thought: Knowledge, Consciousness, and the Politics of Empowerment.* New York: Routledge, 1991. Print.

Cone, James H. *The Spiritual and the Blues: An Interpretation.* Marynoll, NY: Orbis, 1997. Print.

Cordell, Shirley J. "The Black Woman: A Focus on 'Strength of Character' in *I Know Why the Caged Bird Sings*," *Virginia English Bulletin* 36.2 (Winter 1986): 36–9. Print.

Cosgrave, Mary Silva. "Review of *And Still I Rise*," *Horn Book* 55 (1979): 97. Print.

—. "Review of *Oh Pray My Wings Are Gonna Fit Me Well*," *Horn Book* 52 (1976): 78. Print.

—. "Review of *The Heart of a Woman*," *Horn Book* (February 1982): 84. Print.

—. "Review of *Shaker, Why Don't You Sing?*" *Horn Book* 59 (1983): 336. Print.

Cothren, Tim. "Madame Tussauds Fits Maya Angelou," *New York Times* (June 10, 2014): A16. Print.

Cotter, James Finn. "Review of *Oh Pray My Wings Are Gonna Fit Me Well* by Maya Angelou, *The Women and the Men* by Nikki Giovanni, and *The Peacock Poems* by Sherley Williams," *America* 134.2 (February 7, 1976): 103–04. Print.

Coulthard, A. R. "Poetry as Politics: Maya Angelou's Inaugural Poem, 'On the Pulse of Morning,'" *Notes on Contemporary Literature* 28.1 (January 1998): 2. Print.

Courtney-Clarke, Margaret. *Maya Angelou, The Poetry of Living.* New York: Clarkson Potter, 1997. Print.

Crockett, Sandra. "Poetic Angelou Can Sing, Cut a Rug," *Baltimore Sun* (September 9, 1997): E1, 8. Print.

Cronin, Gloria. "Maya Angelou," *Encyclopedia of African-American Literature.* New York: Facts On File, 2007: 12–15. Print.

Cudjoe, Selwyn. "Maya Angelou and the Autobiographical Statement," *Black Women Writers (1950–1980).* Ed. Mari Evans. Garden City, NY: Doubleday, 1984: 6–24. Print.

—. "Maya Angelou: The Autobiographical Statement Updated," *Reading Black, Reading Feminist.* Ed. Henry Louis Gates Jr. New York: Penguin, 1990: 272–306. Print.

Culley, Margo. *Fea[s]ts of Memory: The Autobiographical Writings of American Women.* Madison: U of Wisconsin P, 1992. Print.

Currey, Mason. *Daily Rituals: How Artists Work.* New York: Knopf, 2013. Print.

Dance, Daryl C. "Black Eve or Madonna?" *Sturdy Black Bridges.* Ed. Roseann P. Bell, Bettye J. Parker, and Beverly Guy-Sheftall. Garden City, NY: Doubleday, 1979: 123–32. Print.

Davis, Thulani. "Slam Queen vs. Inaugural Poet," *Village Voice* (September 4–10, 2002): 1–6. Print.

DeGout, Yasmin Y. "The Poetry of Maya Angelou: Liberation Ideology and
Technique," *Bloom's Modern Critical Views: Maya Angelou—New Edition*.
New York: Bloom's Literary Criticism, 2009: 121–32. Print.

Demetrakopoulos, Stephanie A. "The Metaphysics of Matrilinearism in
Women's Autobiography: Studies of Mead's *Blackberry Winter*, Hellman's
Pentimento, Angelou's *I Know Why the Caged Bird Sings*, and Kingston's *The
Woman Warrior*," *Women's Autobiography: Essays in Criticism*. Ed. Estelle
Jelinek. Bloomington: Indiana UP, 1980: 180–203. Print.

Diedrich, Maria, Henry Louis Gates, Jr., and Carl Petersen, eds. *Black
Imagination and the Middle Passage*. New York: Oxford UP, 1999. Print.

Doten, Patti. "Maya Angelou's Rules for Life," *Boston Globe* (September 24,
1997): C1. Print.

"Down in the Delta," *Ebony* (February 1, 1999): 1–4. Paging refers to
EBSCOhost online printout.

Dreher, Kwakluti Lynn. "Spirituality as Ideology in Black Women's Film and
Literature," *Quarterly Review of Film and Video* 26.1 (November 2008):
59–62. Print.

DuCille, Ann. *The Coupling Convention: Sex, Text and Tradition in Black
Women's Fiction*. New York: Oxford UP, 1993. Print.

Ealy, Charles. "Maya Angelou's Film Foray," *Dallas Morning News* (December
21, 1998). Print.

Egan, Susanna. *Patterns of Experience in Autobiography*. Chapel Hill: U of North
Carolina P, 1984. Print.

Elliot, Jeffrey M., ed. *Conversations with Maya Angelou*. Jackson: U of
Mississippi P, 1989. Print.

English, James F. *The Economy of Prestige: Prizes, Awards and the Circulation of
Cultural Value*. Cambridge, MA: Harvard UP, 2005. Print.

Essick, Kathy M. *The Poetry of Maya Angelou: A Study of the Blues Matrix as
Force and Code*. Indiana: Indiana U of Pennsylvania P, 1994. Print.

Estes-Hicks, Onita. "The Way We Were: Precious Memories of the Black
Segregated South," *African-American Review* 27.1 (Spring 1993): 9–18. Print.

Evans, Mari, ed. *Black Women Writers (1950–1980): A Critical Evaluation*. New
York: Doubleday, 1984. Print.

"*Even the Stars Look Lonesome*," *Essence* 28.6 (October 1997): 62. Print.

"*Even the Stars Look Lonesome*," *Philadelphia Tribune* (September 1997): a11.
Print.

"*Even the Stars Look Lonesome*," *Times Literary Supplement* 4963 (May 1998): 32.
Print.

Farr, Cecilia Konchar and Jaime Harker, eds. *The Oprah Affect: Critical Essays on
Oprah's Book Club*. Albany: State U of New York P, 2008. Print.

Felman, Shoshana and Dori Laub. *Testimony: Crises of Witnessing in Literature, Psychoanalysis, and History*. New York: Routledge, 1992. Print.

Felton, Keith. "Womanflight on the Wings of Words," *Los Angeles Times* (December 28, 1975): 70–1. Print.

Ferris, William. *The American South: Its Stories, Music, and Art*. Chapel Hill, NC: Friday Center online course, 2014. Online.

Findlen, Barbara. "*Even the Stars Look Lonesome*," *Ms*. 8.3 (November 1997): 86. Print.

Foster, Frances Smith. "Parents and Children in Autobiography by Southern Afro-American Writers," *Home Ground: Southern Autobiography*. Ed. J. Bill Berry. Columbia: U of Missouri P, 1991: 98–109. Print.

Fox, Margalit. "Maya Angelou, Lyrical Witness to the Jim Crow South, Dies," *New York Times* (May 29, 2014): A1. Print.

Fox-Genovese, Elizabeth. "My Statue, My Self: Autobiographical Writings of Afro-American Women," *The Private Self: Theory and Practice of Women's Autobiographical Writings*. Ed. Benstock, Shari. Chapel Hill: U of North Carolina P, 1988: 63–89. Print.

—. "'Myth and History': Discourse in Origins in Zora Neale Hurston and Maya Angelou," *Black American Literature Forum* 24.3 (Summer 1990): 221–35. Print.

Frank, Arthur W. *The Wounded Storyteller: Body, Illness, and Ethics*. Chicago: U of Chicago P, 1995. Print.

Froula, Christine. "The Daughter's Seduction: Sexual Violence and Literary History," *Signs: Journal of Women in Culture and Society* 11.4 (1986): 621–44. Print.

Fulghum, Robert. "Home Truths and Homilies," *Washington Post Book World* (September 19, 1993): 4. Print.

Fuller, Edmund. "The Bookshelf: The Making of a Black Artist," *Wall Street Journal* (April 16, 1970): 16. Print.

Gabbin, Joanne V. "Maya Angelou: The People's Poet Laureate: An Introduction," *Langston Hughes Review* 19 (Spring 2005): 3–7. Print.

Gates, Henry Louis, Jr. *Reading Black, Reading Feminist: A Critical Anthology*. New York: Meridian, 1990. Print.

—. *The Signifying Monkey: A Theory of African-American Literary Criticism*. New York: Oxford UP, 1988. Print.

Georgoudaki, Ekaterini. "Contemporary Women's Autobiography: Maya Angelou, Gwendolyn Brooks, Nikki Giovanni, Lillian Hellman, and Audre Lorde," *Diavazo* 237 (April 1990): 62–9. Print.

—. *Race, Gender, and Class Perspectives in the Works of Maya Angelou, Gwendolyn Brooks, Rita Dove, Nikki Giovanni, Lillian Hellman, and Audre Lorde*. Thessaloniki, Greece: Aristotle U of Thessaloniki, 1991. Print.

Gergen, Christopher and Stephen Martin. "Follow Angelou's Legacy of Creativity." *Raleigh News & Observer* (July 6, 2014). Print.

Gibson, Donald B. "Individualism and Community in Black History and Fiction," *Black American Literature Forum* 9.4 (Winter 1977): 123–9. Print.

Gilbert, Sandra M. "A Platoon of Poets," *Poetry* 128 (1976): 290–9. Print.

Gilbert, Susan. "Maya Angelou's *I Know Why the Caged Bird Sings*: Paths to Escape," *Mount Olive Review* (1987): 39–50. Print.

Gillespie, Marcia Ann, Rosa Johnson Butler, and Richard A. Long. *Maya Angelou: A Glorious Celebration*. New York: Doubleday, 2008. Print.

Gilroy, Paul. *Small Acts: Thoughts on the Politics of Black Cultures*. London: Serpent's Tail, 1993. Print.

Glover, Terry. "Legend: Dr. Maya Angelou," *Ebony* 65.2 and 3 (December 2009): 66. Print.

Goldberg, Doris. "Poetry of Angelou," *Blade* 5 (November 1978): G10. Print.

Goodman, George, Jr. "Maya Angelou's Lonely Black Chick Outlook," *New York Times* (March 24, 1972): 28. Print.

Goring, Rosemary. "Maya Angelou," *The Herald* (May 29, 2014): 18. Print.

Gottlieb, Annie. "Growing Up and the Serious Business of Survival," review of *Gather Together in My Name*. *New York Times Book Review* (June 16, 1974): 16, 20. Print.

"*Great Food, All Day Long*," *Michigan Citizen* 33.8 (January 2011): A7. Print.

Gropman, Jackie. "Review of *All God's Children Need Traveling Shoes*," *Southern Literary Journal* (August 1986): 113. Print.

Gross, Robert A. "Growing Up Black," review of *I Know Why the Caged Bird Sings, Newsweek* 75 (March 2, 1970): 90–1. Print.

Gruesser, John C. "Afro-American Travel Literature and Africanist Discourse," *Black American Literature Forum* 24.1 (Spring 1990): 5–20. Print.

Guttridge, Peter. "Maya Angelou," *The Independent* (May 30, 2014): 52. Print.

Haaken, Janice. "The Recovery of Memory, Fantasy, and Desire: Feminist Approaches to Sexual Abuse and Psychic Trauma," *Signs* 21.4 (1996): 1069–94. Print.

Hagen, Lyman B. *Heart of a Woman, Mind of a Writer, and Soul of a Poet: A Critical Analysis of the Writings of Maya Angelou*. Lanham, MD: UP of America, 1997. Print.

Harris, Jennifer. "Reading Mobility, Motherhood and Domesticity in Four African American Women's Texts," *Journal of the Association for Research on Mothering* 2.2 (2000): 200–10. Print.

Harris, Joan K. "The Kindness of Strangers," *Times Educational Supplement* (October 19, 1984): 48. Print.

Harris, Trudier. *Saints, Sinners, Saviors: Strong Black Women in African American Literature*. New York: Palgrave, 2001. Print.

Henderson, Stephen E. *Understanding the New Black Poetry: Black Speech and Black Music as Poetic References.* New York: Morrow, 1973. Print.

Henke, Suzette A. "Maya Angelou's *Caged Bird* and Trauma Narrative," *Bloom's Modern Critical Views: Maya Angelou—New Edition.* New York: Bloom's Literary Criticism, 2009: 107–20. Print.

—. *Shattered Subjects: Trauma and Testimony in Women's Life-Writing.* New York: St. Martin's/Palgrave, 1998/2000. Print.

Herman, Judith. *Trauma and Recovery: The Aftermath of Violence—from Domestic Abuse to Political Terror.* New York: Basic, 1997. Print.

Herman, Judith Lewis. *Trauma and Recovery.* New York: HarperCollins, 1992. Print.

Hiers, John T. "Fatalism in Maya Angelou's *I Know Why the Caged Bird Sings,*" *Notes on Contemporary Literature* 6.1 (1976): 5–7. Print.

Hill-Lubin, Mildred A. "The Grandmother in African and African-American Literature: A Survivor of the Extended Family," *Ngambika: Studies of Women in African Literature.* Ed. Carol B. Davies and Anne A. Graves. Trenton, NJ: African World P, 1986: 257–70. Print.

Hine, Darlene Clark. "Rape and the Inner Lives of Black Women in the Middle West: Preliminary Thoughts on the Culture of Dissemblance," *Signs* 14 (1989): 916–20. Print.

Hine, Darlene Clark and Kathleen Thompson. *A Shining Thread of Hope.* New York: Broadway, 1998. Print.

Hinson, Hal. "Poetic Justice," *Washington Post* (July 23, 1993). Print.

Hirsch, Marianne. "Maternal Narratives: 'Cruel Enough to Stop the Blood,'" *Reading Black, Reading Feminist.* Ed. Henry Louis Gates, Jr. New York: Penguin, 1990: 415–30. Print.

—. *The Mother/Daughter Plot: Narrative, Psychoanalysis, Feminism.* Bloomington: Indiana UP, 1989. Print.

Hobson, Fred. "Southern Women's Autobiography," *The History of Southern Women's Literature.* Ed. Carolyn Perry and Mary Louise Weaks. Baton Rouge: Louisiana State UP, 2002: 268–74. Print.

Holden, Stephen. "Film Review: The Healing Power of a Delta Family's Roots," *New York Times* (December 25, 1998). Print.

Holloway, Karla F. C. *Codes of Conduct: Race, Ethics, and the Color of Our Character.* New Brunswick, NJ: Rutgers UP, 1995. Print.

—. *Moorings and Metaphors: Figures of Culture and Gender in Black Women's Literature.* New Brunswick, NJ: Rutgers UP, 1992. Print.

"The Homecoming of Dr. Maya Angelou," Memorial Service, Wait Chapel, Wake Forest University, Winston-Salem, North Carolina. June 7, 2014.

Hord, Fred Lee. "Someplace to Be a Black Girl," *Reconstructing Memory: Black Literary Criticism.* Chicago: Third World P, 1991: 75–85. Print.

Horsford, Victoria. "Maya Angelou, The Gift," *Sun Reporter* (February 10, 2011): L1. Print.

Horvitz, Deborah M. *Literary Trauma: Sadism, Memory, and Sexual Violence in American Women's Fiction*. Albany: State U of New York P, 2000. Print.

Howe, Michele. "Angelou's Poetry Builds Bridges between Peoples," *Star-Ledger* (Newark, New Jersey) (June 3, 1990): C4. Print.

Hull, Gloria T., Patricia Bell Scott, and Barbara Smith, eds. *All the Women Are White, All the Blacks Are Men, but Some of Us Are Brave: Black Women's Studies*. New York: Feminist P, 1982. Print.

Illouz, Eva. *Oprah Winfrey and the Glamour of Misery*. New York: Columbia UP, 2003. Print.

Italie, Hallie. "Writer Maya Angelou Dies," *Charleston Daily Mail* (May 29, 2014): D4. Print.

Jacobs, Janet Liebman. *Victimized Daughters: Incest and the Development of the Female Self*. New York: Routledge, 1994. Print.

Jamison, Kay Redfield. *Exuberance, The Passion for Life*. New York: Random, 2004. Print.

Jelinek, Estelle C. *The Tradition of Women's Autobiography: From Antiquity to the Present*. Boston: Twayne, 1986. Print.

Jimoh, A. Yemisi. *Spiritual, Blues, and Jazz People in African American Fiction*. Knoxville: U of Tennessee P, 2002. Print.

Joeres, Ruth-Ellen Boetcher. "The Passionate Essay, Radical Feminist Essayists," *The Politics of the Essay: Feminist Perspectives*. Ed. Joeres, Ruth-Ellen Boetcher and Elizabeth Mittman. Bloomington: Indiana UP, 1993: 151–71. Print.

Johnson, Charles. *Being and Race: Black Writing since 1970*. Bloomington: Indiana UP, 1988. Print.

Johnson, Guy. *Echoes of a Distant Summer*. New York: One World/Ballantine, 2002. Print.

—. "The Last Oasis." In Program for "The Last Homecoming," June 7, 2014, n.p.

—. *Standing at the Scratch Line*. New York: Stivers Row/Random, 1998. Print.

—. "Tribute to Maya Angelou," *Black Issues Book Review* 1.3 (May 1999): 44–5. Print.

Jones, Gayl. *Liberating Voices: Oral Traditions in African American Literature*. Cambridge, MA: Harvard UP, 1991. Print.

Jones, George E. "Maya Angelou's *I Know Why the Caged Bird Sings* and Black Autobiographical Tradition," *Kansas Quarterly* 7 (1975): 72–8. Print.

Jordan, June. "Review of *Singin' and Swingin' and Getting' Merry Like Christmas*," *Ms.* (January 1977): 40–1. Print.

Joyce, Joyce A. *Warriors, Conjurers and Priests: Defining African-centered Literary Criticism*. Chicago, IL: Third World P, 1994. Print.

Juncker, Clara. "Bodies in Motion: Maya Angelou's *Wouldn't Take Nothing for My Journey Now,*" *Through Random Doors We Wandered: Women Writing the South.* Odense: U of Southern Denmark, 2002: 228–47. Print.

June, Pamela B. *The Fragmented Female Body and Identity.* New York: Peter Lang, 2010. Print.

Kee, Lorraine. "Maya Angelou Offers a Perfect Ending," *St. Louis Post Dispatch* (October 2, 2002). Print.

Kelley, Ken. "An Interview with Maya Angelou," *Mother Jones* (May–June 1995). Print.

Kelly, Ernece B. "*I know Why the Caged Bird Sings,*" *Harvard Educational Review* 40 (November 1970): 681–2. Print.

Kent, George E. *Blackness and the Adventure of Western Culture.* Chicago, IL: Third World P, 1972. Print.

—. "*I Know Why the Caged Bird Sings* and Black Autobiographical Tradition," *Kansas Quarterly* 7.3 (1973): 72–8. Print.

King, Debra Walker. *Deep Talk, Reading African-American Literary Names.* Charlottesville: UP of Virginia, 1998. Print.

King, Sarah E. *Maya Angelou: Greeting the Morning.* Brookfield, CT: Millbrooke, 1994. Print.

Kinnamon, Keneth. "Call and Response: Intertextuality in Two Autobiographical Works by Richard Wright and Maya Angelou," *Studies in Black American Literature: Belief versus Theory in Black American Literary Criticism,* II. Ed. Joe Weixlmann and Chester J. Fontenot. Greenwood, FL: Penkeville, 1986: 121–34. Print.

Kite, Patricia L. *Maya Angelou.* Minneapolis, Minnesota: Lerner, 1999. Print.

Kizis, Sarah. "Two Women: Maya Angelou's Character Sketches," *Writing* 24.6 (April 2002): 16. Print.

Klekner, Olga. "Metamorphosis, Mutations of a Hungarian Continental Drifter into an American Woman," *Private Voices, Public Lives, Women Speak on the Literary Life.* Ed. Nancy Owen Nelson. Denton: U of North Texas P, 1995: 141–52. Print.

Klotman, Phyllis Rauch. *Another Man Gone: The Black Runner in Contemporary Afro-American Literature.* Port Washington, NY: Kennikat P, 1977. Print.

Koolish, Lynda. *African American Writers, Portraits and Visions.* Jackson: UP of Mississippi, 2001. Print/photographs.

Koyana, Siphokazi. "The Heart of the Matter: Motherhood and Marriage in the Autobiographies of Maya Angelou," *Bloom's Modern Critical Views: Maya Angelou—New Edition.* New York: Bloom's Literary Criticism, 2009: 67–83. Print.

Kuehl, Linda. "Review of *Singin' and Swingin' and Gettin' Merry Like Christmas,*" *Saturday Review* (October 30, 1976): 46. Print.

LaCapra, Dominick. *Writing History, Writing Trauma.* Baltimore, MD: Johns Hopkins UP, 2001. Print.

Langellier, Kristin M. and Eric E. Peterson. *Storytelling in Daily Life.* Philadelphia, PN: Temple UP, 2004. Print.

Lanker, Brian. *I Dream a World: Portraits of Black Women Who Changed America.* New York: Stewart, Tabori and Chang, 1999. Maya Angelou, Introduction, 10–11. Print.

Lanser, Susan S. *Fictions of Authority: Women Writers and Narrative Voice.* Ithaca, NY: Cornell UP, 1992. Print.

Lawson, Erica. "Black Women's Mothering in a Historical and Contemporary Perspective: Understanding the Past, Forging the Future," *Mother Outlaws: Theories and Practices of Empowered Mothering.* Ed. Andrea O'Reilly. Toronto: Women's P, 2004: 193–201. Print.

Lehmann-Haupt, Christopher. "Books of the Times: Masculine and Feminine," *New York Times* (February 25, 1970): 45. Print.

Lewis, David Levering. "A Transitional Time: *The Heart of a Woman,*" *Readings on Maya Angelou,* 1997: 152–5. Print.

Lim, Grace. "Spotlight on . . . Maya Angelou," *People* 51.3 (January 25, 1999). Print.

Lindberg-Seyersted, Brita. *Black and Female: Essays on Writings by Black Women in the Diaspora.* Oslo: Scandinavian UP, 1994. Print.

Lionnet, Francoise. *Autobiographical Voices: Race, Gender, Self-Portraiture.* Ithaca, NY: Cornell UP, 1989. Print.

—. "Maya Angelou," *The Oxford Companion to African American Literature,* 18–19. Print.

—. *Postcolonial Representation: Women, Literature, Identity.* Ithaca, NY: Cornell UP, 1995. Print.

Loos, Pamela. *Maya Angelou.* Philadelphia, PN: Chelsea House, 2001. Print.

Lupton, Mary Jane. *Maya Angelou, A Critical Companion.* Westport, CT: Greenwood, 1998. Print.

—. "Singing the Black Mother: Maya Angelou and Autobiographical Continuity," *Black American Literature Forum* 24 (1990): 257–76. Print.

—. "'Spinning in a Whirlwind': Sexuality in Maya Angelou's Sixth Autobiography," *Bloom's Modern Critical Views: Maya Angelou—New Edition.* New York: Bloom's Literary Criticism, 2009: 85–90.

—. "Talking with an Icon: An Interview with Maya Angelou," June 16, 1997, unpublished.

MacKethan, Lucinda H. "Mother Wit: Humor in Afro-American Women's Autobiography," *Studies in American Humor* 4 (1985): 51–61. Print.

Madhubuti, Haki (Don L. Lee). "Toward a Definition: Black Poetry of the Sixties (After LeRoi Jones)," *Within the Circle: An Anthology of African American*

Literary Criticism from the Harlem Renaissance to the Present. Ed. Angelyn Mitchell. Durham, NC: Duke UP, 1994: 213–23. Print.

Mama, Amina. *Beyond the Masks: Race, Gender and Subjectivity*. London: Routledge, 1995. Print.

Manegold, Catherine S. "An Afternoon with Maya Angelou, A Wordsmith at Her Inaugural Anvil," *New York Times* (January 20, 1993): C1. Print.

Manora, Yolanda. "'What You Looking at Me For? I Didn't Come to Stay': Displacement, Disruption, and Black Female Subjectivity in Maya Angelou's *I Know Why the Caged Bird Sings*," *Women's Studies: An Interdisciplinary Journal* 34.5 (July–August 2005): 359–75. Print.

Manuel-Logan, Ruth. "20 Facts about Maya Angelou," *Sun Reporter* (June 5, 2014): L1. Print.

Mason, Mary G. "Travel as Metaphor and Reality in Afro-American Women's Fiction," *Black American Literature Forum* 24 (1990): 337–56. Print.

Matthews, Karen. "Writer Maya Angelou Launches Hallmark Line," Associated Press (February 1, 2002): 1. Print.

"Maya Angelou," *The Commercial Appeal* (2007–Current) (August 25, 2012): 1. Print.

"Maya Angelou," *Daily Telegraph* (May 29, 2014): 27. Print.

"Maya Angelou," *Le Monde* (June 4, 2014): 16. Print.

"Maya Angelou," *The Patriot-News* (September 27, 2012): G20. Print.

"Maya Angelou," *The Plain Dealer* (June 1, 2014): 2. Print.

"Maya Angelou," *Providence Journal* (June 5, 2014): 11. Print.

"Maya Angelou," *Sunday Independent* (June 1, 2014): 31. Print.

"Maya Angelou: Interview," *Harper's Bazaar* (November 1972): 124. Print.

Mayer, Nancy. "Maya Angelou's Poetic Justice," *Philadelphia Daily News* (October 31, 1995): 33. Print.

Mayfield, Julian. "Black on Black: A Political Love Story," *Black World* (February 1972): 55–71. Print.

McCall, Cheryl. "Maya Angelou," *People* (March 8, 1982): 92–7. Print.

McDowell, Deborah E. "Traveling Hopefully," *Women's Review of Books* 4 (October 1986): 17. Print.

McHaney, Pearl Amelia. "Southern Women Writers and Their Influence," *Cambridge Companion to the Literature of the American South*. Ed. Sharon Monteith. Cambridge: Cambridge UP, 2013: 132–4. Print.

McLennen, Karen Jacobsen. *Nature's Ban: Women's Incest Literature*. Boston, MA: Northeastern UP, 1996. Print.

McMurry, Myra K. "Role-Playing as Art in Maya Angelou's *Caged Bird*," *South Atlantic Bulletin* 41.2 (May 1976): 106–11. Print.

McPherson, Dolly A. *Order Out of Chaos: The Autobiographical Works of Maya Angelou*. New York: Peter Lang, 1990. Print.

McWhorter, John. "Saint Maya," *New Republic* 20 (May 2002). Online.

Megna-Wallace, Joanne. "Simone de Beauvoir and Maya Angelou: Birds of a Feather," *Simone de Beauvoir Studies* 6 (1986): 49–55. Print.

—. *Understanding I Know Why the Caged Bird Sings: A Student Casebook to Issues, Sources, and Historical Documents.* Westport, CT: Greenwood, 1998. Print.

"Memorial Honors Poet Maya Angelou," *Charlotte Observer, The Herald* (June 7, 2014). Print.

Merritt, Grace E. "Maya Angelou Charms Audience," *Hartford Courant* (October 25, 2002): B1. Print.

Miller, Alice. *Breaking Down the Wall of Silence: The Liberating Experience of Facing Painful Truth.* Trans. Simon Worrall. New York: Dutton, 1991. Print.

—. *The Drama of the Gifted Child.* Trans. Ruth Ward. 1979, rpt. New York: Harper Basic, 1990. Print.

—. *Thou Shalt Not Be Aware: Society's Betrayal of the Child.* Trans. Hildegarde and Hunter Hannum. 1981, rpt. New York: New American Library, 1986. Print.

Miller, Nancy K. *Getting Personal.* New York: Routledge, 1991. Print.

Minzesheimer, Bob. "Maya Angelou Celebrates Her 80 Years of Pain and Joy," *USA Today* (March 26, 2008). Print.

Mitchell, Lisa. "Maya Angelou: Sometimes She Feels Like a Motherless Child," review of *Singin' and Swingin' and Gettin' Merry Like Christmas. Los Angeles Times* (November 21, 1976): 5. Print.

Moallem, Minoo and Iain A. Boal. "Multicultural Nationalism and the Poetics of Inauguration," *Between Woman and Nation: Nationalisms, Transnational Feminisms, and the State.* Ed. Caren Kaplan, Norma Alarcon, and Minoo Moallem. Durham, NC: Duke UP, 1999: 243–63. Print.

Molotsky, Irvin. "Poet of the South for the Inauguration," *New York Times* (December 5, 1992): A8. Print.

Moore, Opal. "Learning to Live: When the Bird Breaks from the Cage," *Censored Books.* Ed. Nicholas J. Karolides, Lee Burress, and John M. Kean. Metuchen, NJ: Scarecrow, 1993: 306–16. Print.

Mostem, K. *Autobiography and Black Identity Politics, Racialization in Twentieth-Century America.* Cambridge: Cambridge UP, 2004. Print.

Moyers, Bill. "Portraits of Greatness," PBS Home Video, Pacific Arts, 1982. Online.

Murphy, Kate. "Maya Angelou," *New York Times* (April 21, 2013): SR2. Print.

Neale, Larry. "The Black Arts Movement," *Within the Circle: An Anthology of African American Literary Criticism from the Harlem Renaissance to the Present.* Ed. Angelyn Mitchell. Durham, NC: Duke UP, 1994: 184–98. Print.

Nero, Clarence. "A Discursive Trifecta: Community, Education, and Language in *I Know Why the Caged Bird Sings*," *Langston Hughes Review* 19 (Spring 2005): 61–5. Print.

Neubauer, Carol E. "Displacement and Autobiographical Style in Maya Angelou's *The Heart of a Woman*," *Black American Literature Forum* 17 (1983): 123–9. Print.

—. "An Interview with Maya Angelou," *Massachusetts Review* 28 (1987): 286–92. Print.

—. "Maya Angelou: Self and a Song of Freedom in the Southern Tradition," *Southern Women Writers: The New Generation*. Ed. Tonette Bond Inge. Tuscaloosa: U of Alabama P, 1990: 114–41. Print.

Neumann, Thomas. "Maya Angelou in Search of Roots: Sojourn to Ghana," *Houston Chronicle* (July 13, 1986): 17.

Neville, Jill. "Southern Sequel," *Times Literary Supplement* (June 14, 1985): 674. Print.

Nnaemeka, Obioma. *Sisterhood: Feminists and Power from Africa to the Diaspora*. Trenton, NJ: Africa World P, 1989. Print.

Nuba, Hannah, Deborah Lovitky Sheiman, and Michael Searson, eds. *Children's Literature: Developing Good Readers*. New York: Taylor and Francis, 1999. Print.

O'Connell, Daniel C., Annette D. Sahar, and Sebastian M. Brenninkeyer. "Maya Angelou's Inaugural Poem," *Journal of Psycholinguistic Research* 26.4 (1997): 449–63. Print.

Oliver, Stephanie Stokes. "Maya Angelou: The Heart of a Woman," *Essence* 14 (May 1983): 112–14. Print.

Omolade, Barbara. "Hearts of Darkness," *Powers of Desire: The Politics of Sexuality*. Ed. Ann Snitow, Christine Stansell, and Sharon Thompson. New York: Monthly Review P, 1983: 350–70. Print.

O'Neale, Sondra. "Inhibiting Midwives, Usurping Creators: The Struggling Emergence of Black Women in American Fiction," *Feminist Studies/Critical Studies*. Ed. Teresa de Lauretis. Bloomington: Indiana UP, 1986: 139–56. Print.

—. "Reconstruction of the Composite Self: New Images of Black Women in Maya Angelou's Continuing Autobiography," *Black Women Writers (1950–1980)*. Ed. Mari Evans. Garden City, NY: Doubleday, 1984: 25–36. Print.

Pascal, Sylvia. "Review of *The Heart of a Woman*," *Southern Literary Journal* (December 1981): 88. Print.

Paterson, Judith. "Interview: Maya Angelou," *Vogue* 172 (September 1982): 416–17, 420, 422. Print.

"Phenomenal Woman" celebration, Carrboro [NC] Arts Center, November 9, 2014.

Plimpton, George. "The Art of Fiction CXIX: Maya Angelou," *Paris Review* 32.116 (1990): 145–67. Print.

"Poet and Author Maya Angelou Dies," *BreakingNews* (May 28, 2014). Print.

Popova, Maria. "Maya Angelou on Courage and Facing Evil," *brainpickings* (August 19, 2014). Online.

Premo, Cassie. "When the Difference Becomes Too Great: Images of the Self and Survival in a Postmodern World," *Genre* 16 (1995): 183–91. Print.

Rampersad, Arnold. *The Life of Langston Hughes.* Vol. 2. New York: Oxford UP, 2002. Print.

Ramsey, R. Priscilla. "Transcendence: The Poetry of Maya Angelou," *Current Bibliography of African Affairs* 17.2 (1984–5): 139–53. Print.

Reames, Kelly Lynch. *Women and Race in Contemporary U. S. Writing.* New York: Palgrave, 2007. Print.

Reed, Ishmael. *Writin' Is Fightin'.* New York: Atheneum, 1988. Print.

Rehm, Diane. "Maya Angelou: *Letter to My Daughter,*" *The Diane Rehm Show* (November 22, 2008). Online.

Rigney, Barbara Hill. *Lilith's Daughters, Women and Religion in Contemporary Fiction.* Madison: U of Wisconsin P, 1982. Print.

Robinson, Kathryn. "Review of *Singin' and Swingin' and Gettin' Merry Like Christmas,*" *Southern Literary Journal* (Summer 196): 144. Print.

Rody, Caroline. *The Daughter's Return: African-American and Caribbean Women's Fictions of History.* New York: Oxford UP, 2001. Print.

Rosenblatt, Paul C., and Beverly R. Wallace. *African American Grief.* New York: Routledge, 2005. Print.

Rosenfield, Paul. "Angelou: The Caged Bird Still Sings," *Los Angeles Times,* Calendar (May 29, 1985): 7. Print.

Ruddick, Sara. *Maternal Thinking: Toward a Politics of Peace.* New York: Ballantine, 1989. Print.

Rushdie, Salman. "Introduction," *The Paris Review Interviews,* IV. New York: Picador 2009: ix–xiii. Print.

Russell, Anna and Alexandra Alter. "Author, Poet Maya Angelou Dies," *Wall Street Journal* Eastern Edition (May 29, 2014). Print.

Russell, Sandi. "The Silenced Speak: Maya Angelou, Alice Walker," *Render Me My Song: African-American Women Writers From Slavery to the Present.* New York: St. Martin's, 1990.

Ryan, Judylyn. *Spirituality as Ideology in Black Women's Film and Literature.* Charlottesville: U of Virginia P, 2005. Print.

Sample, Maxine. "Gender, Identity, and the Liminal Self: The Emerging Woman in Buchi Emecheta's *The Bride Price* and Maya Angelou's *I Know Why the*

Caged Bird Sings," North-South Linkages and Connections in Continental and Diaspora African Literature. Ed. Edris Makward, Mark Lilleheht, and Ahmed Safer. Trenton, NJ: African World, 2005: 213–15.

Sanchez, Sonia. *Blues Book for a Blue Black Magical Woman*. Detroit: Broadside P, 1974. Print.

Sarler, Carol. "A Life in the Day of Maya Angelou," *Sunday Times Magazine* (December 27, 1987): 50. Print.

Saunders, James Robert. "Breaking Out of the Cage: The Autobiographical Writings of Maya Angelou," *Hollins Critic* 28.4 (October 1991): 1–11. Print.

Scheiber, Andrew. "Blues Narratology and the African American Novel," *New Essays on the African American Novel*. Ed. Lovalerie King and Linda F. Seltzer. New York: Palgrave, 2008: 33–49. Print.

Schmich, Mary. "Maybe Poetry Has a Chance After All," *Chicago Tribune* (January 22, 1993): 2C, 1. Print.

Schmidt, Jan Zlotnik. "The Other: A Study of the Persona in Several Contemporary Women's Autobiographies," *CEA Critic* 43.1 (1980): 24–31. Print.

Schnall, Marianne. *What Will It Take To Make a Woman President? Conversations about Women, Leadership, and Power*. Berkeley, CA: Seal, 2013. Print.

Schramm, Katharine. "Imagined Pasts-Present Confrontations: Literacy and Ethnographic Explorations into Pan-African Identity Politics," *Africa, Europe, and (Post) Colonialism: Racism, Migration and Diaspora in African Literatures*. Ed. Susan Arndt and Marek Spitezok von Brisinki. Bayreuth, Germany: Bayreuth UP, 2006: 243–56. Print.

Schultz, Elizabeth. "The Insistence Upon Community in the Contemporary Afro- American Novel," *College English* 41.2 (October 1979): 170–84. Print.

—. "To Be Black and Blue: The Blues Genre in Black American Autobiography," *Kansas Quarterly* 7.3 (1975): 81–96. Print.

Seaman, Donna. "*Even the Stars Look Lonesome*," *The Booklist* 93.22 (August 1997): 1842. Print.

Seay, Jorian L. "Grand Slam: Maya Angelou and Alice Walker Always Deliver," *Ebony* 68.7 (May 2013): 35. Print.

Seidel, Kathryn Lee. "Myths of Southern Womanhood in Contemporary Literature," *The History of Southern Women's Literature*. Ed. Carolyn Perry and Mary Louise Weaks. Baton Rouge: Louisiana State UP, 2002: 429–38. Print.

Showalter, Elaine. *A Jury of Her Peers: American Women Writers from Anne Bradstreet to Annie Proulx*. New York: Knopf, 2009. Print.

Shuker, Nancy. *Maya Angelou*. Englewood Cliffs, NJ: Silver Burdett P, 1990. Print.

Smelstor, Marjorie and Marion M. Tangum. "Hurston's and Angelou's Visual Art: The Distancing Vision and the Beckoning Gaze," *Southern Literary Journal* 31.1 (October 1998): 80–97. Print.

Smiley, Tavis (with David Ritz). *My Journey with Maya*. Boston: Little, Brown, 2015. Print.

Smith, Candace. "*Mom & Me & Mom*," *The Booklist* 109.19 and 20 (June 2013): 120. Print.

Smith, Dinitia. "A Career in Letters, 50 Years and Counting," *New York Times* (January 23, 2007). Online. http://www.nytimes.com/2007/01/23loom.html.

Smith, Sidonie. "Autobiography," *The Oxford Companion to Women's Writing in the United States*. Ed. Cathy N. Davidson and Linda Wagner-Martin. New York: Oxford UP, 1995: 85–90. Print.

—. *A Poetics of Women's Autobiography: Marginality and the Fictions of Self-Representation*. Bloomington: Indiana UP, 1987. Print.

—. "The Song of a Caged Bird: Maya Angelou's Quest after Self-Acceptance," *Southern Humanities Review* 7 (1973): 365–75. Print.

—. *Where I'm Bound: Patterns of Slavery and Freedom in Black American Autobiography*. Westport, CT: Greenwood, 1974. Print.

Smith, Sidonie, and Julia Watson. *De/Colonizing the Subject: The Politics of Gender in Women's Autobiography*. Minneapolis: U of Minnesota P, 1992. Print.

Smith, Valerie. *Self-Discovery and Authority in African-American Narratives*. Cambridge, MA: Harvard UP, 1987. Print.

Sorel, Nancy Caldwell. "Maya Angelou and Billie Holiday," *Atlantic Monthly* (September 1990): 61. Print.

Southern, Eileen. *The Music of Black Americans: A History*. New York: Norton, 1971. Print.

Spacks, Patricia Meyer. "Stages of the Self: Notes on Autobiography and the Life Cycle," *Boston University Journal* 25.2 (1977): 7–17. Print.

—. "Women's Stories, Women's Selves," *Hudson Review* 30 (1977): 29–46. Print.

Spigner, Nieda. "Review of *The Heart of a Woman*," *Freedomways* l (1982): 55. Print.

Stepto, Robert B. *From Behind the Veil: A Study of Afro-American Narrative*. Urbana: U of Illinois P, 1979. Print.

—. "The *Phenomenal Woman* and the Severed Daughter (Maya Angelou, Audre Lorde)," *Parnassus: Poetry in Review* 8.1 (Fall–Winter 1979): 312–20. Print.

Stone, Albert E. "Patterns in Recent Black Autobiography," *Phylon* 39.1 (March 1978): 18–34. Print.

Streitfeld, David. "The Power and the Puzzle of the Poem," *Washington Post* (January 21, 1993): D11. Print.

Sudarkasa, Niara. *The Strength of Our Mothers: African and African American Women and Families*. Trenton, NJ: Africa World P, 1996. Print.

Sukenick, Lynn. "Review of *Gather Together in My Name*," *Village Voice* (July 11, 1974): 31. Print.

Sutherland, Zena. "Review of *I Know Why the Caged Bird Sings*," *Saturday Review* 9 (May 1970): 70. Print.

Tal, Kali. *Worlds of Hurt: Reading the Literatures of Trauma*. Cambridge: Cambridge UP, 1996. Print.

Tally, Justine. *Toni Morrison's Beloved: Origins*. New York: Routledge, 2009. Print.

Tate, Claudia. *Black Women Writers at Work*. New York: Continuum, 1983. Print.

Tawake, Sandra Kiser. "Multi-Ethnic Literature in the Classroom: Whose Standards?" *World Englishes: Journal of English as an International and Intranational Language* 10.3 (Winter 1991): 335–40. Print.

Taylor, Helen. *Circling Dixie: Contemporary Southern Culture through a Transatlantic Lens*. New Brunswick, NJ: Rutgers UP, 2001. Print.

Terry, Gayle Pollard. "Maya Angelou: Creating a Poem to Honor the Nation," *Los Angeles Times* (January 17, 1993): M 3. Print.

Thomas, Trudelle. "'You'll Become a Lioness': African-American Women Talk About Mothering," *Journal of the Association for Research on Mothering* 2.2 (2000): 52–65. Print.

Thompson, Lisa. *Beyond the Black Lady: Sexuality and the New African American Middle Class*. Urbana: U of Illinois P, 2009. Print.

Thursby, Jacqueline S. *Critical Companion to Maya Angelou*. New York: Facts on File, 2011. Print.

Tinnie, Wallis. "Maya Angelou," *The History of Southern Women's Literature*. Ed. Carolyn Perry and Mary Louise Weaks. Baton Rouge: Louisiana State UP, 2002: 517–24. Print.

"To Come: Maya Angelou," *Economist* 411.8890 (June 2014): 98. Print.

Todorov, Tzvetan. *Genres in Discourse*. Trans. Catherine Porter. Cambridge: Cambridge UP, 1990.

Traylor, Eleanor W. Foreword to *Order Out of Chaos*. New York: Lang, 1990: xi–xiii. Print.

—. "Maya Angelou Writing Life, Inventing Genre," *Bloom's Modern Critical Views: Maya Angelou—New Edition*. New York: Bloom's Literary Criticism, 2009: 91–105. Print.

Umstead, R. Thomas. "Cable Remembers Maya Angelou," *Multichannel News* 35.21 (June 2014): 30. Print.

Valentine, Victoria. "*Even the Stars Look Lonesome*," *Emerge* 9.1 (October 1997): 74. Print.

Van der Kolk, Bessel A. "The Body Keeps Score: Approaches to the Psychobiology of Posttraumatic Stress Disorder," *Traumatic Stress: The Effects of Overwhelming Experience on Mind, Body, and Society.* Ed. Bessel A. Van der Kolk et al. New York: Guilford, 1996: 214–41. Print.

Vermillion, Mary. "Reembodying the Self: Representations of Rape in *Incidents in the Life of a Slave Girl* and *I Know Why the Caged Bird Sings*," *Biography* 15 (1992): 243–60. Print.

Viceroy, Laurie. *Trauma and Survival in Contemporary Fiction.* Charlottesville: U of Virginia P, 2002. Print.

Voice of America, Interviews with Eight American Women of Achievement: Grace Hopper, Betty Friedan, Nancy Landon Kassebaum, Mary Calderone, Helen Thomas, Julia Montgomery Walsh, Maya Angelou, Nancy Clark Reynolds. Washington, DC: Voice of America, United States Information Agency, 1985. Print.

Wagner-Martin, Linda. *A History of American Literature from 1950 to the Present.* Malden, MA: Wiley-Blackwell, 2013. Print.

—. "Lillian Hellman: Autobiography and Truth," *Southern Review* 19 (April 1983). Print.

—. "*Still* Telling Women's Lives," *Writing Lives: American Biography and Autobiography.* Ed. Hans Bak and Hans Krabbendam. Amsterdam: VU UP, 1998: 283–99. Print.

—. *Telling Women's Lives, The New Biography.* New Brunswick, NJ: Rutgers UP, 1994. Print.

—. *Toni Morrison and the Maternal, from The Bluest Eye to Home.* New York: Peter Lang, 2014. Print.

Waldron, Karen A., Laura M. Labatt, and Janice H. Brazil, eds. *Risk, Courage and Women: Contemporary Voices in Prose and Poetry.* Denton: U of North Texas P, 2007. Interview and poems by Angelou. Print.

Walker, Pierre A. "Racial Protest, Identity, Words, and Form in Maya Angelou's *I Know Why the Caged Bird Sings*," *College Literature* 22.3 (October 1995): 91–108. Print.

Wall, Cheryl. "Maya Angelou," *Woman Writers Talking.* Ed. Janet Todd. New York: Holmes & Meier, 1983: 59–67. Print.

—. "Maya Angelou, Toni Morrison, Alice Walker," *A New Literary History of America.* Ed. Greil Marcus and Werner Sollers. Cambridge, MA: Harvard UP, 2009: 968–72. Print.

—. *Worrying the Line: Black Women Writers, Lineage, and Literary Tradition.* Chapel Hill: U of North Carolina P, 2005. Print.

—, ed. *Changing Our Own Words: Essays on Criticism, Theory, and Writing by Black Women.* New Brunswick, NJ: Rutgers UP, 1989. Print.

Wanzo, Rebecca. *The Suffering Will Not Be Televised: African American Women and Sentimental Political Storytelling.* Albany: State U of New York P, 2009. Print.

Warga, Wayne. "Maya Angelou: One-Woman Creativity Cult," *Los Angeles Times*, California section (January 9, 1972): 1. Print.

Washington, Teresa N. *Our Mothers, Our Powers, Our Texts: Manifestations of Aje in Africana Literature.* Bloomington: Indiana UP, 2005. Print.

Watkins, James H. "Contemporary Autobiography and Memoir," *The History of Southern Women's Literature.* Ed. Carolyn Perry and Mary Louise Weaks. Baton Rouge: Louisiana State UP, 2002: 447–54. Print.

Wedin, Carolyn. *How To Write about Maya Angelou.* New York: Bloom's Literary Criticism, 2012. Print.

Weeks, Linton. "Hallmark of a Poet," *The Washington Post* (May 11, 2002): C1, C3. Print.

Weller, Sheila. "Work in Progress/Maya Angelou," *Intellectual Digest* (June 1973). Print.

Werner, Craig Hansen. *Playing the Changes: From Afro-Modernism to the Jazz Impulse.* Urbana: U of Illinois P, 1994. Print.

Weston, Carol, and Caroline Seebohm. "Talks with Two Singular Women," *House and Garden* 153 (November 1981): 128–9, 190, 192. Print.

Whitehouse, A. "*Wouldn't Take Nothing for My Journey Now,*" *New York Times Book Review* (December 1993): 18. Print.

Wilentz, Gay. *Healing Narratives, Women Writers Curing Cultural Dis-Ease.* New Brunswick, NJ: Rutgers UP, 2000. Print.

Williams, Mary E., ed. *Readings on Maya Angelou.* San Diego, CA: Greenhaven P, 1997. Print.

Williams, Roland L., Jr. *African American Autobiography and the Quest for Freedom.* Westport, CT: Greenwood, 2000. Print.

Williams-Forson, Psyche. *Building Houses Out of Chicken Legs: Black Women, Food, and Power.* Chapel Hill: U of North Carolina P, 2006. Print.

Willis, Susan. *Specifying: Black Women Writing the American Experience.* Madison: U of Wisconsin P, 1987. Print.

Winfrey, Oprah. Foreword to *Maya Angelou, A Glorious Celebration.* Ed. Marcia Ann Gillespie, Rosa Johnson Butler, and Richard A. Long. New York: Doubleday, 2008: 1–3.

—. Foreword to *Maya Angelou, The Poetry of Living.* Ed. Margaret Courtney-Clarke. New York: Clarkson Potter, 1999: 9–11. Print.

—. "What I Know for Sure," column on Maya Angelou's being presented her portrait at the Smithsonian's National Portrait Gallery, *Oprah* (June 2014): 160. Print.

—. "What I Know for Sure," column on her friendship with Maya Angelou—
    with photos—and references to her "spiritual" influence, *Oprah* (August
    2014): 128. Print.

—. *What I Know For Sure*. New York: Flatiron, 2014. Print.

Yeager, Patricia. *Dirt and Desire: Reconstructing Southern Women's Writing,
    1930–1990*. Chicago: U of Chicago P, 2000. Print.

Young, John K. *Black Writers, White Publishers: Marketplace Politics in
    Twentieth- Century African American Literature*. Jackson: UP of Mississippi,
    2006. Print.

Younge, Gary. "No Surrender," *Guardian* (May 25, 2000): 16. Print.

Zakariya, Sabahat. "The Courage of Maya Angelou," *The Nation* (May 30, 2014).
    Print.

Zauditu-Selassie, Kokahvah. *African Spiritual Traditions in the Novels of Toni
    Morrison*. Gainesville: UP of Florida, 2009. Print.

Index